Exploring
AUSTRIA

OTHER BOOKS IN THE *EXPLORING RURAL* SERIES

Series Editor: Andrew Sanger

England & Wales : Christopher Pick
France : Andrew Sanger
Germany : John Ardagh
Greece : Pamela Westland
Ireland : Andrew Sanger
Italy : Michael Leech
Spain : Jan S. McGirk

Forthcoming: Scotland

Exploring Rural
AUSTRIA

GRETEL BEER

PASSPORT BOOKS
a division of *NTC Publishing Group*
Lincolnwood, Illinois USA

This edition first published in 1990 by Passport Books,
a division of NTC Publishing Group, 4255
West Touhy Avenue, Lincolnwood (Chicago), Illinois
60646-1975 U.S.A. Originally published by Christopher
Helm (Publishers) Ltd.

Printed in Great Britain

CONTENTS

Contents

ACKNOWLEDGEMENTS

With many thanks . . .

. . . to old and new friends at local tourist offices throughout Austria and in particular to Norbert Burda of the Austrian National Tourist Board in Vienna, to the Austrian Agricultural Association, to Austrian Airlines for flying me (and my heavy-weight documentation) and to Denzel-Europcar/IR, but above all, to Alison Starling of Christopher Helm Ltd. for her infinite patience.

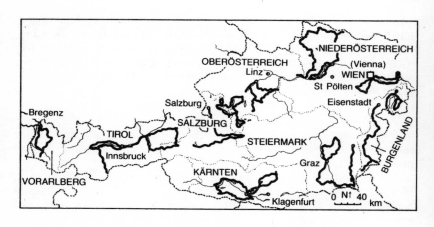

Austria: the provinces and the routes

INTRODUCTION

'Autriche, c'est ce qui reste', Clémenceau said during the peace negotiations after the First World War: 'Austria, that's what is left over.'
'Twixt the child that's Italy and the man that's Germany you stand, a
gallant lad with warm red cheeks,' said Grillparzer over a hundred years
ago referring to thirteenth-century Austria at the beginning of the
Habsburg reign. 'May God preserve the heart of youth in you; may he
make good what others have destroyed.'

Austria is a small country, measuring just 580 km from west to east,
about 270 km at its broadest and only 34 km at its narrowest (about twice
the size of Switzerland). It is a country of nine provinces, where one
province (Vienna) sits inside another (Lower Austria).

Bordering seven other countries (Italy, Germany, Switzerland,
Hungary, Yugoslavia, Czechoslovakia and Liechtenstein), Austria is the
heart of Europe—in fact the geographical centre of the continent is a
gentle mountain called Honigkogel—'the honeyed hill' on Lake Zell in
the province of Salzburg. Appropriately it also marks one of the most
beautiful spots in Europe.

For many people, Austria means Vienna and Salzburg, ski-ing in
winter and possibly the lakes in summer—yet there is so much more to
explore and discover. High mountains and Alpine villages in the west
(and superb roads to get you there), dark forests and fierce fortresses in
the north, the Hungarian Puszta in the east with a salt lake, sand dunes
(and tarantulas—as someone rather helpfully pointed out), medieval
strongholds and Renaissance palaces, Baroque castles and Gothic
churches, village festivals and local customs (and costumes)—Austria is a
lovely part of the world.

How best to explore it? Since it is not possible to take you there in
person—and what an enjoyable task this could be, stretching over
months—I have worked out, travelled and described a number of routes,
literally showing off the best of Austria. They are based on leisurely driving, leaving plenty of time for sightseeing, for meals, and for admiring the
lovely scenery *en route*. All the itineraries can be cut short—or extended.
In fact I rather hope you will be tempted to do the latter and in places
suggestions for excursions have been included.

Looking at a map, you may sometimes wonder why I have taken a particular small road or made a certain detour—until you actually take that road and make that detour. It will invariably lead to a secluded castle, an unusual church, or an especially pretty view which might otherwise have been missed. I cannot pretend to have shown the way to all that is beautiful in Austria—there's simply too much—and quite frankly, I still feel guilty about not including St Florian in Upper Austria, leaving out the spectacular Silvretta group in the west, and the historic Herzogstuhl in the south and for not insisting on (though at least suggesting it as the best approach to Carinthia) the magnificent Grossglockner road . . . Next time!

Getting There

From Britain to Austria
The fastest and most direct route for the Tirol, Salzburg and all points east and south is the motorway starting at Ostend, via Brussels, Cologne, Frankfurt and Munich. Since Dover/Ostend is the longer crossing, it may be preferable to use the Dover/Calais crossing (ferry 1¼ hours, Hovercraft 35 minutes) and travel the short distance to Ostend to join the motorway.

For Vorarlberg, Austria's westernmost province, the best route is from Calais, via Rheims, Strasbourg, Basle and Zurich: again, motorway all the way to Bregenz in Vorarlberg.

Motorail
Putting the car on a train (and travelling on the same train) is the easiest and most comfortable way for the long overland journey. German Railways (Deutsche Bundesbahn) run a number of services such as Brussels to Salzburg and Villach, 's-Hertogenbosch to Salzburg and Villach, Cologne to Basle, Cologne to Lindau on Lake Constance and others. In all cases you travel with your car on the ferry and drive to the loading point (Brussels, Cologne, etc.) on the other side. Prices include ferry for car and passengers as well as Motorail (though Motorail can be booked without cross-Channel ferry, booking this separately if you prefer) and sleepers as well as couchettes are available where appropriate.

For full information and booking contact **DER Travel Service**, 18, Conduit Street, London, W1R 9TD (01 408 0111) or 230, Park Avenue, New York, N.Y. 10169 (212 8180150).

Motorail is also available within Austria where services run between Vienna and Villach; Vienna and Graz; Vienna and Lienz; Graz and Feldkirch; Linz and Feldkirch; Vienna and Bischofshofen. DER handle bookings and information for these as well, but in Austria information is available from **Austrian Railways** (01 56500) and **ÖAMTC** (Austrian Automobile Motorcycle and Touring Club), Vienna 1010, Schubertring 1-3 (01 72990) and their offices throughout Austria.

Routes are included which start from Villach, Salzburg and Graz.

If you want to add extra days to your holiday, 'fly-drive' is of course the answer and there are direct non-stop flights to Salzburg and Vienna, as well as flights to Graz, Klagenfurt, Innsbruck and Linz where hire-cars can be picked up at the airport.

Roads and Maps

Practically all the routes described in this book are on minor roads—not on motorways or 'Schnellstrassen' (trunk or 'fast' roads). All motorways in Austria are prefixed with 'A', trunk roads with 'S' and some roads also have an alternate 'E' numbering, standing for 'European' route, presumably preparatory to Austria joining the EEC!

Roads are built with lightning speed in Austria and they are excellent, but the numbering (other than on motorways and trunk roads) is erratic to say the least and likely to be changed with equal speed. There is no explanation for instance why road 50 running south from Eisenstadt and marked as such on one map, should start off as 59a on another map, change numbers to 331 and then to 61—only to 'remember' that it is the good old 50 after all a little further south, whilst on yet another map it is alternately marked 50 and E69 (when in fact 'E' numbers are usually set next to ordinary road numbers). I have tried to cover all eventualities, but just in case numbers have been changed once again—or new ones added—follow the route and directions according to towns and villages! (Watch out for identical and similar town names: there's Pettnau and Pettneu, Igls and Ischgl, Telfs and Telfes—two towns called Gmünd, several Altenmarkts ...) This having been said, ÖAMTC (Austrian Automobile Motorcycle and Touring Club) issue a set of maps (4 sheets) in a neat folder, covering the whole of Austria and this is available from their offices throughout Austria. It has a scale of 1:200,000, is very detailed and also lists some landmarks such as farmhouses and inns. ÖAMTC also sell a variety of other maps, including special ones for hikers (Touristen Wanderkarten), town plans, etc.

Driving

Austrian traffic regulations are similar to those in force in other European countries. Children under the age of twelve are not allowed to sit next to the driver (they must be on the back seat). Seat belts are obligatory, including for back-seat passengers. Driving is, of course, on the right-hand side of the road; at intersections without traffic lights the vehicle approaching from the right has right of way. There are, however, certain exceptions such as emergency vehicles and vehicles on rails always having priority, also when approaching from the left, vehicles on priority streets have the right of way over vehicles from intersecting streets and vehicles leaving 'residential' streets ('Wohnstrassen') must yield their priority to passing traffic (there should be a sign 'Ende einer Wohnstrasse' to warn of this).

Speed limits

Maximum speed on trunk roads and roads outside built-up areas:
100 km (62 mph)
on motorways: 130 km (81 mph)
in built-up areas: 50 km (31 mph)
There are hefty on-the-spot fines for speeding, drunkenness, not wearing a seat-belt and even driving through a yellow light!

Parking

Short-term parking zones

These are outlined in blue and are marked 'Kurzparkzone' by means of a street sign which also gives the maximum parking time allowed. In towns such as Graz, Villach, Klagenfurt, Innsbruck, Feldkirch, St Veit an der Glan (the list is being enlarged constantly) parking in these zones is 'gebührenpflichtig' (subject to a fee) and this is stated on the street sign. Parking tickets (which are valid only in the town of purchase) can be bought from tobacconists, banks, ÖAMTC offices (in Innsbruck and some other towns also from vending machines) and have to be marked in pen or pencil with date, time of arrival, etc. and displayed against the windscreen. Some of the 'Kurzparkzonen' are 'frei' (free of charge) in which case a parking clock has to be displayed against the windscreen, set at the time of parking the car. Parking clocks are (supposedly) available free of charge from tobacconists (Tabak Trafik), but on a recent visit I had to pay a small sum for mine. Please remember that, particularly in small towns, everything closes for lunch and get your parking tickets and/ or parking clock (keep it in the car) in time! In Feldkirch (and possibly in some other towns as well) short-term parking is free between noon and 1 pm—no doubt to allow for a quick lunch—and this is also marked on the street sign.

Car parks

These operate pretty much the same as in Britain: on extracting a ticket the barrier is lifted, **but** you pay, before collecting your car, at a cash desk where the ticket is marked (or in some cases a token given) which is inserted at the gate on leaving, to lift the barrier again. In some car parks there are automatic cash points: you insert the parking ticket, the amount due shows up and you insert the money (most machines take 100S notes and give change). The stamped ticket (or token) is then returned for use at the exit.

Stores in quite a number of towns will refund parking fees, though they do not always advertise this—you have to ask for it. In other words, if you go shopping in a town such as Innsbruck, park in a car park and ask about refund of the parking fee in the shop. You may be given some parking vouchers (depending on the value of your purchases) which you can use for payment when collecting your car.

Where to Stay

Austria abounds in good hotels and inns, ranging from the very simple to the simply luxurious—with prices to match. Hotels and inns are graded from one to five stars, but there are also many excellent 'Pensionen' (bed and breakfast places) and—increasingly popular in recent years—farmhouses, listed as 'Urlaub am Bauernhof' (holidays in a farmhouse), details of which are available from local tourist offices. The term 'Gasthof' (Inn) is not always to be taken literally: it can mark the understatement of all time (as in 'Gasthof Hotel Post' at Lech, one of the really 'great' hotels with a five-star rating!).

Austria also has about 450 campsites and a list of these is available from ÖAMTC offices, local tourist offices and the **Austrian Camping Club**, A.1010 Vienna, Johannesgasse 20 (01 7299 1356).

Except during high season it is usually not essential to book far ahead—a telephone call a few days in advance being sufficient—but it is wise to check for local events such as fairs and other celebrations which could easily fill a small rural place to bursting point!

Hotel accommodation is charged per person (according to the room) and room prices must be displayed (often on the inside of wardrobe doors). Prices usually include breakfast except for a few rather grand, American-influenced hotels where there is a separate (and often very high) charge for breakfast.

As a rule the breakfast charge only applies in towns. You can either 'grin and bear it' or, much better, repair to the nearest coffee house—and there is always a coffee house near—for a delicious 'Wiener Frühstück' (Viennese Breakfast, known as such even in towns other than Vienna). It consists of really good coffee (or tea, chocolate, etc.), a marvellous selection of breads and crisp rolls, butter, jam, a soft-boiled egg—and all the magazines and newspapers you could possibly want. These coffee houses will also provide a cooked breakfast to order and, in the 'superior' establishments, foreign language newspapers are available as well.

At hotels where breakfast is included this will vary from 'Continental breakfast' consisting of coffee (or tea, chocolate, hot milk, etc.), rolls, croissants and/or bread, butter and jam (and possibly fruit juice as well) to 'Extended breakfast' usually with cheese, a bit of pâté and some sausage as well. Some hotels, too, offer a 'Full Buffet breakfast' which can come close to a banquet (so much so that some hotels have had to put up discreet notices to the effect that, whilst they are delighted for their guests to eat as much as they like, have second and even third helpings, taking away of food from the buffet for picnic lunches, etc. is definitely not on!). Incidentally, Austrian croissants ('Kipferl') are not like French croissants (though French croissants are frequently served): they are drier, crisper and can be absolutely marvellous—no doubt to make up for the tea which is invariably of the 'tea bag' variety. (There are a number of places where this is not the case, such as Haas and Haas in Vienna, the Sheraton in Salzburg, Sir Richard at Seefeld, Tennerhof at Kitzbühel, Post at Lech, Bleiberger Hof at Bad Bleiberg—a list to which I am adding constantly!)

Dinner at your hotel is not obligatory, except in hotels which only let rooms on a half-board or full-board basis (usually only at holiday resorts and at high season). Some hotels, again mostly in holiday resorts and at high season, like to let their rooms only on a longer term basis (say a minimum of three days) and there is often a reduction in price for stays over three days (or, to put it boldly, you will pay more if you only stay for one night).

Hotel Federations and Associations

There are a number of hotel federations and associations, the most interesting of which I have listed below. Note that inclusion in one group does not exclude from another: for example, Tennerhof in Kitzbühel is a Schlosshotel as well as a Romantik Hotel, Grüner Baum at Badgastein belongs to Relais et Chateaux as well as to Romantik hotels, etc. Wherever one of these hotels has been recommended in this book I have also indicated their inclusion in the respective group.

Relais et Chateaux
French-based association covering independently owned, very luxurious hotels all over the world which also include **Relais Gourmand** (restaurants only): of a very high standard (and sometimes price, though not necessarily so). All four and five stars.

Schlosshotels and Herrenhäuser in Österreich und Südtirol
Extremely comfortable and often luxurious, independently-owned hotels in Austria and South Tirol (Italy) set in manor houses, hunting lodges, castles as well as in minor—and major—palaces, ranging from three to five stars. Very—and very delightfully—Austrian. Moderately to high-priced.

Silence hotels (Relais de Silence)
Good quality hotels in particularly quiet situations, ranging from four to five stars.

Romantik hotels
Voluntarily linked group of carefully chosen historic hotels and restaurants in various European countries (including Britain), under personal management of the owner. Mostly four stars.

Telephones

Most hotel bedrooms, even in quite modest inns, are equipped with a direct-dial telephone, but charges can be exorbitant. The local Post Office will provide a clean, comfortable and well-lit cubicle, often with a chair and a shelf. No coins are needed—you make as many calls as you like and pay on leaving. Austrian phone numbers are subject to frequent change, but all are correct in this book at time of going to press.

Eating Out

Food in Austria can be excellent and portions are invariably enormous, but a few guidelines are needed.

'Menu' means the fixed-price set meals (there is usually a selection of two or three at different prices, varying in number of courses). What, in English, we would call 'Menu' (i.e. a list of *à la carte* dishes) is known in Austria as the 'Karte', short for 'Speisenkarte'. This usually comes in two parts—a list of dishes, sometimes covering several pages, and the so-called 'Tageskarte' featuring dishes of the day.

Menus, Tageskarte and, sometimes, also the long list of dishes are always displayed outside restaurants and you can often tell quite a lot from this. (I was trained from an early age by a discriminating aunt who would happily spend hours comparing notes and invariably come up with the right choice.) A large, printed and sometimes elaborately illustrated menu in a small country place—particularly with headings such as 'Gemma's an' (slang for 'let's start' instead of *Hors d'oeuvres*)—usually augurs badly, whilst a small, obviously freshly-typed list is a good sign. Fixed-price menus—particularly in towns and particularly at lunchtime—are usually excellent value. Portions will of course not be as large as if you ordered the same dish *à la carte*, but still huge by other (non-Austrian) standards.

Austria likes to lunch early and if a restaurant—except in a holiday resort out of season—is half empty by 12.30 pm, this is a bad sign. (At the Bayrischer Hof in Salzburg all seats are usually taken by noon!). Opening times vary: quite a few restaurants, though open all day, serve hot food only between noon and 2.30pm (though others start serving at 11.30am and even at 11 am) and again from 6 pm until 10 pm or 11 pm. Others proudly proclaim 'ganztägig warme Küche' (hot food served throughout the day), often starting at 8 am and going on until midnight. This applies particularly to good old-fashioned country inns where they think nothing of frying a crisp spring chicken for you in the middle of the afternoon or producing a giant mixed grill preceded by a delicious bowl of hot soup long after other restaurants have closed. (At some restaurants 'hot food throughout the day' may mean a restricted choice of dishes out of ordinary eating times, but it will still be freshly cooked).

Speciality restaurants, particularly where there is a 'Star Chef', like you to book in advance. Not only is seating limited as a rule, but their day of closure is liable to change. (Almost without exception, even quite expensive restaurants offer a moderately priced set meal at lunchtime).

Eating places and hotels have been recommended all along the routes in this book, but there is one particular phenomenon of Austrian gastronomy that deserves special attention: **Rosenberger motorway restaurants**. These were started in 1970 by two brothers who felt that motorists 'deserved better' than the usual motorway restaurants (which at that time were as mediocre in Austria as elsewhere). Word got round in no time that 'food at Rosenbergers' was excellent and that you could dine there in great comfort (the farther you go into the restaurant, the more elegant it gets—the front, though very pleasant, is for motorists in a hurry).

The success of the Rosenberger restaurants has been staggering (about 70 per cent of the clientele are Austrians). There are now thirteen Rosenberger motorway restaurants—some with very comfortable accommodation—as well as hotels in Salzburg and Wels and a restaurant in Linz. Standards in other motorway restaurants have improved as a result, though there is nothing to compare with Rosenberger. They bake their own bread and pastries and people will travel from Innsbruck to the motorway restaurant at Ampass just to buy the bread which is sold at the shop adjoining the restaurant. Definitely worth stopping for if you are travelling on one of the motorways and 'straying onto' if you detour from one of the routes.

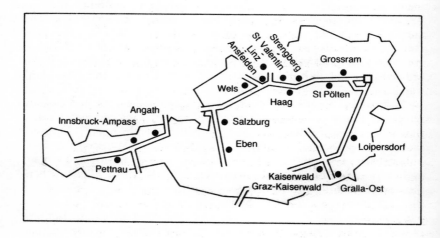

Rosenberger hotels and restaurants:
Inntalautobahn
at Angath (05332 4375—78) incl. Motor-Hotel
at Ampass (0522 46431)
at Pettnau (05238 87350)

Tauernautobahn
at Eben (06464 8404)

Südautobahn
'Kaiserwald' nr. Graz (03136 3972)
at Loipersdorf, Burgenland (03359 2572) incl. Motor Hotel

Phyrnautobahn
at Gralla—Ost (03452 4771)

Westautobahn
at Haag (07434 2180)
at Ansfelden (07229 87166)
at St. Valentin (07435 2002, 2005) incl. Motor Hotel
at Grossram (02773 6651) incl. Motor Hotel
at Strengberg (07432 2274)
at St. Pölten (02749 2298)

Hotels
Wels Hotel Rosenberger (0742 82236)
Salzburg Hotel Rosenberger, Bessarabierstrasse 94 (0662 39516)

Restaurant at New Town Hall at **Linz** (0732 231378—9)

Hotel and Restaurant Guides
There is no red Michelin for Austria, but there is the **Guide Gault–
Millau** (in German) listing some 600 restaurants, inns, etc. (500 hotels,
inns and pensions) and awarding 'toques' (chefs' hats). Typically Gault
Millau and highly subjective, it makes good—and often entertaining—
reading, listing heavily towards French tastes. **Eating out in Austria**
(Grafton) was compiled by this author and recommends about 150
eating places, ranging from good small inns to speciality restaurants, as
well as some patisseries and coffee houses. Written in English, it also
includes a list of Austrian dishes (with translation) and recommendations
as to what to order where.

Shops and Banks

Most shops in Austria are open from Monday to Friday from 8 am to 6 pm
(with more often than not a lunchtime break, particularly in small towns
and villages) and from 8 am until noon (sometimes 12.30 pm) on Saturday.

There is now a new law which allows shops to stay open on Saturday
afternoon on one Saturday of the month (usually the first Saturday of the
month, but choice is left to the shop owner) and one late closing day per
week (usually 8pm). Food shops usually open at 7 am. Hairdressers usually
close on Mondays, except for hairdressers at large hotels (and Dietmar in
Graz). Tobacconists are usually open from 6.30 am. In Vienna shops do
not close for lunch (except in rare cases), but banks surprisingly do!

Principal credit cards are usually accepted, as are travellers cheques
and Eurocheques.

Foreign visitors making purchases of over 1001S in any one shop can
receive a refund of Austrian VAT on leaving the country. Any shop will
give details (and provide the necessary form) but you must not use the
purchase whilst in Austria—in other words if you buy clothes do not wear
them on your holiday, they must be taken out of the country unworn.
Refunds of VAT can be obtained either at border stations on leaving the

country or you can send back the form, duly stamped by Austrian Customs, to the shop where the goods were purchased and they will send you the refund. If you buy goods amounting to over 1001S at a Duty Free Shop at one of the airports, VAT will be deducted on the spot.

Banks are open 8 am to 12.30 pm and from 1.30 pm until 3 pm, except on Thursdays when they are usually open until 5.30 pm, closed on Saturdays.

Useful Services
Medical
The Drogerie is not the place to buy medicines—you will need an Apotheke. They operate a rota system at night and on Sundays and holidays. When closed there is a notice giving the address of the nearest Apotheke which is open.

Information about medical emergency services (Ärztenotdienst) is obtainable from the local police station as well as from the telephone directory.

Car Breakdown
Dial 120 wherever you are.

Emergency messages
These are transmitted on VHF (UKW) station 'Autofahrer unterwegs' (motorists on the road) in German between 11.30 am and 12.45 pm from Monday to Saturday and between 12.03 am and 1 pm on Sundays and holidays. Messages are co-ordinated by ÖAMTC Vienna until 10.45 am daily. No fee. (01 7299, ext. 7).

Foreign language broadcasts
Austrian radio broadcasts news bulletins in French and English in the First Programme every day from 8.05 am to 8.15 am.

Public holidays

1 January
6 January
Easter Monday
Labour Day (1 May)
Ascension Day
Whit Monday
Corpus Christi Day
15 August
26 October (National holiday)
1 November (All Saints)
8 December
Christmas Day and Boxing Day

Tourist Information

Austrian National Tourist Office (ANTO) in Britain is at 30, St Georges Street, London, W1R 0AL (01 629 0461). In the United States at 500 Fifth Avenue, Suite 2009-2022, New York, NY 10110 (212 9446880); and at 11601 Wilshire Blv., Suite 2480, Los Angeles, California 90025 (213 477-3332). Each of the nine provinces of Austria has its own tourist office, and so has even the smallest hamlet, usually found in the main square. The office will be called anything from 'Kurdirektion' (in spas) to 'Fremdenverkehrsverein' and is quite often marked with a green 'i'.

Metric Conversion Tables

All measurements are given in metric units. For readers more familiar with the imperial system, the accompanying tables are for quick conversion to metric units. Bold figures in the central columns can be read as either metric or imperial: e.g. 1kg = 2.20lb or 1lb = 0.45kg.

mm		in	cm		in	m		yds
25.4	1	.039	2.54	1	0.39	0.91	1	1.09
50.8	2	.079	5.08	2	0.79	1.83	2	2.19
76.2	3	.118	7.62	3	1.18	2.74	3	3.28
101.6	4	.157	10.16	4	1.57	3.66	4	4.37
127.0	5	.197	12.70	5	1.97	4.57	5	5.47
152.4	6	.236	15.24	6	2.36	5.49	6	6.56
177.8	7	.276	17.78	7	2.76	6.40	7	7.66
203.2	8	.315	20.32	8	3.15	7.32	8	8.75
228.6	9	.354	22.86	9	3.54	8.23	9	9.84

g		oz	kg		lb	km		miles
28.35	1	.04	0.45	1	2.20	1.61	1	0.62
56.70	2	.07	0.91	2	4.41	3.22	2	1.24
85.05	3	.11	1.36	3	6.61	4.83	3	1.86
113.40	4	.14	1.81	4	8.82	6.44	4	2.48
141.75	5	.18	2.27	5	11.02	8.05	5	3.11
170.10	6	.21	2.72	6	13.23	9.65	6	3.73
198.45	7	.25	3.18	7	15.43	11.26	7	4.35
226.80	8	.28	3.63	8	17.64	12.87	8	4.97
255.15	9	.32	4.08	9	19.84	14.48	9	5.59

ha		acres	*Metric to imperial conversion formulae*	
0.40	1	2.47		multiply by
0.81	2	4.94	cm to inches	0.3937
1.21	3	7.41	m to feet	3.281
1.62	4	9.88	m to yards	1.094
2.02	5	12.36	km to miles	0.6214
2.43	6	14.83	km² to square miles	0.3861
2.83	7	17.30	ha to acres	2.471
3.24	8	19.77	g to ounces	0.03527
3.64	9	22.24	kg to pounds	2.205

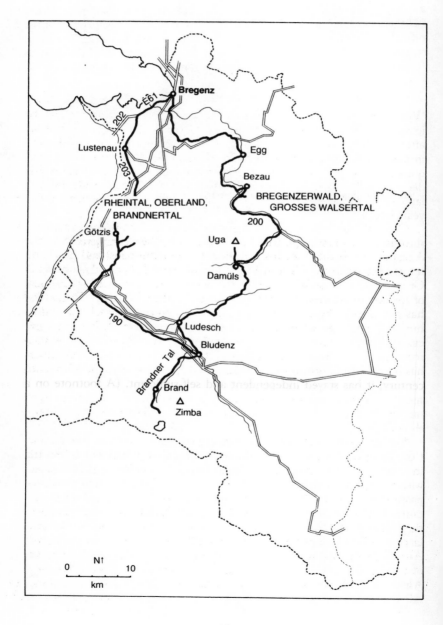

1 VORARLBERG

'Vorarlberg is an independent state' it says in the constitution 'which joined the Austrian Federal Republic of its own free will.' True, but only after a plebiscite in 1919 in which 80 per cent of the population had voted in favour of joining Switzerland instead—an offer which the Swiss, with quite a lot of help from the League of Nations, more or less graciously declined. (The man who had most promoted the alliance with Switzerland—a Vorarlberger, of course—became Austrian prime minister a few years later.)

Certainly the people of Vorarlberg are closer to the Swiss in every way: the country was first populated by the Raetians, then conquered by the Alamanni (when the Raetians withdrew to the mountains) and later on settlers came from the Canton Wallis in Switzerland (hence the name of Grosses and Kleines Walsertal). Even neighbouring Tirol, to say nothing of the rest of Austria, would be considered foreign territory: 'What God has put asunder by a mountain, let no man join by a tunnel' they said a hundred years ago when the Arlberg Tunnel was started. It was to give easier access to and from the rest of Austria than could the mountain road, which was impassable for part of the year. And although Vorarlberg has been part of Austria—albeit with interruptions—since the fourteenth century, it has stayed independent and self-sufficient. (A footnote on a menu in Röthis points out that 'in the parish of Röthis there is no drink tax on coffee and the alcohol tax on wine is merely 5 per cent. That'll show those in Vienna'!)

Yet, to the rest of Austria, Vorarlberg—fondly known as the 'Ländle' ('the little country'; it is in fact the second-smallest province)—is 'Austria in a nutshell'. This is certainly true as far as the landscape is concerned, with the plains of the Rhine Valley and the Walgau, the rich meadows, pastures and gentle hills of the Bregenzerwald, the valleys and high mountains of the Montafon, Grosses Walsertal and Brandnertal, and the gigantic glaciers of the Silvretta. There are thirty protected nature reserves, the largest lake in Europe (of which admittedly only a small part belongs to Austria), pretty towns and ancient villages. (There's also the slight oddity of the Kleines Walsertal which cannot be reached from Vorarlberg—or Austria—at all, only via Germany, its currency being the German mark.) All ideal touring country, with particularly easy access from the west.

Bregenzerwald, Grosses Walsertal

1-3 days/about 95 km/from Bregenz to Bludenz

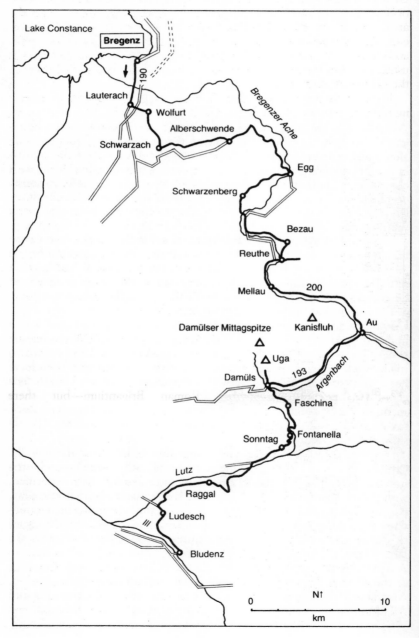

This route discovers the different aspects of Vorarlberg—the beautifully terraced valley called Bregenzerwald—gentle pastures framed by high mountains, rising gently to the mountain villages and gorges of the Grosses Walsertal, descending to the river Ill and the charming old town of Bludenz. (If you look at a map of Vorarlberg you will note that only the area along the river Lutz is marked 'Grosses Walsertal'—it does however encompass the whole region up to Au and including Faschina, Fontanella and Damüls. Walsertal is not named after a river or a mountain as is usual, but after the farmers from the Canton Wallis who settled there in the fourteenth century.)

It would be quite easy to complete the route in a day or even in a morning or afternoon—roads are excellent throughout—but to appreciate the full beauty of the various regions I would suggest that you allow three days. One day for the attractive villages of the Bregenzerwald, going as far as Schwarzenberg and staying at the Hirschen (few country inns anywhere can match its charms), then travelling perhaps as far as Damüls on the next day to watch the sun set (and rise) from the top of the world! And another day to amble gently down to Bludenz, arriving in time to explore the little town.

Bregenz: the parish church of St Gallus

Bregenz (pop: 25,000) the capital of Vorarlberg was first mentioned at the turn of the first century as Brigantion—later to become the Roman Brigantium—but there were settlements here as far back as the Bronze Age. Just big enough for a city, yet small enough to be a lakeside resort, Bregenz gets the best of all worlds—and the Summer Festival with enormous auditorium and stage built into the lake greatly adds to the attraction.

To see: medieval fortifications with St Martin's tower; parish church St Gallus; Seekapelle (chapel) in centre of Bregenz; Mehrerau monastery; and more. Tourist Office: Inselstrasse 15 (05574 23391) for Bregenz, but visit to Vorarlberg Tourist Office,

15

Römerstrasse 7 (05574 225250) could also prove useful. Take a cable car up the Pfänder mountain (good views from top, also a very good restaurant).

Hotel Weisses Kreuz (05574 22488) in the town centre is particularly pleasant (near-soundproof windows!) and **Hotel Heidelberger Fass** (05574 22463), though more modest, equally commendable; **Ilge Weinstube** (05574 23609) is very pleasant with excellent food; and there have been good reports about **Neptun** (05574 26325). If you want to stay on the lake—and near the festival stage—there is **Hotel Mercure** (05574 26100).

Leave Bregenz on 190 (direction Dornbirn) and drive as far as **LAUTERACH** where turn left, marked Bezau, Bregenzerwald (two Roman roads are still recognisable in Lauterach). Continue through **WOLFURT** which seems endless (villages in Vorarlberg have a habit of running into each other—village signs often being placed barely a yard apart). The thirteenth-century Burg Wolfurt, destroyed by fire in 1939 and rebuilt, was the French Headquarters after the Second World War. Drive to Schwarzach where turn left for Alberschwende (not particularly well signposted, but turn is at corner of Mobil station and Löwenstube). **ALBERSCHWENDE** is a pretty, typically Bregenzerwald village, known for an 800 year old Linden tree, its St Wendelin Chapel (built on the spot where Merbod was murdered in 1120), and as the birthplace of Hermann Gmeiner (founder of SOS Kinderdorf childrens' village) after whom the splendid new village hall is named. In Alberschwende join 200 to Egg (at first just marked 200—no direction—but later on marked Bezau). Keep on this very pleasant road over undulating hills—do not wander to the left (marked Moselbach) which would take you straight to Germany.

Drive on to **EGG**, the largest village in Bregenzerwald (pop: 2,800) and one of the oldest. The parish church was built in 1275, destroyed by fire and rebuilt in 1890, but there are some charming old houses in Egg as well as a little (unobtrusive) industry. The Capo hat factory on the hill (05512 23810) is well worth a visit for ex-factory sales (at practically wholesale prices) not just of splendid be-feathered Alpine hats, but rather fashionable headgear as well.

From Egg take the road between Gasthaus Ochsen and Gasthaus Löwen (direction Bödele and Schwarzenberg), past the church on the right. Follow directions to **SCHWARZENBERG** which is one of the most delightful Bregenzerwald villages. Angelika Kaufmann, though born at Chur, considered it her home town (her father was born at Schwarzenberg) and she painted the pictures of the Twelve Apostles for Schwarzenberg parish church when she was only sixteen (the altar picture, also one of her works, came later). The local museum has one room dedicated to Angelika Kauffmann (Open Tuesday, Thursday, Saturday and Sunday from 2 pm to 4 pm). The village has some lovely old houses; not the oldest of them, but one of the nicest, is No. 14, **Gasthof zum Hirschen** (05512 29440) which really is perfect in every way—and with most reasonable prices.

Schwarzenberg, Goldener Hirsch

Leave Schwarzenberg direction Bezau, re-joining 200, then follow directions for Bezau to the right. **BEZAU**, now a sprawling village with a surprisingly large church (built at the beginning of this century in place of a much older one), was the centre of the 'Bauernrepublik' (farmers' republic) between 1400 and 1806 (with courts at Egg and Andelsbuch). Meetings were held at the old town hall which stood on four stilts and could only be reached by a ladder. As soon as the 24 councillors had assembled, the ladder was taken away and only replaced when they had all agreed! The Bauernrepublik remained in force until 1805 when Vorarlberg was ceded to Bavaria (courtesy of the Pressburg Peace Treaty) and a county court was established at Bezau which remained even after Vorarlberg became Austrian once again in 1814—and there is now only the 'Bezegg column' on a hill to remind of this. See: local museum in 300 year old house (Open Tuesday, Thursday, Saturday from 2 pm to 4 pm; and Wednesday from 10 am to 12 noon 05514 2220); St Leonhard chapel; monastery and church. **Hotel Gams** (05514 2220), in a building which dates back to the seventeenth century, has nice rooms and excellent food, all reasonably priced.

Drive through Bezau, direction Bizau, rejoining 200 at the end of village, then turn left direction Mellau, Au, Damüls. (Almost immediately afterwards a road forks off to left for Bizau and **Reuthe**, a pleasant little spa with one of the oldest churches in Bregenzerwald—remarkable fifteenth-century frescoes—a short diversion well worth taking). The 200 closely follows the Bregenzer Ache river, with good views of Kanisfluh and Mittagspitze mountains on the way to **MELLAU** and **AU** where the famous Vorarlberger builders guild was started in 1651 (over the next hundred years some 1,800 young builders received their training there). There were several families in the Bregenzerwald—mostly intermarried— who produced notable architects, starting with Michael Beer and his son Franz (the only one to become a sort of eighteenth-century 'tycoon' and be duly enobled as 'Wohledler Herr von Bleichten'), followed by Michael Thumb from Bezau and his younger brother Christian and Andreas Moosbrugger from Au—their work can mostly be seen in Germany and Switzerland.

At Au, opposite the church (fifteenth-century with later additions) take right fork for Damüls and Fontanella, leaving 200 and crossing the Bregenzer Ache, then take right fork onto 193. The road narrows and twists a bit, but is rewarding, with marvellous views and a lovely feeling of driving towards the top of the world! Follow directions for Damüls and, just after the road fork having taken right fork for Damüls, turn right at Sporthaus Madlener and drive up to the Uga mountain (past parking area and station for chair-lift on left). Go as far as **Gasthaus Walisgaden** (05510 214) which sits at an altitude of 1,700 m—the road leads further still, but this will do very nicely for the most wonderful view of Damüls and the galleried tunnel past Damüls. The terrace of the Walisgaden is an absolute suntrap during the afternoon and it is exactly the sort of place one never wants to leave (you can in fact stay very comfortably at the inn).

Return to Sporthaus Madlener and then follow directions for **DA-MÜLS** (pop: 320). At an altitude of 1,430 m, Damüls is now a popular winter sports resort (and pretty popular in summer too) but it was the first of the settlements by farmers from the Canton Wallis in the fourteenth century. The parish church—the third one to stand on this spot—was built in 1484, baroquised later, and has some remarkable fifteenth-century frescoes which were only discovered some thirty years ago. A walk up the Mittagspitze—called 'Trista' (haystack) locally—is a favourite Damüls recommendation, but you are just as likely to be told that the air at an altitude of 1,500 m has a 'training effect' and that you can 'jog' just by laying back in a deckchair! Damüls is also known for its rich alpine flora—highly protected with an illustrated list of what may be picked singly, in small bunches or not at all.

Hotel Mittagspitze (05510 211—open from December to October) is a good family hotel; **Damülser Hof** (05510 210) is 'tops' in altitude as well as in price, though by no means exorbitantly so. The Tourist Office is in the centre of Damüls (05510 253).

Double back the way you came up to Damüls and after crossing the little bridge turn right, back onto 193 for Faschina gallery leading to **FASCHINA** and **FONTANELLA** (which means 'little well' in Romansch) descending gently—and very beautifully—to **SONNTAG** which is the name of the village as well as of a small district (Old Sonntag church was partly destroyed by an avalanche and rebuilt in the nineteenth century). Take right turn at Sonntag (direction Bludenz, Raggal) driving along the little river Lutz until you have passed a huge sawmill and a VW garage, then take left fork at Stutz (signposted Bludenz and Ludesch, also Raggal and Marul) crossing the river, then follow signs for Raggal (ignore left fork for Marul). **RAGGAL** is a particularly charming village with remarkably reasonable accommodation: **Hotel Nova** (05553 222) is about the 'grandest' and **Pension Nilla** (05553 221) one of the cosiest (also self-catering apartments).

From Raggal—with views of St Gerold monastery across the river—take direction 'Ludesch 4 km' which will seem the longest in the world to **LUDESCH** (old parish church St Martin on the hill was mentioned in 840, enlarged 1480—note the seventeenth-century altar, also so-called 'rosary' altar in choir and fifteenth-century frescoes). From Ludesch follow signs for Bludenz.

BLUDENZ (pop: 13,120) at the junction of five valleys, is a town of late seventeenth-century houses where—if the wind blows in the right direction—you are all but enveloped in the scent of hot chocolate (one of the largest chocolate factories in Austria sits in Bludenz). It is a lovely old town, full of hidden charms, with its narrow streets and arcaded court-yards where you least expect them. Make a point of seeing: Schloss Gayenhofen (now local government offices); parish church St Laurentius; Spitalkirche (particularly beautiful seventeenth-century altar); old town fortifications; and lots of beautiful old houses. Tourist Office: Werden-berger Strasse 42 (05552 62170). **Hotel Herzog Friedrich** (05552 62703) named after Duke Friedrich who granted a number of privileges to Bludenz in the fifteenth-century is modern and very moderately priced. **Schloss Hotel** (05552 63016) sits rather grandly above town, with beauti-ful views of mountains and valleys. It is slightly more expensive than the Herzog Friedrich, but still perfectly reasonable.

Rheintal, Oberland, Brandner Tal

1-2 days/about 75 km/from Bregenz

The beginning of this route leads through the valley of the Rhine, the river which, except for the Rhine Delta where Austria extends to both river banks, forms the border between Austria and Switzerland. The route then makes its way to Lustenau and romantic Hohenems, and farther to the Oberland where fruit trees vie with vines and where a frame of high mountains acts as a reminder that you are, after all, in an alpine region. (The reeds and marshes around the Rhine Valley may have made you forget it temporarily.) Here you find lovely sleepy villages, and the best cherries, especially around Fraxern where they grow twenty different kinds in an altitude up to 1,000 m and make pretty potent Eau de Vie from it too!

The Brandner Tal branching off from Bludenz is something else again, a valley embedded between Switzerland and Tirol and when you arrive at

Brand you may think that you have come to the end of the world—and a very lovely world at that. Until you realise that there is another 7 km of road ahead, right up to the cable car station for the Lünersee—and there the world really stops!

Leave **BREGENZ** (see Bregenzerwald route for details) on 202, direction Switzerland, which leads through the industrial suburb of Bregenz on Rheinstrasse; Wolford have their factory at No. 68 (05574 38500) with a special 'ex-factory' shop (parking directly opposite entrance—follow signs for 'Detailverkauf') where you can buy tights, stockings, socks and knitwear—mostly 'seconds' at wholesale prices (Open 8 am to 12 pm and 1.30 pm to 5 pm; Saturdays 8 am to 12 pm). It is like being at a permanent sale, only more comfortable. Stay on 202 through **HARD** (marvellous lakeside beach behind which stretches the heathland of the Harder Ried), then take the left turning for Chur (Schweiz) and Lustenau onto 203. At a crossroads carry straight on, first signposted Feldkirch and then Lustenau and Chur, still on 203.

LUSTENAU on the Rhine is the widest spread town in Vorarlberg. It extends over 22 km² and there are 18,000 inhabitants living in 4,000 houses surrounded by some 45,000 fruit trees, which gives a fair picture of the town. Sometimes you cannot see the houses for the blossoms—or the fruit! The inhabitants of Lustenau are sometimes referred to as 'gipsies' or as having gipsy blood and it is quite true that they are not at all like the rest of the people in Vorarlberg. The reason for this is very simple: unlike all other towns in Vorarlberg, which were ruled by some feudal lord or other, Lustenau was an Imperial Free Town from the Middle Ages until 1805 which meant that anyone could take up residence without special permission from the local ruler. Great use was made of this freedom, and not at all to the detriment of present-day Lustenauers ... In 1805 Lustenau, like the rest of Vorarlberg and Tyrol, was ceded to Bavaria, only to return to Austria in 1814. Lustenau is a noted centre for embroidery. This is not immediately obvious, for much of the work is done by small firms, sometimes with a showroom on the ground floor of a private house. A visit to the Embroidery Museum (Pontentstrasse 20, 05577 3234) is most rewarding, as is a visit to one of the firms, small or large, where they have ex-factory sales (come armed with your window measurements for it is often possible to pick up bargain curtain lengths). Tourist Office: Town Hall (05577 2281). On Fridays you can pick up another Lustenau speciality, freshly-baked cheese bread. The best can be found at **Bäckerei Wund**, Steinackerstrasse 27, but other bakers also sell it. **Gasthof Krönele**, Reichsstrasse (05577 2118, closed Monday), is a nice solid place at which to eat or stay. **Sporthotel Huber** (05577 3831) on the outskirts of Lustenau, a modern hotel complex with all sorts of sporting facilities, may be better for longer stays. See the town's seventeenth-century Loreto chapel and also its parish church built in 1830 (the plans were drawn by Negrelli better-known for the Suez Canal!)

Pick up 203 out of Lustenau, direction Feldkirch. At the roundabout take the road for Feldkirch and Hohenems. After about 6 km, leave 203, taking a left turning for Hohenems, then follow signs to the Zentrum (one-way system operates in part of Hohenems). Follow directions for 190 (Feldkirch and Götzis) and park as near the church as you can. **HOHENEMS** (pop: 13,500) is mostly known for the magnificent Schubertiade which takes place in June every year when the little town tends to get overcrowded with visitors. At other times you can actually see the place! The sixteenth-century palace is the centre of attraction (a former guest house it is now the town hall) where manuscripts A and C of the Nibelungenlied came to light in the archives in 1755 and 1779, though how they got there will probably remain a mystery forever. Other things to see include the parish church (magnificent Renaissance high altar); fortress ruins Alt Ems and Neu Ems (if you fancy the climb for the beautiful views from the top); and the seventeenth-century Jewish cemetery. Tourist Office: Town Hall (05576 4647). Schubertiade: Schweizertalstr. 1 (05576 2091). **Gasthaus zum Schäfle** (05576 2343, closed Tuesday) serves good, typically Austrian, or rather Vorarlberg food at reasonable prices.

From Hohenems follow 190 to **GÖTZIS** (late-Gothic parish church St Ulrich, sixteenth-century Jonas Schlösschen) where take left fork for Rankweil, leaving 190, through **KLAUS** with its so-called 'Heidenhäuser' (built in sweet chestnut wood) wreathed in flowers.

A short excursion you may like to take begins after Klaus where a turning on the left leads up to **FRAXERN**; here even the village sign consists of cherries carved in wood. They grow twenty different kinds of cherries in Fraxern and the local Eau de Vie called 'Kriasi' is pretty potent.

Drive on to **WEILER** (trace of Bronze-Age settlements, fortress ruins Alt-Montfort on the way to Fraxern) and thence to **SULZ/RÖTHIS**, always mentioned in the same breath although they are really two separate villages. This particular road to Rankweil is infinitely prettier than the 190—and you may care to divert once more—to the left for **VIKTORS-**

BERG with the oldest (former) monastery in Vorarlberg (see also parish church). Vines grew on the slopes near Sulz and Röthis a thousand years ago and are growing there once again. Note also the seventeenth-century Rothner Schlösschen, now a farmhouse.

Follow road to **RANKWEIL** (pop: 9,000) clustered very prettily round the hill on which sits Rankweil's famous pilgrimage church, built on the old fortress ruins. Rankweil assizes, dating back to Charlemagne, were held in the open originally and withdrew to 'the castle on the hill' only in later years. The parish church was built in the fourteenth-century, renewed in the fifteenth and again in the seventeenth-century (one of the few works by Michael Beer, founder of the Bregenzerwald school of builders, to be seen in Vorarlberg), and is the most popular pilgrimage church in Vorarlberg—much favoured for weddings. See particularly the Loreto Chapel, and Romanesque Cross (some other relics at present not on show, but may be again). There are beautiful views from the ramparts. In Rankweil itself see Romanesque St Peter's parish church (baroquised) and charnel house, also lots of interesting nineteenth-century and turn-of-the-century houses.

Leave Rankweil taking direction Feldkirch, joining 190 and entering Feldkirch through Altenstadt. In Feldkirch follow 'i' sign for Information: first left and almost immediately sharp right (before tunnel) for Zentrum. Park where you can — some of the centre is a pedestrian zone and in any case Feldkirch is best explored on foot. You will find the Tourist Office at

Rankweil

Herrengase 12 (05522 23467) well signposted and a first call there for maps and guidance will prove very useful.

FELDKIRCH (pop: 25,000) is built in a triangle around the Ardetzenberg, but the old part, the actual centre, snuggles very cosily on the north shore of the river Ill, between Blasenberg, Ardetzenberg and Felsenau Gorge. Mostly medieval, with a lot of the old fortifications still intact, there have been additions and alterations through the centuries and quite a lot of Feldkirch's charm lies in that curious mixture of periods and cultures. Certainly it does not look like a grim medieval town, far less an alpine one. There is almost a southern touch, particularly in the arcaded squares where almost anything is sold, from the latest fashions to freshly-baked bread and cakes. (There is also a market every Tuesday and Saturday, quite apart from special market days during the year which come close to being a carnival).

Wine grows on the Ardetzenberg and at the beginning of the sixteenth century Emperor Maximilian I (the one they called 'the last knight') bought Schloss Amberg (now a *hotel garni*; 05522 22419) for Countess Anna von Helfenstein so that — as they say in Feldkirch — she could 'help him' sample the wine (the first part of her name 'Helfen' translates as 'help'). Feldkirch was founded by Count Hugo von Montfort, sovereign lord of the region, who had first built the Schattenburg fortress in the

Feldkirch

Festive procession outside Feldkirch

thirteenth century. Count Rudolf von Montfort, one of his descendants, sold the town to the Habsburgs in 1377, having granted special privileges to the citizens, the year before the sale, which were recognised by the Habsburgs. Feldkirch is also a border town, sitting in what is always referred to as the 'three country corner' formed by Switzerland, Austria and Liechtenstein. You could easily visit all three countries in one afternoon!

There's a lot to see: fortifications with towers and gates (there are quite a few of these towers like the Katzenturm — canons being called 'cats', Wasserturm, Churertor, Pulverturm, Mühletor, etc.); fourteenth-century town hall; Domkirche (cathedral, as Feldkirch is also a bishopric); Schattenburg Fortress (accessible by car; with museum of local history and culture open July/August, closed Monday). There is also a restaurant at the Schattenburg, reputed to serve the largest Wiener Schnitzel, if not in Austria, then certainly in Vorarlberg!; Dominican convent and church at Altenstadt; and more. A wine festival is celebrated during the second week in July at Feldkirch; this is an event not to be missed. **Hotel Alpenrose** (garni) 05522 22175 is one of the best small hotels I know — so much so that it almost hurts to recommend it lest it should get overcrowded. **Hotel Illpark** is very modern and in the same complex as the concert hall to which the Hohenems Schubertiade extends (05522 24600). **Restaurant Treff**, Mühletorplatz (05522 28746) fairly new, very light and modern with excellent food to match. Schäfle, Marktgasse 15 (05522 22339, closed Sundays and Mondays until 18.00) offers splendid food in a marvellous old setting. There are plenty more excellent places at which to eat, or just sit under the arcades and sip a coffee or a glass of wine: hospitality in Feldkirch is certainly writ large!

Take 190 out of Feldkirch, direction Bludenz. The road is dual carriage for a bit with the motorway to the left, driving mostly along the river Ill, through the area known as Walgau, past **FRASTANZ** (mostly known for a fierce battle which was fought there in 1499) and **NENZING** (at the beginning — or end, depending which way you look at it — of the beautiful Gamperdonatal the top of which is known as 'Nenzinger Himmel', the heavens of Nenzing) until you come to a sort of spaghetti junction outside Bludenz. Just after the town sign for Bludenz — brewery on left, railway station below on right — you will find a sign for Brand directing you to the right, past the Suchard factory. You will eventually come to face the railway station, where turn left and left again (signposted Brand, but not all that easily spotted) then take the right fork for Brand. (Since my recent visit the authorities may have added bigger and better signs, or even altered the roads so that the route to Brand is easier to find, in which case just follow signs for Brand throughout.)

Having got onto the road for Brand, simply follow it. This is a beautiful road rising gently to 1,037 m at Brand, leading through deep dark woods and high pastures, first to **BÜRS** (from where a footpath leads through the Bürs Gorge) with **BÜRSERBERG** up high on the right, reaching Brand after 10 km.

BRAND (pop: 650), at an altitude of 1,037 m, is scattered along the river Alvier. A typical alpine village framed by high mountains it is prettier than most, because although there are plenty of new buildings, mostly guest houses and hotels, these are so completely covered by cascades of flowers that one can barely see them. (In winter soft clouds of snow greatly help too.) Brand gives the impression of being 'at the end of the world' — that the road leads thus far and no further and that from now on there will be only high mountains for company (and not a bad thing at that!). In fact though the road does lead farther: another 6 km or so up to the station from which a cable car climbs to 1,979 m and the Lünersee — and then farther up still, if you would like to put on your mountain boots!

There are some excellent hotels in Brand of which the **Scesaplana** (05559 221) is the grandest, very comfortable and not too expensive. **Hotel Valschena** (05559 331 and 332) is more modest but excellent value. And there are masses more on which the Tourist Office (05559 555) will gladly advise.

2 TIROL

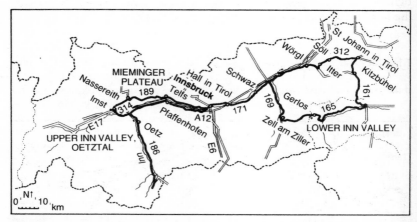

The red eagle, heraldic figure of Tirol, was first adopted as insignia by the Counts of Vintschgau in the twelfth-century when they had completed building Burg Tirol near Merano, thereafter calling themselves Counts of Tirol. In the fourteenth century one of their descendants, Margarethe Margravine of Tirol (perhaps better known as Margarethe Maultasch, the 'ugly duchess'), bequeathed Tirol to the Habsburgs. The capital transferred to Innsbruck and, later on, Emperor Maximilian ruled the Holy Roman Empire from there, calling Tirol 'des Reiches Schatzkästlein' (the Empire's treasure chest). It has stayed fiercely loyal to Austria at all times. When Tirol was ceded to Bavaria in the Peace Treaty of Pressburg in 1805 the Tiroleans, led by Andreas Hofer from the Passeier valley in the south, three times defeated Napoleonic and Bavarian troops (they lost the fourth battle and Hofer was executed at Mantua); the Andreas Hofer hymn is still the National Anthem of Tirol.

Tirol was returned to Austria at the Congress of Vienna and Austrian it remained, until after the First World War when the entire country south of the Brenner Pass—some 15,000 km²—was ceded to Italy. Thus there are now three 'Tirols': the province Tirol in Austria, stretching from the Arlberg in the west to the borders of Salzburg in the east and south to the Brenner; an area called Osttirol—officially part of the province of Tirol, but situated south-east of Salzburg (if you want to reach it from Tirol you have to cross into Salzburg first or go via Italy); and South Tirol in Italy where it is called Südtirol.

The routes suggested are concerned only with Austrian Tirol, probably the country's most popular 'tourist' region. Surprisingly, it is also the least-populated province in Austria—and a quarter of the inhabitants live in its capital Innsbruck. Breathtaking scenery and Baroque churches, pretty villages and medieval towns—and quite spectacular brass bands: 'Tirol has more Kapellmeister (band leaders) than Bürgermeister (mayors)' a TV commentator said as yet another splendid band in regional costume—leather breeches and hats with sweeping feathers this time, for they all differ slightly—appeared on the screen. Of course he was right—a town can only have one Bürgermeister, but there's no limit to the number of brass bands!

Upper Inn Valley and Oetztal

3 days/about 240 km/from Innsbruck

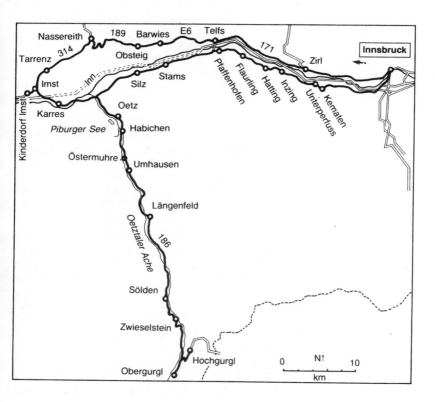

A very rural route this, following the Inn river where the rockface practically comes down to meet the road, then branching off, not to fashionable Seefeld, but to the Mieminger Plateau with its rich meadows and tiny hamlets framed by high mountains. From there the route sweeps through deep forests to ancient Imst and then leads to the Oetztal—50 km of magnificent scenery—the road closely following the river, rising to an altitude of 1.927 m at Obergurgl, the highest church parish in Austria. The return journey on the south bank of the Inn leads to the Cistercian monastery Stams and through small, completely unspoiled villages back to Innsbruck.

INNSBRUCK (pop: 117,000) is the capital, of the Tirol and the most beautiful town in the Alps. There is a slight touch of Ruritania about Innsbruck—not surprising when you remember that it was the residence of sovereign princes who could certainly be called 'colourful'. Friedrich, fondly called 'Friedl mit der leeren Tasche' (with the empty purse) who for centuries was believed to have built Innsbruck's famous 'Golden Roof' (made in fact of gilded copper) just to show that his pockets were not that empty! His son Sigmund 'of the many coins' (how quickly family fortunes can change—particularly with the discovery of a silver mine or two!) was succeeded by none other than the Emperor Maximilian I, dubbed 'the last knight' who ruled his great empire from Innsbruck. When at the end of his life he returned to Innsbruck after a meeting at Augsburg, he found that the local innkeepers would not put up his suite because of the unpaid bills he had left behind. Deeply offended he went on to Wels where he died; he was buried at Wiener Neustadt. His grandiose tomb at Innsbruck is empty, but the 28 statues which he commissioned are there for all to admire: enormous figures in bronze (some designed by Albrecht Dürer) including England's King Arthur and of course Maximilian's entire family.

Innsbruck ceased to be an Imperial residence in 1665, but the Habsburgs still guarded it with a benevolent eye: Leopold I founded Innsbruck University in 1669 and the Empress Maria Theresia rebuilt the Imperial residence. Tirolean freedom fighters in 1809 fought three times victoriously against Napoleon's troops from nearby Bergisel and when the American Army reached Innsbruck at the end of the Second World War, they found that Innsbruck had already managed to liberate itself from the Germans!

Innsbruck is best explored on foot—most of the old part is a pedestrian zone—but there are also guided tours by bus lasting one or two hours, leaving from the Imperial Palace and Bozner Platz respectively. Tourist Office: Burggraben 3, 05222 760500. Make a point of seeing the sixteenth-century Hofkirche with Maximilian's empty tomb and bronze statues, also 'Silver Chapel'; Wilten Basilica—the most beautiful rococo church in the Tirol; Wilten Deanery Church; Imperial Palace; Schloss Ambras (outside town, but well worth the excursion); Gothic town hall with tower; eighteenth-century Landhaus—Baroque palace; Goldenes Dachl (the famous 'golden roof'); seventeenth-century Mariahilfkirche—

Cenotaph of Emperor Maximilian I at the Hofkirche, Innsbruck

and much, much more besides. **Goldener Adler**, Herzog Friedrich-strasse 6 (05222 26334) is not only a fine old building, but a historic hostelry ('everybody' stayed there including Goethe on his way to Italy). **Hotel Europa** (05222 35571) is the best hotel in Innsbruck and their **Philippine Welser Restaurant** is certainly excellent. **Hotel Central** (05222 24886) is a particularly pleasant hotel with rooftop swimming-pool and a good old-fashioned 'Viennese' coffee house. **Grauer Bär** (512 5924) is another sturdy, typically Tirolean hotel with good restaurant. **Hotel Maximilian** (05222 37577—open December to October) a family hotel, family-run. **Weinhaus Jörgele** (05222 571155) is just the place for a comforting meal after exploring the old town.

Leave Innsbruck on 171, direction west, mostly signposted Arlberg, past airport and Kranebitten. The road runs along the river and at one point there seems barely enough room for it to squeeze through, where the steep mountain face reaches right down. This is the Martinswand where Emperor Maximilian I was trapped whilst hunting chamois and—according to legend—guided back to safety by angels (or, according to a less popular legend, hoisted by some sort of crane/ropes!) To commemorate this event, there is a plaque on the roadside and also the Kaisergrotte up high; the ascent is very steep, but rewarding with magnificent views across the Inn Valley (very impressive also viewed from below, particularly from certain points on the return journey of this route). Schloss Martinsbühel between the river and Martinswand was built almost on the spot of the Roman Teriolis (remains of old Roman walls still in existence) probably around 1290, but enlarged and transformed into a hunting lodge by Maximilian I. (St Martin's Chapel built around 1500 on foundations of Roman church).

Continue to **ZIRL**—thirteenth-century fortress ruins Fragenstein high above village, which has the only vineyard in the Tirol (all the others are in South Tirol which is now in Italy) and you can sample the wine at the

Zirler Weinhof on the main road, just before coming into Zirl. Stay on 171 (do not stray onto road for Seefeld or the autobahn which after Zirl runs parallel to river and 171 to **TELFS** with its many painted and richly-decorated houses. (Dürer painted Telfs from high above Mösern, known as the 'swallow's nest'.) Every five years Telfs celebrates carnival with the Schleicherlaufen, a masked dance procession (some of the ancient masks can be seen at the local museum).

In Telfs main street (still on 171) turn right onto E6 (189) signposted to Mieming and Obsteig, and drive as far as Barwies where turn right, following signs for Hotel Römisch Deutscher Kaiser which leads on to the **Mieminger Plateau**—a series of hamlets dotted about deep lush meadows with a marvellous backdrop of high mountains. With a particularly mild climate—a sun trap of the first order—it is a paradise for walkers. **Hotel Römisch Deutscher Kaiser** (05264 5668) is marvellously situated, very comfortable, with a large indoor swimming pool (an outdoor pool belongs to the village, but practically adjoins the hotel) and is not expensive for what is offered.

Double back to E6 (189). On the right going back there is the **Hotel Schwimmbad** which is simpler, but still very comfortable: the last time I was there it had a Sunday morning Frühschoppen (very jolly singing with beer mugs being lifted in time with the music) still going in full swing at 1 pm on a fine September day—and delicious smells wafting over from the kitchen.

Continue westwards on E6 (189), direction Nassereith (romantically poised Burg Klamm near Frohnhausen was originally thirteenth-century, but has been heavily restored and rebuilt) to **OBSTEIG**, a sprawling little village with nice inns and a large hotel complex called **Tyrolhotel** (05264 8181) set a little aside from the road.

The road rises through tiny hamlets and deep dark woods—an altogether lovely journey—to come down again at the outskirts of Nassereith where turn left onto 314 for Imst. Drive through **TARRENZ** (fortress ruins Altstarkenberg and also Burg Neustarkenberg, now a brewery) and at fork turn right for Imst.

IMST (pop: 7,000), butterfly-shaped and built against a hill so that

Mieminger Plateau

30

in parts it rises to an altitude of nearly 1,000 m, has often been called the 'Merano of the North Tirol' because of its gentle climate. Mentioned as far back as the eighth century, it reached the peak of its prosperity from the fifteenth to the seventeenth century, due to the nearby mines (silver, copper and lead). Between the seventeenth and nineteenth century Imst was also the home of the famous 'Birdsellers' who were trading as far afield as Russia and Spain and even had their own depot in London. (Rather charmingly described in a novel and—more generally known— an operetta by Zeller, where birdseller Adam sings about making gifts of roses in the Tirol and the romantic implications thereof). Every three to four years Imst has its 'Schemenlaufen' (similar to the Schleicherlaufen in Telfs) with old masks which can be seen at the local museum. See: the fifteenth-century parish church Maria Himmelfahrt (fifteenth to eighteenth-century frescoes; St Michael's Chapel, fifteenth century; calvary hill church St Lorenz; numerous decorative fountains and lots of beautiful old houses. Tourist Office: Johannesplatz 6 (05412 2419) **Hotel Post** (05412 2554), formerly Schloss Sprengenstein and a hostellerie since 1637, is a Romantik hotel. 'Z' Imscht in der Poscht da gibt's a guate Koscht' they say in the Tirol—meaning that you will fare well at the Post.

The first ever SOS Kinderdorf was built at Imst in 1948 at the instigation of Hermann Gmeiner. Anyone can visit the village—in fact visitors are welcome (at the end of Imst take right fork for Arlbergpass and Landeck and then right again at next fork for Landeck, then right for Gunglgrün and SOS Kinderdorf). The village is lovely and peaceful, the original 'mothers', having been elevated to grandmothers, still live in the village, the trees planted in 1948 are sturdy and strong and (in season) laden with fruit. There are now hundreds of similar childrens' villages throughout the world—living proof of how much one man's faith can achieve. (Near SOS Kinderdorf—at Gunglgrün—there is also the pretty rococo chapel of Maria Schnee—worth seeing if you are there.)

Retrace your steps from SOS Kinderdorf to the bottom of the hill, then turn left, direction Imst and 171. Keep on 171 (having reached it), following direction Garmisch and Innsbruck (ignore pointers to Reutte and Fernpass, and also ignore the fork to Pitztal) after which signs varyingly say Innsbruck and Oetztal (or both) until you come to the fork for 186 and Oetztal on the right, after which fork left onto 186 signposted Oetztal, Meran and Timmelsjoch.

The Oetztal is about 50 km long and called the valley of the 'six steps' because it rises in six well-defined plateaux. The first one is still lush meadows, maize fields and sweet chestnut trees with one of the warmer bathing lakes—the Piburger See—well sheltered by trees on the right after Sautens (follow directions). **OETZ** (pop: 2000)—and there will forever be a dispute as to whether it should be spelled Oetz or Ötz—has been a popular resort since the late nineteenth century, a typical Tirolean village with its attractive painted houses like **Gasthof Stern** (05252 6323), its parish church perched on a rock high above the village (Gothic altar, charnel house in tower) and St Michael's Chapel (beautiful

Baroque altar). There are lovely walks in the neighbourhood and the chair-lift to Ober-Oetz greatly adds to the attraction.

Continue on 186 (there are imposing waterfalls in an adjacent gorge) through **HABICHEN** (seventeenth-century Grassmayrhaus with painted facade), to **UMHAUSEN** (altitude 1016 m), the oldest village in the valley—and the largest waterfalls in the Tirol, with a pleasant walk through the woods to get there. See its fifteenth-century parish church St Vitus; its eighteenth-century parsonage with painted facade; and the octagonal St Johannes Chapel with ceiling fresco.

The road now closely hugs the Oetztaler Ache all the way to **LÄNG-ENFELD** (an interesting museum is housed in an old farmhouse at Lehn on the way) which divides into 'Unter' (Lower) and 'Ober' (Upper) Längenfeld. Their combined population totals 3,000, making it the largest village in the valley. Längenfeld is also the centre of the Oetztal and—as if to mark the point—it has the church with the highest steeple. (Look also at the little Schneiderkapelle at Unterlängenfeld which expands into an adjoining farmhouse.)

Rocks get steeper, and tall mountains closer, as the road rises to 1,377 m at **SOLDEN**, a popular ski-ing and summer resort and known as the widest-spread community in Austria, stretching over 4,68 km² right up to Obergurgl and Vent on the other side. Sölden is 'tops' in many respects: start of the highest glacier road in Europe—the Oetztaler Gletscherstrasse—and the highest cable car (up to the 3,058 m high Gaislachkogel). And the Wildspitze—Tirol's highest mountain at 3,768 m—is also close on the right.

Still on 186 drive on to **ZWIESELSTEIN** (parish church with early

Baroque altar), from where a road branches off to the right to **VENT**. When Duke Friedrich was declared an outlaw in 1415, he fled to the so-called 'Rofenhöfe', farmhouses high up in the mountains near Vent. The farmers hid him and when the citizens of the Tirol refused to accept the new prince (Friedrich's brother), Friedrich reassumed sovereignty, removed his residence from Merano to Innsbruck and built himself a new castle there. To 'his' farmers near Vent he promised that they would live without paying any taxes whatsoever—forever. Surprisingly, 'forever' did last until 1850!

Continue on 186. The road rises 15 per cent to **UNTER-GURGL** and thence to **OBER-GURGL** which, at 1,927 m, is the

Church in Vent

highest church parish in Austria. Its church was built in 1726 in place of a previous chapel, enlarged in 1924 and again in 1967 (by Clemens Holzmeister). Obergurgl had its 'sensation' on 27 May 1931 when Professor Auguste Piccard, having ascended to 15,781m in a balloon, made a surprise landing on the Gurgl glacier. (Most appropriate, everybody at Obergurgl agreed—where else to drop in from the skies but the highest church parish?)

This is the end of the road—time to relax, count the glaciers if you like and perhaps stay at one of the excellent hotels like the friendly **Bellevue** (05256 228) or the traditional **Edelweiss und Gurgl** (05256 223) before starting on the return journey. After leaving Obergurgl you might care to turn right after about 3 km for **HOCHGURGL**—only 4 km away at an altitude of 2,145 m—for another lovely view of the Oetztal and the glaciers. There is a magnificently sited hotel called simply **Hochgurgl** (05256 266) which is like a self-contained fortress with all modern amenities. (From there the road leads via Timmelsjoch into Italy—the border is a mere 11 km away).

Return to 186 and retrace your steps down the Oetztal—it will of course look quite different as you 'step down' from bare mountains into lush pastures once more (you might also care to stop at Oetz at cosy **Konditorei Heiner**). At the 'end' of 186 follow signs for Innsbruck and Telfs which brings you onto 171.

Drive, direction Innsbruck/Telfs, through holiday village Silz—passing Schloss Petersberg on a hill, surrounded by Linden trees and further along the road you will see the pilgrimage church Maria Hilf (on a hill north of the river, near Mötz). It was built around 1900, and looks rather endearing from below.

Still on 171 (which calls itself E17 a little further on) you come to **STAMS** Monastery (follow signs 'Zum Stift') which alone warrants a journey to the Tirol. A guided visit is advisable, for details which you might otherwise miss (like the delicate 'rose trellis'), but will also take you to the Bernardisaal where concerts are held during the summer months (and gives details of performances). Whilst at Stams see also the fifteenth-century St Johann parish church, a little way up the hill, with an outstandingly beautiful Baroque interior.

From Stams take 171 to **RIETZ** with its interesting late-Gothic parish church St Valentin (Gothic frescoes on church wall with tombstone of one Hans Reindl and his wife, 'Oberjägermeister' to Emperor Maximilian I, dated 1522) and from there until the beginning of **PFAFFENHOFEN** (parish-church built 1414 on sixth-century foundations, also fortress ruins—thirteenth-century Burgruine Hörtenberg—with keep and observatory tower) taking the road signposted Pfaffenhofen and Kematen. This leads through a number of charming villages which are not at all touristy.

First there is **FLAURLING** with Riseneck (also known as Risgebäude), a former hunting lodge of Archduke Sigmund and later turned into a parsonage with chapel added (Gothic altar), also Gasthof Goldener Adler with Baroque facade painting. Continue driving on this country road (after Flaurling there is a particularly good view of the

Martinswand) through **HATTING** and **INZING**. The former is a particularly pretty village with typical farmhouses, fifteenth-century parish church (completely preserved Gothic wall paintings in choir). Go past Unterperfuss towards **KEMATEN**, with more splendid views of the Martinswand. Just before Kematen follow directions for Innsbruck and Kematen (cross straight over). In Kematen there's a fourteenth-century church with remains of Gothic frescoes and Baroque Madonna, and a Gothic corn market. Turn left for Innsbruck.

Continue on this road, direction Innsbruck, then follow signs for Innsbruck west. Confusingly the final sign just outside Innsbruck says 'Arlberg Brenner'—nothing else—but leads into Innsbruck (provided you watch out and do not go too far).

Lower Inn Valley and Gerlosplatte

3-4 days/about 280 km/from Innsbruck

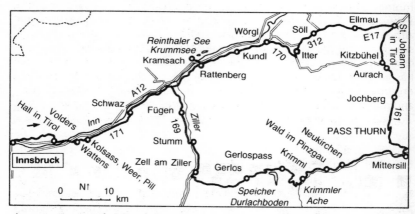

A journey into the Tirol's past—to the ancient towns Hall and Schwaz, then through that most typical of all Tirolean valleys, the Zillertal—right into the present on the splendid modern roads via the Gerlos Pass and Pass Thurn—and a brief excursion into the province of Salzburg. Return via Kitzbühel and St Johann—and a few far lesser known places, including medieval Rattenberg and the lakes near Kramsach.

Leave **INNSBRUCK** (see Upper Inn Valley and Oetztal route for details) on 171, direction east for Hall in Tirol. The road leads through or partly skirts what are known as the 'Martha' villages—Mühlau, Arzl, Rum Thaur and Absam—their initials spelling out the name Martha. Near Arzl the Innsbrucker Küchenschelle (also known as Easter Bluebell) grows in profusion, whilst around Thaur you will find a special kind of primrose—both heavily protected! **THAUR** was the first village in the Inn Valley to be mentioned in chronicles (as Turane in 827) and there have also been Bronze Age finds. A number of interesting churches—St

Ulrich (Romanesque, rebuilt 1612, later additions) and little Romedi-kirchl on a hill north of Thaur (with fortress ruins nearby, reputed birth-place of St Romedius). At **ABSAM** there is one of the most popular pilgrimage churches in the Tirol (late-Gothic, rococo and later additions; right side altar with Gothic fresco). For a closer look at all these, turn left at Rum: the road leads through Thaur and Absam straight to Hall in Tirol. Otherwise stay on 171.

HALL IN TIROL (pop: 13,000), not to be confused with Hall in Upper Austria, grew rich on shipping and the local salt mines (first mentioned in 1244, but closed in 1967) and prosperity increased even further when the Mint was transferred from Merano to Hall, possibly because of the silver mines at nearby Schwaz. The first coins were struck in Sparberegg Castle in 1477, to the delight of Duke Sigmund, called 'der Münzreiche' (the one rich in coins). He loved to be feted by the popu-lation, throwing handfuls of coins to the poor—though in later years his pleasure consisted in merely running his hands through bowls full of gold and silver. The Taler—forerunner of the dollar—takes its name from the Inntal and it will be pointed out to you that the first dollar was struck in 1486 in Hall. The Mint was later transferred to Burg Hasegg and although it ceased as an official mint in 1809, you can still have a medal struck in the old way at the 'Alten Münze'. Hall's present prosperity comes from other sources, but the old, mostly medieval, part of the town has been preserved *en bloc* and is easily (and most pleasurably) explored on foot. Tourist Office: Wallpachgasse 5 (05223 6269) in the old town and a first call there (even to arrange a guided tour) could prove helpful. To see: parish church St Nicholas (late-Gothic 'Hallenkirche', baro-

Hall in Tirol

quised); Allerheiligenkirche (formerly Jesuitenkirche, seventeenth-century); fifteenth-century Salvatorkirche; Damenstift (convent) with Stiftskirche and Sommerhaus (one of the most beautiful Baroque interiors); Nagglburg; town hall; Geisterburg (former arsenal, now an inn); Burg Hasegg with Münzertor—and much, much more besides.

Return to 171 and continue eastwards, crossing the Inn just before **VOLDERS**. Karlskirche (Servite monastery church) immediately on the right after crossing the bridge, has a rather exotic, almost Eastern appearance. Built in the seventeenth century, it has a rococo interior (with a fine central fresco). The story is told that during its construction a huge piece of rock got loose and was about to crash down, killing farmers working beneath, when one of the workmen cried out 'Stop—for God's sake!' which it promptly did, staying suspended until the men had fled to safety. The stone can still be seen in the church. Also at Volders: Burg Friedberg with keep, built thirteenth century, present form around 1500, good frescoes; Schloss Aschach; and some attractive old houses on the main road.

Still on 171 you come to **WATTENS**, completely dominated by the huge Swarowski works (there is also a large paper mill). It's worth a stop though for a visit to **Kristall**, Innstrasse 1 (05224 3086—open also on Sundays during summer and at times astonishingly crowded) where you can not only buy glass and porcelain, but watch glass cutting and blowing and, especially interesting, cutting of precious stones (on first floor). Also at Wattens: swimming pool with 'underwater' coffee house.

Continue on 171 past **KOLSASS** (parish church with Gothic apsis and frescoes) through **WEER** (parish church St Gallus with stunning Baroque interior) and **PILL** (pretty pilgrimage church Heiligenkreuz on roadside where road joins river) to Schwaz.

SCHWAZ (pop. 11,000) has sometimes been called 'the mother of all mines' which is perhaps overstating the case. Silver and copper have certainly been mined there since 1420 and whilst reports as to the quantities extracted vary, they were evidently considerable; enough, for example, to finance the election campaigns of future emperors Maximilian I and Charles V. In 1500 Schwaz was by far the largest settlement in the Tirol. It was rich, extremely well-run (with a free health service for the miners!) and immensely cultured. Fine churches and beautiful houses were built, most of which still stand today. Following a visit of Hans Sachs a school for Mastersingers was established; in 1515 Paracelsus visited Schwaz and was initiated into the art of smelting; in the ducal residence of Sigmundslust (there are quite a few of these around the Tirol—Sigmundsfreud, Sigmundberg and so on—all named after the Sigmund who was 'rich in coins') the first Tirolean printing press was established. Emperor Maximilian I wanted Schwaz to achieve city status (granted only in 1899), but the rich town fathers declined. They feared, or so they said, for their spacious municipal gardens; more likely, they were worried about the cost of fortifications! At the end of the sixteenth century the mining industry began to decline and the mines were finally exhausted by 1780. Schwaz fell on hard times, suffering greatly during the Napoleonic Wars and again at the end of the Second World War, but today it is a flourishing town once more. A little more austere than Hall, and the treasures of her shining past have to be searched out, but it is well worth the effort. Among the most notable 'sights' in Schwaz is the parish church. It is the largest Gothic Hallenkirche in Tirol, roofed entirely in copper, with 15,000 tiles. In 1490 it was enlarged so that really two churches were constructed under a single roof: one for the miners, the other one for the burghers, with a wooden wall between. Then it was baroquised and the partition was removed. Other things to see in Schwaz: Franciscan monastery and church; Schloss Freundsberg; Fugger Haus; town hall and much more besides. Tourist Office: Franz Josefstrasse 26 (05242 3240). **Lendbräu**, Innsbrucker Strasse 39 (05242 38392) is a very good restaurant with a friendly host, serving local as well as other specialities at reasonable prices.

Back on 171, past Buch and Rotholz (and imposing Schloss Rotholz), follow signs for 171 to Salzburg and then take right fork signposted Gerlos 165 which brings you onto the 169 for Zillertal.

The Zillertal has often been called the most typical of all Tirolean valleys, known as much for its beauty as it is for its happy atmosphere, its garnets—and its musicians. The Rainer singers were well known not only throughout Europe, but also in America which they toured frequently during the last century. They sang 'Auf der Alm da gibts koa Sünd' (translating it swiftly to 'On the Alp no sin is found') for Queen Victoria in London and when presented to the Emperor Franz Josef whose greeting was 'Grüss Dich Gott, Rainer', Rainer simply replied 'Grüss Dich Gott, Kaiser.' The Rainer singers were the first to start spreading the fame of 'Silent Night' throughout the world (local Karl Mauracher had gone to repair the church organ at Oberndorf where it was written and first performed and brought back the song to the Zillertal). They sang it for Tsar Alexander and Franz I of Austria in 1822, at Schloss Fügen in the pretty village of the same name. **FÜGEN** is a very pleasant spot, never overcrowded as tend to be some of the more popular places in the Zillertal and the church is probably the most important Gothic church in the valley.

A narrow gauge (760 mm) railway runs from Jenbach to Mayrhofen, the whole length of the Zillertal, and is much favoured by railway buffs. Stay on 169 for an equally leisurely view of the valley by road, driving along the Ziller river, past Kaltenbach and Stumm (typical sixteenth-century castle) to **ZELL AM ZILLER**. In 1650 a gram of pure gold was found near Zell, after which a sort of gold rush set in. It lasted long enough for the gold hunters to build a pilgrimage church in 1658 at Hainzenberg. Zell is enchanting, a typical Tirolean village complete with solidly-rounded pink village church (a favourite for weddings) and thick-walled, cosy inn **Zum Bräu** (0528 2313) in the main square. Good food, charming rooms and moderate prices. As the name implies, they have their own brewery, which is very important on the first Sunday in May when Zell celebrates the Gauderfest, a 400 year old custom with special parades and special beer called 'Gauderbier'.

From Zell follow 165 marked Gerlos and Gerlos Pass. The road is a little bumpy at first (when I was last there, local residents were literally sweeping it with a broom!), but soon improves. The road climbs gently, and very prettily, through **HAINZENBERG** (where seventeenth- and eighteenth-century gold prospectors built a pilgrimage church) high above Zell, at the beginning of the Gerlos valley. Signposts suddenly only state Mittersill, which is perfectly in order as long as you realise that this is where you are ultimately going, and the view gets lovelier every minute. **GERLOS** (altitude 1245 m) is a good holiday spot for anyone keen on walking tours (possibilities are endless) and almost anywhere on this route would be ideal for a picnic, the best placed probably being near the top—like the Durlassboden (altitude 1376m) with magnificent views of the Wildgerlostal and lake below. The top of the Gerlospass (altitude 1507 m) marks the border between Tirol and Salzburg and here the road forks. Take the right fork, signposted Mittersill 38 km and Krimmler Wasserfälle (leaving 165 to the left which is signposted roughly the same—Mittersill 33 km). The road to the right is the splendid Gerlospass road for which a toll has to be paid. It's well worth it, as you will come to appreciate when you descend in elegant sweeps towards **KRIMML** and its famous water-falls. Claimed to be the largest waterfalls in Europe, they cascade down some 400 m and are certainly impressive. You can admire them at a comfortable distance from an observation platform to the right on the road down. For a really close look, follow directions in Krimml.

You are of course in the province of Salzburg now, rejoining 165 at **WALD IM PINZGAU** where **Walderwirt und Märzenhof** (06565 8216) provide the best of both worlds: a sturdy old inn with good food on one side of the road and, connected by underground passage, a modern hotel on the other side. It is reasonably priced. Schlosshotel **Jagdschloss Graf Recke** (06565 6417—follow signs from road. Closed 20 March to 20 May and 2 October to 19 December) is more secluded, more exclu-sive, and more expensive (but still reasonable).

Follow directions for Mittersill on 165 through pleasant little villages such as **ROSENTHAL** (fourteenth-century fortress ruins Hieburg high up on left, twelfth-century Friedburg ditto on right), **NEUKIRCHEN** (sixteenth-century castle, now retirement home), Bramberg, Mühlbach, and Hollersbach. The real attraction is not the villages though, pretty as they are, but the mountains: the Kitzbühler Alpen on the left, and on the right the Hohe Tauern with Austria's shiniest, glossiest and highest (3,797 m) glacier, the Grossglockner. Not that the Grossvenediger—practically opposite Neukirchen—is any less impressive!

MITTERSILL (pop: 5,000) lies on the route to practically every-where—to East Tirol (via the Felber Tunnel), to Kitzbühel and of course to the start of the gigantic Grossglockner road. **Schloss Mittersill** (06562 4523—open December to October) built in the twelfth century, severely damaged by fires and rebuilt several times, is now a hotel. The chapel in 'Hexenturm' (witches tower) at the castle is well worth a look.

Take 161 out of Mittersill, marked Kitzbühel and Innsbruck. This is another splendid road leading across a mountain pass—the Pass Thurn (no toll this time though)—with wonderful views on the way. At almost the highest point (1,230m) there is an excellent restaurant, the **Tannenhof** (06562 8385) where everything is home-made, even the bread. A good shop sells fierce mountain spirit below the restaurant and almost next door (same owners) there's a good, moderately priced pension, the **Tauernblick** (06562 8380).

At the top of Pass Thurn is the border, after which you are back in the Tirol once again. Continue on 161 through **JOCHBERG**, where the local swimming pool contains health-giving moor (a suspension of mud in water) and **AURACH** (fifteenth-century parish church with baroque 'hat') to **KITZBÜHEL** (pop: 8000). Well-known (one might almost say too well-known) as a winter sports centre, it is in fact a charming summer resort too (romantic, moor-containing Schwarzsee is nearby) and a delightful old town when most of the visitors have gone. Many of its buildings date back to the sixteenth century when Kitzbühel was a prosperous mining town. There's plenty to see: fifteenth-century parish church St Andreas (beautiful high altar by local sculptor Benedikt Faistenberger, 663) with Rosa Chapel (rococo stucco and ceiling painted by a later Faistenberger); fourteenth-century Liebfrauenkirche (baroquised with frescoes by the later Faistenberger, beautiful Baroque altar); fourteenth-century St Katharina; buildings in Vorderstadt and Hinterstadt (road in centre of town) and much more besides. The sixteenth-century **Schloss Lebenberg** (05356 4301) and fifteenth-century **Schloss Münichau** (05356 2962—at Reith, about 1km from Schwarzsee) are both luxurious Schlosshotels hotels as is the **Tennerhof** (05356 3181) which is also a Romantik hotel. **Sporthotel Reisch** (05356 33660) is a good, comfortable family hotel. **Unterberger Stuben** (05356 2101), a Relais Gourmand, counts as one of the best restaurants in the Tirol (priced accordingly). Tourist Office: Hinterstadt 18 (05356 2272 and 2155).

Still on 161, drive through the peaceful holiday village **OBERNDORF**, splashed against the Wilde Kaiser mountain (eighteenth-century parish church—altar and ceiling frescoes by the Faistenbergers) to **ST JOHANN IN TIROL** (pop: 7,000). This is a charming resort with many painted house facades—if one could but see them for the many visitors! St Johann certainly attracts the crowds during the season and inevitably new buildings have been added, dwarfing the old ones—like the **Goldener Löwe** (05352 2251) a good family inn which is overshadowed by the rather grand (and admittedly very comfortable) new building of the same name. Imposing Baroque church Maria Himmelfahrt (where yet another Faistenberger—Georg this time—joined the family team).

Leave St Johann, taking direction Wörgl on E17 (312 later on), also signposted Innsbruck, Kufstein. Just outside St Johann, right on the road, you will find the Spitalskirche in der Weitau (see fifteenth-century glass painting in presbytery). Farther along E17 you come to **GOING**, another picturesque Tirolean village silhouetted against the Wilde Kaiser, with its onion-domed Baroque church; and farther on to **ELLMAU**. All these are much-favoured and much-frequented holiday resorts, each with a faithful clientele who book not only in the same place, but the same room in the same hotel every year. Ellmau not only has the almost obligatory Baroque church and nice old farmhouses, but also very superior **Hotel Der Bär** (05358 2395, closed 2 November to 18 December and 9 April to 20 April) with excellent food, accommodation and service. Not exactly cheap, but prices are certainly appropriate. Relais et Chateaux.

Continuing on 312 which by-passes **SÖLL** (eighteenth-century parish church with imposing interior; Baroque houses) to Mühltal where turn left for **ITTER** which has one of the prettiest unspoilt village centres in the Tirol. Schloss Itter, guarding the village from the west, was largely rebuilt in the nineteenth century and was until recently a very luxurious hotel (hopefully it will be again).

Leave Itter in the direction of Hopfgarten which will bring you onto 170 where turn right, direction Innsbruck. This road by-passes Wörgl and joins 171 just outside the town. Continue on 171, direction Innsbruck, to **KUNDL** where the sixteenth-century Gasthof Post and eighteen-century Auerwirt have particularly attractive painted facades. Here too is a Baroque parish church (frescoes by Simon Benedict Faistenberger), and Kundlburg Fortress ruins perched on top of craggy rock. 'Perchtenlaufen' during Advent is a Kundl speciality: a procession with historic (some horrendous) masks. The real treasure of Kundl however is a little farther west on 171: the pilgrimage church St Leonhard, also known as 'St

Auerwirt at Kundl

Leonhard auf der Wiese' (in the meadow), one of the most interesting medieval churches in the Tirol. The present building dates from 1481 but according to legend there was an earlier church built by King Henry II who had vowed that he would have a church erected and then promptly forgot to honour the promise. He was then thrown by his horse in precisely the spot where the church now stands, duly remembered his vow and hastily built the church. There is in fact no trace of an earlier building, but it is a nice legend, and the church is certainly worth seeing (note statuary, trellis), as is the traditional 'Leonhardiritt' which takes place every November.

Heading further west on 171 you come to **RATTENBERG**. With a population of under 700, this is the smallest town in the Tirol. A town since 1393, Rattenburg has not changed much since it was prosperous and important in the fifteenth and sixteenth centuries—when the population was about the same. Cradled between the Inn and the fortress hill, Rattenberg looks slightly unreal and were it not for the thousands of visitors (and alas, their cars) passing through it every year, one could well believe oneself to be back in the Middle Ages. See particularly: Hassauerstrasse, Inngasse, Sparkassenplatz (No. 67 reputedly birthplace of St Notburga) Klostergasse and Südtirolerstrasse (Glass Museum at No. 41), also the fifteenth-century parish church, Servitenkirche, with former monastery and Gothic cloister, sixteenth-century Spitalkirche and much more besides. Tourist Office: Klostergasse 94 (05337 3321). Fortress ruins above the town are a grim reminder of the tragedy of Wilhelm Biener, Chancellor of the Tirol in the seventeenth century, who was victim of political intrigue and executed there in 1651 (he has been immortalised in several plays). It is said that his widow, known as the 'Bienerweibl' still haunts the place—and I would not be a bit surprised (anyone passing through Rattenberg at night would readily agree).

After Rattenberg turn right, following directions for Kramsach and A12, and at the junction turn right again for Kramsach Zentrum (do not stray onto A12). **KRAMSACH**, almost opposite Rattenberg, is a sprawling village at the confluence of the Brandenburger Ache and the Inn, and an important centre of glass manufacture since the seventeenth century. Visits to the specialist glassworks school can be arranged (05357 2623 for appointment) and the **Kramsacher Glas Stüberl** is an absolute treasure trove, where almost anything can be made to order (05357 2697—follow directions for Sonnwendjoch Bergbahn). Immediately outside Kramsach there are some pretty lakes (follow signs 'Zu den Seen'), one of them covered with waterlilies. The lakes are surrounded by meadows and forests, a charming scene, and are reputedly the warmest bathing lakes in the Tirol. Also just outside Kramsach there is an open air museum with old Tirolean farmhouses (May to October), including **Rohrerhof Restaurant** with Tirolean specialities.

To return, follow signs for A12 out of Kramsach and then either follow this or directions onto 171 for return to Innsbruck.

3 SALZBURG

Exploring Rural Salzburg

3-4 days/about 230 km/from Salzburg to Zell an See

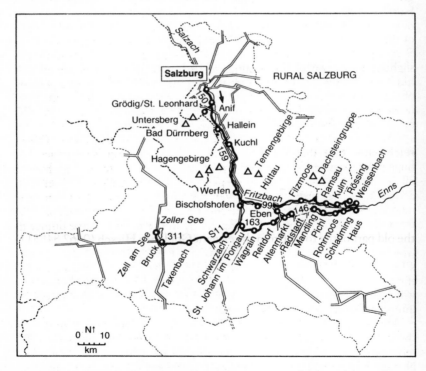

This route leads through four of the five regions which make up the tri-angular-shaped province of Salzburg. It starts from the top at Salzburg in the rather inaptly named Flachgau—the 'flat' region which is in fact studded with high mountains, yet full of warm lakes and highly-scented meadows. The Tennengau due South is slightly different—the name stems from 'Tanne', the fir tree which grows there in profusion. Hallein is the centre of that region where salt, the 'white gold', has been mined for over four thousand years and where stalwart medieval houses remind of a glorious past. Pinzgau, Pongau and Lungau form the base of the triangle. The Grossglockner, Austria's highest mountain, may have its peak firmly set in Carinthia, but it presents its most stunning profile to the province of Salzburg—a fact well taken into consideration when planning this particular route. This has meant leaving out altogether the Lungau, which links—through tunnels—far more naturally with Carinthia in any case, but to make up for this the route includes a brief excursion into Styria and the delightful Alpine pastures of the Ramsau.

SALZBURG (pop: 140,000) 'How everything is so simple in its grandeur' wrote Bettina von Arnim about Salzburg and 'One sees a symphony' said Erich Kästner (alas, known outside Austria mostly for **Emil and the Detectives** and not for the enchanting, but never translated **Der kleine Grenzverkehr** which is as much a slightly unusual guide to Salzburg as it is a declaration of love for that town). If you arrive by road or rail, you may wonder what they—or all those who voted Salzburg one of the most beautiful towns in the world—were talking about, for entering Salzburg from any direction is disappointing and does not give the slightest indication of the beauties to be found. In fact they are all well hidden (arriving at Salzburg by air is different—one gets at least a preview of the beauty to come). There are two 'instant' introductions to Salzburg however which are infallible—one expensive, the other one costing as much as you care to spend.

The first is to book a room facing the river at the **Hotel Oster-reichischer Hof** (0662 75421), preferably on the top floor which has huge plate-glass windows, and get your first view of the town at night with all the most important buildings picked out by floodlights. Then walk across the bridge spanning the river Salzach and explore the town—the magnificent squares like giant ballrooms leading into each other, the spray from the Baroque fountain swaying gently in the breeze—have dinner in the old part of the town (from the elegant **Goldener Hirsch** (0662 848511) which is expensive but excellent, to its realistically priced 'relation' **s'Herzl** (0662 848517/889) next door—the name means 'the little heart' of the Goldener Hirsch). By now Salzburg will have you enthralled—and you will be more than ready for serious sightseeing—such as the Residenz, interior of churches, etc.—in broad daylight!

The second introduction is to take the lift up to the **Cafe Winkler** on the Mönchsberg and view the town from the top. You can sit on the terrace, eat at the restaurant—or simply take a good look at the town. Not quite as dramatic as the first suggestion, but still very impressive and it will certainly leave you wanting to explore further. A visit to the Tourist Office, Auerspergstrasse 7 (0662 80720) should be your next step. They will supply all the necessary information, maps, etc., but there are certain 'musts' which should not be missed on any account: Mirabell Palace (built by Prince Archbishop Wolf Dietrich for Salome Alt—it was originally called 'Altenau', but his successor Marcus Sitticus changed it to Mirabell in honour of another beauty! See particularly the famous 'Angel staircase' by Raphael Donner and the Marble Hall. The latter is a favourite place for weddings and you may notice that one of the putti on the staircase taps his head—some say as a last minute warning before entering the state of matrimony!); Fortress Hohensalzburg (reached on foot or by funicular from Festungsgasse—the largest completely preserved fortress in Europe); Mozart's birthplace with Mozart Museum, also Mozart's residence; Residenz (state rooms decorated under the direction of Lukas von Hilde-brandt, frescoes and paintings by Rottmayr and Altomonte); 'New' Resi-denz—with carillon tower; Salzburg Cathedral (much of the ancient Salzburg was demolished at the direction of Wolf Dietrich to make room for 'his' Renaissance Salzburg, but the original cathedral was partly destroyed by fire—said not to have displeased Wolf Dietrich at all!); Franciscan church with high altar by Fischer von Erlach, containing a Gothic Madonna by Michael Pacher; St Peter's Abbey and Benedictine monastery with tombs of St Rupert and Michael Haydn—and St Peter's Cemetery where the gravestones read like a book of Salzburg's history, and early Christian catacombs (conducted tours). St Peter's Stiftskeller also deserves a visit; Collegiate church by Fischer von Erlach, with altar paintings by Rottmayr; Salzburg's Marionette Theatre (hopefully they will not be on one of their world tours!); Hellbrunn Palace outside town—beautiful early Baroque country palace, famous also for its ornamental gardens and 'trick' fountains, as well as the Stone Theatre—and this is only the beginning!

Not surprisingly, there are many excellent hotels in and around Salzburg and prices are high (and rooms difficult to get) during the princi-pal festival seasons. There are however considerable reductions during the rest of the year, particularly at week-ends. Ask the Tourist Office for special 'package' leaflet. **Bayrischer Hof** (0662 541700) though un-glamorously situated near the railway station, is extremely comfortable and moderately priced (with an excellent restaurant). The new **Rosenberger Hotel Salzburg** (Bessarabierstrasse 94) has all the typically Rosenberger luxuries and attention to detail—at very reasonable prices.

In the old days the restaurant at **Salzburg railway station** was known for its excellent food, and this still holds good today, though it has been swiftly overtaken in popularity by the **Airport restaurant**! There are of course plenty of superb restaurants in Salzburg—**Mirabell** at the **Sheraton Hotel** (0662 793210) being particularly good value for their fixed price lunch—but I wanted to mention the first two for their unusual venue. **Schatz Konditorei** (passage off Getreidegasse 3) and **Ratzka** (Imbergstrasse 45) are two of the best patisseries in Salzburg, but there is much to be said for the cakes and pastries at **Cafe Bazar** (Schwarzstrasse 3) and **Cafe Tomaselli** (Alter Markt 9)—and for the delightful old-world atmosphere.

Leave Salzburg on 150 (direction Hallein and Anif), travelling along the river out of Salzburg. Just before you get to Anif you will find directions for Hellbrunn to the right and if you have not made a special excursion to **Schloss Hellbrunn** from Salzburg, now is your chance—and one that should not be missed! Otherwise continue on 150 to **ANIF** with Schloss Anif on the left, surrounded by water, rather like a giant swan preening itself and admiring its reflection in the lake. Schloss Anif dates back to the sixteenth-century, but was almost completely rebuilt during the last century 'in the English style'. Once the property of the bishops of Chiemsee, it is now privately owned, so you will have to be content with admiring it from afar. You will however be more than welcome at the **Schlosswirt** (06246 2175, closed February) an elegant inn and Romantik hotel (part of the building dates back to the seventeenth-century), but during Festival time the rush of guests can be overwhelming and advance booking is advisable; not exactly cheap, but reasonable for what is being offered. **Friesacher** (06246 2075) is a good, sturdy family hotel with restaurant and particularly pleasant garden.

There is a cable car station at nearby Grödig/St Leonhard (follow directions from Anif) from which you can be whisked up to the top of the gigantic **Untersberg** (1776m) in about ten minutes flat. There you discover glorious views and a fairly remarkable restaurant, the Hochalm— particularly when you consider that everything has to be hauled to the top by cable car! According to legend, Barbarossa—though sometimes it is Charlemagne—sleeps in one of the caves in the Untersberg and when his beard has grown seven times (or is it ten?) round the table, he will awaken, emerge and heaven only knows what will happen! Better continue on 150, which changes number to 159 after Anif (but not direction) to **HALLEIN** (pop: 14,000) where salt has been mined at Dürrnberg above the town since the early Stone Age. Hallein, at one time known as 'little Hall' ('big' Hall being Reichenhall just across the border in Germany), is now mostly looked upon as an industrial town and the charming old part tends to get ignored which is a great pity. A fire in 1943 did much damage, but there is still a lot which deserves attention. The river Salzach runs through the town—divides and meets again, thus forming a small island opposite the ancient part of Hallein which is centred around the Deanery church (rebuilt after the fire with remaining Gothic choir, eighteenth-century altars and statuary—see also Gothic St Peter's Chapel adjoining deanery). Particularly notable: town fortifications with tower and gate; seventeenth-century Salinengebäude (former administrative office for the salt mines which now houses excellent Celtic Museum as well as memorabilia of Franz Gruber, including the original score of 'Silent Night'); medieval houses between deanery church and river, such as the old bath house at Obere Badgasse 1, Schloss Wiespach in North Hallein. There's plenty more to see. Ask at the Tourist Office, Unterer Markt 1 (06245 2546/7).

A road as well as a cable car lead from Hallein up to Dürrnberg—or rather **BAD DÜRRNBERG**—for in place of the Stone Age settlement there is now a modern little spa. Dürrnberg's great attraction however is the very professionally arranged tours down the salt mines which are conducted with great aplomb: you even have your photograph taken when sliding down one of the chutes, and the little salt lake adds to the interest. The mines are open between 1 May and 30 September and during that period there are usually about 150,000 visitors! See also the pilgrimage church built entirely in local marble during the sixteenth and seventeenth centuries; see, too, the sixteenth-century marble fountain.

Continue on 159 to **KUCHL**—one of the very few places marked on the world map of Cartorius (as Cucullae)! It has an interesting late-Gothic parish church with Romanesque portal as well as a Gothic church on Georgenberg which has a marble pulpit on the outside especially for pilgrims.

Farther on 159 you come to **GOLLING**, with its nice solid houses grouped around a medieval castle (now museum). From here the road winds upwards, still mostly along the river, to Pass Lueg. 'Lueg' means as much as 'Look out' and for centuries this was one of the most important guard posts in the land. Largely demolished now, it is still a splendid 'look out' for a fine view of the river gorge between Hagen and Tennengebirge. (The little rococo pilgrimage church, shaped like a four-leafed clover, is known as the 'motorists' chapel'). Continue on 159 (direction Werfen) and although you may be well pleased with the beautiful landscape, the 'unseen' below ground is even more spectacular: about 150 caves, the largest and most gigantic of which are the 47 km-long Giant Ice Caves near Werfen—the largest in the world. (To get there either take the bus from Werfen centre or follow directions to Fallstein and Eisriesenwelt, also from Werfen—it is about 20 minutes walk from the parking area to the cable car station and a short walk to the entrance at the other end. Guided tours every hour from May to October, duration two hours. Stout shoes and warm clothing, please!)

WERFEN (pop: 3,100) is completely overshadowed by the enormous and forbidding fortress Hohenwerfen—fortified over and over again through the centuries and although restorations in the nineteenth-century had a slight softening effect, it still looks what it has been for centuries: a grim and gaunt prison holding some rather important prisoners at times. There are guided tours, but it is one of those romantic fortresses which look far more romantic if viewed from afar! Werfen has some pleasing old buildings, notably the sixteenth-century Brennhof (and probably the simplest Baroque parish church seen anywhere!) as well as one of the best restaurants in Austria, **Lebzelter** (06468 212 and 210, closed from 3 pm Tuesdays and all day Wednesday.) Its prices are remarkably modest in relation to the superb food, though the place is by no means 'undiscovered'. There are a few very pleasant rooms in the same house as well as at the **Erzherzog Johann** (owned by the same family) a few doors farther on. Advance booking advisable.

Continue on 159 from Werfen (direction Bischofshofen) through Imlau, and after about 4 km turn left onto 99 (direction Radstadt via Hüttau), practically following the old Roman road from Juvavum to Aquileia. Continue on 99 (direction Eben) and just before Eben follow directions for Filzmoos (left and left again). There is a sign saying 'Grüss Gott in **Filzmoos**' about 4 km before the actual village—an agreeable holiday resort with magnificient views of the Dachstein mountain which almost make up for some not so attractive (though very comfortable)

Werfen

modern hotel buildings. Stay on this road, direction Ramsau, crossing the border into Styria at Hachau—a stunningly beautiful drive facing the Dachstein—and at times feeling that the road is about to lead straight into the mountain!

RAMSAU is the name of the enormous plateau stretching along for about 16 km of high pastureland which always seems to be streaked with sunshine—as well as the name of a pretty little village (and incidentally the first place in Styria to have a Lutheran church). **Pehab Kirchenwirt** (03687 81732) is a good, moderately-priced country inn right in the centre of the village where all the local celebrations from weddings to wakes take place. **Hotel Peter Rosegger** (03687 81223, closed four weeks after Easter and November) is something else again, set amidst woodlands (turn right before getting to Ramsau, direction Pichl, then follow signposts to left) and exceptional in every way. Its superb cooking is reserved for hotel guests, though light snacks are available to casual visitors and altogether delightful. Owner Fritz Walcher also runs the local climbing school and this greatly adds to the attraction.

From Ramsau follow direction Weissenbach and Vordere Ramsau—you may care to deviate by about 1 km and take the first turning on the right to **KULM** which has a particularly interesting parish church with fifteenth-century statue of St Rupert, part of a Gothic triptych. Continue in direction Weissenbach and after about 4 km you will see a sign to left for 'Lodenwalke' and 'Silberkarklamm'. **Lodenwalke** is almost immediately on the right after that turning—the oldest Loden manufacture in Styria (founded 1434) and a lovely, tranquil spot in which to select real Loden at leisure (and at reasonable prices). There is even a restaurant on the premises (open Monday to Friday).

(This is also the starting point for the romantic Silberkarklamm—about 40 'Styrian' minutes to the Silberkarhutte at 1,250 m, 'Styrian' minutes being slightly longer than ordinary minutes when listed on a waysign, but not as long as 'Tirolean' minutes where the accepted ratio is usually about 1:2!!.)

Return to the main road taking direction Weissenbach along the little Ramsaubach with the clearest of clear waters and through lovely woods. At **WEISSENBACH** turn right (direction Schladming/Haus; the sign is rather hidden) to reach 146, where turn right again for **HAUS IM ENNSTAL** (if you have taken the wrong turning at Weissenbach you will still come to 146, but a little further east). HAUS (pop: 2,300) has gained popularity as a ski-ing resort in recent years (shades of glory from championships held at nearby Schladming) and it is worth taking a left turn off the main road and driving through the village, rejoining 146 at the end—there are some nice old houses in Kirchengasse and Kaibling-gasse, as well as a very good Baroque parish church (paintings by Kremser Schmidt), an early Romanesque crucifix at the Katharinenkapelle in the cemetery, seventeenth-century silo with frescoes and an excellent little museum in one part of the parsonage.

Continue on 146 (direction Schladming) through **OBERHAUS** (good, though partially rebuilt parish church with eighteenth-century 'dragon's' pulpit) to **SCHLADMING**, then follow signs for centre. Schladming (pop: 4,000) now mostly known as a very reasonably priced winter sports resort—and for the excellence of its locally brewed beer—was a rich and important mining town in the Middle Ages. The 'Schladminger Bergbrief' (Mining Law) created in 1408 was exemplary and by the beginning of the sixteenth century about 1,500 men were working in the nearby silver, lead, copper and cobalt mines. Schladming suffered badly during the 1525 Peasant Revolution—the rebels took the town (there is a memorial to this effect in the main square) which was subsequently recaptured and set on fire and when 'peace' reigned once more Schladming lost all privileges, including the town rights. Rebuilding started soon afterwards and market rights were restored in 1530, but town rights had to wait until 1925! There were big fires in practically every century, yet despite all this—or possibly because of it—Schladming is a rather endearing little town, sturdy and solid, appearing much greater than its actual size. The Protestant church is the largest in Styria (altar made up of part of a sixteenth-century triptych). The Catholic church was rebuilt in the sixteenth-century; its tower is late-Romanesque, but the onion dome was added in 1814. Note also the town hall, the former Palais Coburg, built as a hunting lodge in the late nineteenth century. One of Schladming's most appealing buildings is the **Hotel Alte Post** in the main square (03687 225710, closed 26 October to 5 December) a Romantik hotel which has been a hostelry since the seventeenth-century, with splendid cooking and marvellous atmosphere. Moderately priced and everything a good country hotel should be. Tourist Office: Hauptplatz (03687 23310).

Return to 146 (direction Salzburg), passing the famous Schladming Brewery on left and Rohrmooser Schlössl up high. The fortifications over the mining valley, built in the thirteenth century, are now mostly in ruins, but the Schlössl survives as a restaurant with exceptionally good views. The road runs fairly close to the Enns river, past Rohrmoos where some of the old mines can be visited. Unless you particularly want to do this, stay on 146, since Rohrmoos is one of the very few truly *unattractive* places in Austria. Beautifully situated, this is where planning has run riot, with a series of 'modern' hotel buildings, all looking alike, all equally ugly!

Continue on 146 to **PICHL** which consists, more or less, only of the old parish church (rococo interior) and the huge **Pichlmayrgut** set well back from the road (06454 305, open December to October). This large hotel complex is built around the former administrative building for St Peter's in Salzburg. Most of the hotel is as recent as 1978, but there are some relics from the past such as wrought iron window 'cages' and sandstone statuary of the Four Seasons—as well as the room in which Styrian peasants, mostly Protestant at the time, were told of Emperor Josef II's 'Toleranzpatent' in 1782, granting freedom of religion. To return to the present—and Hotel Pichlmayrgut—it is ideal as a resting point whilst touring the country or if you do not want to move at all, since everything is on the spot, and reasonably priced.

Return to the province of Salzburg by continuing on 146 (direction Salzburg), to **MANDLING**. Here a roadstone dated 1677 in the centre of the village reminds of the times when this was a strictly controlled border point between the Bishopric of Salzburg and Austrian Styria! Still on 146, drive towards Radstadt, where just outside the town the road number changes to 99 (note Schloss Mauer, now a brewery, on right). Take care just here because 99 runs to left and right—you want the right fork for Radstadt, then follow directions for Zentrum.

RADSTADT (pop: 4,100) was built on a terrace high above the river to protect the Salzburg Enns Valley and could be considered—at least historically—the exact opposite of Schladming (except for the fires which they seem to have shared with 'centenary' regularity!) Radstadt was unsuccessfully beleaguered during the 1525 Peasant Revolt, and so earned the prefix 'forever faithful' plus a number of other highly-desirable privileges such as the right to trade in wine, iron and salt. Prosperous, medieval and moated just about sums up Radstadt, most of today's prosperity stemming from tourism—Radstadt is immensely popular summer and winter. It's a happy little town, with a splendid farmer's market and lots of local activities like the annual 'dumpling feast' which is celebrated with great aplomb! (More about Radstadt's history at Schloss Lerchen which houses a good local museum).

From Radstadt follow directions for **ALTENMARKT IM PONGAU**, a charming little market town—probably built on the site of the Roman Ani—completely dominated by the Deanery church and famous for the 'beautiful Madonna of Altenmarkt', a fine statue of Mother and Child in the so-called 'soft' style. The 1393 original is mostly 'on tour' however and you can only see a copy (at left side, altar). **Markterwirt** (06452 420, closed 7 November to 8 December and 11 April to 29 April) is also worth a visit, a lovely old inn with comfortable rooms and a good restaurant; likewise **Lebzelter Stub'n** (06452 503), with excellent food and remarkably low-priced set menus.

From Altenmarkt continue (direction Reitdorf) through Reitdorf and at junction turn right into 163 for Wagrain. **WAGRAIN** really is an Austrian mountain village at its beautiful best: wreathed in flowers (Wagrain seems to have won every possible prize for flower decoration), set amidst magnificent scenery, a great parish church with an interestingly slanted nave as well as a charming Baroque church built by Solari (who also built Salzburg Cathedral). Josef Mohr, who wrote the verses for 'Silent Night', is buried in the local churchyard. A very traditional village this, where local festivals are still celebrated with due ceremony—like the 'Linden Fete' in July and lots of others. As one would almost expect of such a place, there are some excellent local inns such as **Grafenwirt** (06413 8230) and the **Tatzlwurm** (06413 8359) both with good accommodation.

Continue on 163 (direction St Johann im Pongau)—a wonderful drive along a deep gorge, crossing and re-crossing the little river and arriving virtually on top of **ST JOHANN IM PONGAU** (pop: 7,800) which looks rather picturesque from this vantage point. Once a typical small Alpine village with a huge church (known as 'Pongau Cathedral'), it is now the principal town of the region. Whether the growth has added to the attraction is a debatable point, but at least the planners have been sensible enough to set aside a separate little holiday village—the Alpendorf—leaving St Johann to bask in comparatively new-found glory of being a proper little town, albeit with some large hotels as well. Probably I am prejudiced, but every time I arrive at the top of the hill and see the little town nestling round the church I expect to find the 'old' St Johann—and then it turns out like a meeting with an old friend who has suddenly grown too rich and too suave! Some of the old traditions still hold—like the Pongauer Perchtenlauf, a procession with some horrendous masks which takes place on the 4 January, though only every fourth year! And nothing can take away the grandeur of the nearby **Liechtensteinklamm**, a magnificent ravine with waterfall—there are small, hanging bridges which make access (comparatively) easy. (Open May to October—about 45 minutes.)

Turn left out of St Johann onto 311 direction Lend. Drive past Schwarzach and Lend (for a short while 311 changes into S11 meaning that it is a 'Schnellbahn'—fast road, in fact here just a much needed widening of an existing road) to **TAXENBACH** where a road branches off to the left for the Rauris Valley. (After about 1 km on that road you would come to the **Kitzlochklamm**—another ravishing gorge, open May

The national costume of St Johann im Pongau

to October. Perhaps not quite as 'grand' as the Liechtensteinklamm, but rather endearing with a small, very local restaurant at the entrance, serving robust local fare.)

Continue on 311 direction Zell am See—try not to stray onto the motorway to Bruck, but follow signs for Zell am See. (If you inadvertently find yourself on the motorway, simply watch out for directions to Zell am See and follow them!)

Here I must plead partiality and admit deliberately planning this route so that it finishes at **ZELL AM SEE** which I consider to be the most beautiful place in Austria—whichever way you look at it. And there are many ways of looking at Zell am See: from the top of the Schmittenhöhe which towers over the little town (to watch the sun rise over the mountains would even warrant the ascent on foot—and there is of course a very efficient cable car to take you up there, plus a very comfortable hotel from which to watch the sunrise) or from the centre of the lake (take one of the small motorised boats and switch off the engine when you have reached the best vantage point). There are even people who prefer to stay at Thumersbach across the lake—all the better to look at Zell am See (in all fairness it should also be said that Thumersbach gets all the afternoon sun which makes for longer hours on the beach). Admittedly there are other—and very beautiful—lakes and small lakeside towns in Austria, but none that can measure up to Zell am See or the mountains that surround it: the craggy cliffs of the Steinerne Meer (the 'stony sea') glowing pink in the setting sun—the Kitzsteinhorn with its seemingly endless glacier—and from the centre of the lake there is also the Grossglockner and the Grossvenediger showing in the background. Some years ago it was pointed out to me that the gentle hill called Honigkogel (the 'honeyed mound') behind Thumersbach is the geographical centre of Europe and this seemed only right: the most beautiful spot marks the centre!

There are of course plenty of places at which to stay (though Zell am See is not nearly as touristy as its beauty would warrant) ranging from good simple Pensionen like **Gudrun** (06542 2369) or the time-honoured **Wilhelmina** (06542 2607) to stately hotels like **Zum Hirschen** (06542 2447) grown from a local village inn, with particularly good food or the elegant **St Georg** (06542 3533) and the excellent **Salzburger Hof** (06542 28280). Zell am See is partly built on a promontory reaching out into the lake with the **Grand Hotel** (06542 2388) at its farthest tip. It was completely rebuilt in recent years, the exterior exactly as it had been before (and looking a bit like an iced wedding cake)—but if you get a room as far out into the lake as possible, it is marvellous and exactly like being on board ship (prices are fairly moderate as some of the apartments are let on a time-share basis).

Zell am See's 'hidden' treasures are numerous—jeweller Kröpfl who makes wondrous things out of mountain crystal and semi-precious stones; a pastry shop with a garden set in a small orchard; a ladies' hairdresser in the outlying district of Schütt where one can relax in reclining chairs and watch the incomparable mountain panorama; and a town hall set in a sixteenth-century castle.

Should you wish to go to Carinthia from Zell am See there is of course the marvellous mountain road via the Grossglockner or travel from Lend to the Gastein Valley through the Tauerntunnel (from Böckstein by train which will take the car as well), but if you want to return to Salzburg the shortest way is via the 'German corner', leaving Zell am See on 311 to Bad Reichenhall in Germany and then onto E11 for Salzburg.

4 CARINTHIA
(Kärnten)

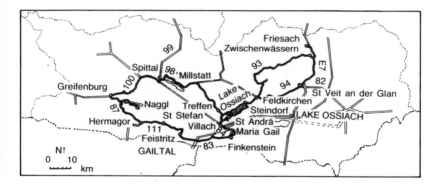

Carinthia is Austria's southernmost province, well protected by mountains on all sides, none lower than 2,000m, but mostly snow-topped giants like the Grossglockner, at 3,797m Austria's highest peak (strictly masculine—'der' Glockner, whilst its only marginally less taller companion is 'die' Glocknerin!). This is the South transplanted into an Alpine setting, with numerous lovely warm lakes (1,270 at the last official count!). The lakes range from tiny tarns to the huge Wörthersee, often called the Austrian Riviera, with its fashionable lakeside resorts and a motorway running high above the lake like a sort of miniature Corniche. The water temperature often rises to 28 degrees and more in summer; and even the exquisite turquoise Weissensee at an altitude of 1,000m does not lag far behind that. There are Renaissance palaces, Alpine villages with Gothic churches, a completely medieval town and tiny hamlets with Roman remains—as well as the fortress straight out of Snow White.

The year of birth for Carinthia is reckoned as 976 when Otto II made it into a separate Duchy—and one which reached as far south as Verona and spread over parts of what is now Lower Austria and Styria as well. There were settlements in the area long before that date though—in fact one of the theories is that the original name of Carontani which first appeared around 660 goes back to the Illyrian Caranto which means stone or rock—and there certainly are plenty of those around in the shape of mountains! The other, and more likely, theory is that the name stems from the Celtic Carantum or Caranta which means 'friend'. This version is much approved by the people of Carinthia who like their country to be known as 'the country of friends'—being quick to point out that Carinthia was the only province not conquered by the Romans, becoming part of the Roman Empire by way of a Trade Agreement!

Many ways lead into Carinthia from the neighbouring provinces, the quickest being to load the car onto a train at Böckstein, south of Badgastein in the province of Salzburg (you stay in the car and the journey takes about nine minutes). Then there is the swish motorway over the Pack mountain from Styria—or the old, twisty and immensely appealing (and almost parallel) road flanked by undulating green hills and meadows where the grass seems to grow taller and smell sweeter than anywhere else in the world. All these have their special attraction, but for sheer dramatic effect there is nothing to beat the approach from Salzburg on the magnificent Tauernstrasse or the spectacular drive across the Grossglockner, Either way you reach Carinthia through a tunnel—which you may well enter through a dense mist at the Salzburg end, or with sleet streaking across the windscreen as you reach the Hochtörl on the Grossglockner—only to emerge in brilliant sunshine on the other side—with a soft, silken wind gently shaking the spring blossoms . . .

Gailtal, Gitschtal, Drautal and Western Lakes

3-4 days/about 190 km/from Villach

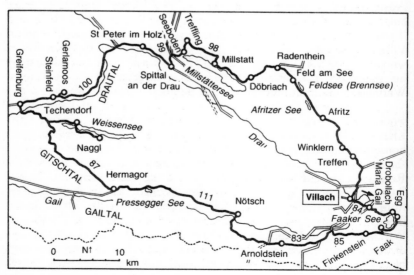

Take a swimsuit, a large beach towel and some suntan lotion—for sooner or later (probably sooner) on this route you will want to stop and settle for a swim in one of the lakes. You may care to take a picnic as well—food shops in Villach are particularly tempting and I have often eyed the enticing displays at the local butchers, almost regretting that there are so may good restaurants in Carinthia! (Sausages and pâtés and freshly-cooked ham, sliced and slipped into a crisp roll whilst still warm—to say nothing of all sorts of ready-to-cook delicacies which would turn a barbecue into a feast).

This is a route introducing at least some Carinthian highlights: wide river valleys and a fjord-like lake (Weissensee), the ancient monastery of Millstatt and Renaissance Schloss Porcia at Spittal; and if you are travelling in June and stray south of Hermagor to the Gartnerkofel, you may encounter that rare plant, the blue Wulfenia, otherwise found only in Syria, Afghanistan and the Himalayas.

'Carinthia has three capitals', runs an old ditty, 'a new one (Klagenfurt), an old one (St Veit an der Glan) and one that might be.' The last one is **VILLACH** (pop: 55,000) often called Carinthia's 'real' or 'secret' capital. The original settlement dates back to 1800BC—there are tumuli on what is now known as 'Napoleon's meadow' at nearby Warmbad Villach. The Romans built a bridge across the river Drau which eventually emerged again as 'pons Uillah' from which Villach takes its name. From 1007 Villach was the property of the see of Bamberg, until the Empress Maria Theresia bought it for one million Gulden in 1759. A solid and prosperous town, though not without its share of disasters: a terrific earthquake in 1348, great fire in 1524 and tremendous destruction during the Second World War (Villach was the second most bombed town in Austria)—yet Villachers are known as 'Viel Lacher' (people of much laughter) and their Carnival is the grandest in all Austria, as is the annual 'Kirtag' (Kermis) which takes place on the first Saturday in August. Villachers will also tell you that theirs was the town in which Karl V—in whose empire the sun never set—sought refuge, where Paracelsus spent his youth and that Napoleon liked so much that he wanted to turn Warmbad Villach into the spa to end all spas . . .

Villach is best explored on foot from the main square (Hauptplatz) where one of the most splendid houses—No. 26, the former Palais Khevenhüller—saw many royal visitors, but the first royal visitor after the house became a hostelry in 1748 was the Empress Maria Theresia when she bought Villach. It is now the very elegant and extremely comfortable **Romantik Hotel Post** (04242 26101) with excellent restaurant. To see: Baroque Trinity column; Parish church St Jakob which was Protestant from 1526 to 1596, in fact the first Protestant church in Austria (sixteenth-century pulpit, rococo altar); parish and pilgrimage church St Peter (known as Heiligenkreuzkirche) in Peraustrasse on the river—one of the few Baroque churches in Carinthia and an absolute jewel; Hauptplatz 14 where Paracelsus lived; and much else. Above all walk through the small streets on either side of the Hauptplatz, look into arcaded courtyards and stroll along the riverside promenade. Tourist Office: Europaplatz 2 (04242 244440). **Gasthof Krapfenbacher** (04242 24817) Peraustrasse 39 near the Heiligenkreuzkirche is a typical and very good

Carinthian inn with lots of local specialities, moderately priced and there are also a few bedrooms.

WARMBAD VILLACH (about 3 km south of Villach), where 40 million litres hot water gush out daily, was known as a spa even in Roman times and probably before that. One of its 'specials' is the 'Maibacherl'—the little May river—a hot spring which emerges usually between Easter and Whitsun, often through the snow and where people 'take the waters' freely—and free of charge! There are a number of excellent hotels of which the **Warmbader Hof** (04242 255010) is the grandest (the best rooms overlooking 'Napoleon's meadow').

The route starts with a slight detour to the east to include the Faaker See, considered one of the prettiest of Carinthia's 1,270 lakes (there are five near Villach alone!)

Leave Villach direction Faaker See to **MARIA GAIL** where the Romanesque parish church with its superb late-Gothic triptych altar certainly warrants a stop. Then continue on 84 towards the lake to **DROBOLLACH** and **EGG** (the wayside shrine you pass a few kilometres after Maria Gail is one of the most photographed landmarks in Carinthia—irresistible to photographers with its background of lake and mountains!). This is the 'favoured' side of the lake with good beaches and excellent hotels such as **Kleines Hotel** Kärnten (04254 2375, open Easter to end October), **Silence Hotel Karnerhof** (04254 2188, open end April to end October) and my own great favourite **Tschebull** (04254 2191, open all year) which styles itself 'an inn with beds' and where the cooking is exceptional.

Take the right fork after Egg—leaving 84 and following the road close to the lake. At the southern tip you will find a sign '**Kärntner Bauerndorf Seeleitn**' which leads to a charming, typically Austrian village right on the lake—timbered houses, balconies hung thick with geraniums in a hundred different hues, a village inn complete with tiled stove—Seeleitn is all that and a lot more, though strictly speaking it should be termed an 'artificial' village: the houses, old Carinthian farmsteads (the oldest fifteenth-century, the 'youngest' eighteenth-century) transplanted from their original sites, lovingly restored and put into place, have been converted into modern apartments, yet none of the village character has been lost. And superbly comfortable apartments they are too, all with tiled stoves (wood supplied free) as well as central heating (should you choose to stay early or late in the season). There are downy duvets with checked covers, fully equipped kitchens—you can opt for full hotel service or just take the apartment and have fresh crisp rolls, milk and whatever else you want for breakfast delivered at your doorstep every morning. Schönleitn—another 'Bauerndorf'—is only a few kilometres away and there are several others, mostly in Carinthia—all good, solid, genuine and very moderately priced. Full details from **Kärntner Bauerndörfer**, Widmanngasse 43, Villach (04242 23387 and 26329).

There is a small island in the centre of the Faaker See, surrounded by waterlilies, with the romantically sited **Insel Hotel** (04254 2145) occupying a favourite spot. To get there, skirt round the lake to **FAAK** village where you will find a sign 'Zum Insel Hotel'. This leads onto a meadow/ parking space where stands a small boat house. Press the 'Boot' button and a small sign will light up, indicating that the boat is on its way. All very improbable—the first time I went through this rigmarole I quite expected the swan from Lohengrin to appear—in fact the boat arrived in no time at all! There is a small fee for the boat transfer which is deducted from the restaurant bill at the Insel Hotel. One word of warning though: the hotel has recently changed hands and there were rumours that it might be turned into a school or training college. Check beforehand.

Stay on the lakeside road, then turn left onto 85 where turn right for **FINKENSTEIN**. (**Burg Altfinkenstein** lies a few kilometres south of the 85—now only the ruins of the twelfth-century fortress remain, but it is beautifully situated with magnificent views and a perfect setting for the concerts which are held there every summer.) Continue on 85 to junction where turn left onto 83 direction Arnoldstein, being careful not to stray onto the motorway—or for that matter onto 109 which leads across the Wurzenpass straight into Yugoslavia. **ARNOLDSTEIN** is on the gateway to Venice—close to the Italian as well as the Yugoslav border—the famous 'three country corner'. Only ruins remain of the former monastery—once a fort from which the Eppenstein Dukes of Carinthia ruled the land—and the tombstones of former abbots in the parish church. Continue on 83 after Arnoldstein, then take right fork which will bring you onto 111 for Feistritz, Nötsch and Hermagor. (A little care is needed here, otherwise you will land on one of the roads to Italy or back to Villach!) Drive on to **FEISTRITZ AN DER GAIL** where on Whit Monday the 'Kufenstechen' takes place—a rather dashing type of tournament—riders attacking the 'Kufen' (a kind of barrel) and a splendid occasion to see the old Gailtal costumes.

You are now in the Lower Gail Valley—the road is the Karnische Dolomitenstrasse named after the stunning mountain range on the left. The mountain on the right—Villacher Alpe—is also called Dobratsch, Slav for 'good mountain', for this is where all the thermal springs originate. It is a mountain wreathed in folklore; at the time of the 1348 earthquake it literally 'burst' and huge quantities of rock tumbled into the valley, causing floods and destruction. Now a comfortable mountain road leads up the Dobratsch from Villach—well worth a separate excursion not only for the view, but also for the terraced Alpine garden on the way—a small and beautiful world on its own.

Continue on 111 to **NÖTSCH**—Schloss Wasserleonburg looming up on the right—built in place of a castle destroyed by the earthquake (in more recent years the Duke of Windsor was a frequent visitor).

Still on 111, continue to **ST STEFAN**, a quiet and charming village with a very old church (part of a Gothic triptych built into the Baroque high altar) and a particularly well-preserved wayside shrine south of the church. About 2 km after St Stefan take the left fork marked 'Pressegger

See' which runs along the lakeside, parallel to 111, rejoining it at Hermagor (note rather beautiful Gothic church between railway line and shores of the lake). Pressegger See is a favourite bathing lake known for its crystal-clear waters—it is fed by underground springs—with romantically reeded shores to the east and west. **HERMAGOR** (pop: 7,100) consists of several small and larger hamlets, set prettily amidst flowering meadows—all very rural, but with lots of good shops.

Take right fork at Hermagor onto 87 (direction Weissbriach and Weissensee), which leads through the Gitsch Valley and **ST LORENZEN**, spread over a high plateau, to Weissbriach, once the centre of gold and silver mining. The road rises gently at first—Weissbriach is 802 m above sea-level—and then more sharply to the Kreuzberg at 1,074 m. After this take right turning for Weissensee which, just for once, is only the name of the lake and not also that of one of the villages!

The northern shore is disappointing at first—there are some decidedly ugly buildings. But all this changes once you get to Techendorf and cross the 800-year old wooden bridge which leads over the narrowest part of the lake, to follow the road up to Naggl. The **Weissensee** lies 1,000 m above sea-level—yet it is warm enough for bathing—a deep, turquoise beauty (the colour is caused by millions of tiny chalk particles and the light reflecting through the water). There is no road round the lake, though it can be reached from the other side and the Lower Drau Valley. The eastern end really looks like a Scandinavian fjord. Stone eagles and white-headed vultures live in the craggy mountains and there is an abundance of fish (pike, carp, perch and rainbow trout) in the lake—an angler's paradise. **NAGGL** really consists mostly of farmhouses and a few hotels sprinkled around the meadows sloping to the lake. **Sporthotel Alpenhof** (04713 2107) is about the 'grandest', originally a 300-year old farmhouse, renewed and enlarged after a fire in recent years and very comfortable with its own little 'spa' centre and lots of other activities. **Nagglerhof** (04713 2106) and **Haus Tischler** (04713 2376) are more modest (and more modestly priced) country inns, but all have their own beaches on the lake below.

Retrace your steps to the lake and across the bridge to Techendorf and back onto 87 where turn right for **GREIFENBURG** with its Romanesque castle and late-Gothic church. Here the climate is so mild that sweet chestnuts grow in profusion.

Turn right at Greifenburg onto 100 (direction Spittal an der Drau) to **STEINFELD**, which according to legend was once called Schönfeld (beautiful field) and was an important and large mining town. Good fortune proved too much for the citizens of Schönfeld who aimed at silver skittles with golden globes—until one night when a bird flew over the town crowing 'Schönfeld today—Steinfeld (stony field) to-morrow.' There was a terrific thunderstorm that night, flooding the little river which in turn loosened huge rocks and devastated the town—thus truly turning it into a 'stony field'. It took a long time for the new, much smaller, settlement to be built and the present church is supposed to stand precisely where one could just discern the spire of the previous church buried under the rubble.

Road 100 will lead on to Spittal, but almost immediately after Steinfeld you will find a sign to the left for **GERLAMOOS**. Take it—it is only a very short detour—and it leads to one of the great treasures of Carinthia, the superb frescoes by Thomas of Villach (whom art historians called the Master of Gerlamoos for a long time because of this particular work) at the village church of St Georg. (You will not be able to drive right up to the church—it is about 30 minutes' walk through orchards to the church surrounded by fir trees and the key has to be obtained in the village before setting out—but it is certainly worth the effort, and is a very pleasurable walk.)

Return to 100 and continue towards Spittal—about 4 km before Spittal turn right for **ST PETER IM HOLZ** (not to be confused with St Peter south of Spittal), a small village on the site of the Celtic-Roman town Teurnia. A bishopric under Aquileia at the beginning of the fifth century and 'metropolis Norici', it became 'Tiburnia' after the fall of the Roman Empire and later on a modest farming community called 'Liburnia'—hence the name 'Lurnfeld' for the whole district. The present late-Gothic church probably stands over the original cathedral, but the cemetery church has been excavated and there is a marvellous mosaic floor glowing with multi-coloured stones, with an inscription that 'Ursus and his wife Ursina' commissioned this work. Probably in the last quarter of the fifth century.

Back to 100 which leads straight into **SPITTAL AN DER DRAU** (pop: 15,000) and Renaissance Schloss Porcia. There is parking in the inner courtyard, but be careful when you drive in for the entrance is extremely narrow. Make straight for the 'Arkadenhof', the magnificent arcaded courtyard after which you will need no further encouragement to explore Schloss Porcia—though in all fairness it is by far the best part of the Schloss. (During the summer months plays and concerts are performed there—absolute magic, even if you do not understand a word or if the performance is slightly below par!) Schloss Porcia also harbours a museum: exhibits range from simple farmhouse furniture and equipment to the gilded Renaissance bed (with rococo additions) in which slept the Empress Maria Theresia—and later on Napoleon. There is a beautiful old park surrounding the Schloss with (what else in Austria?) the almost obligatory Schlosscafé—sit on the terrace if the weather allows (and it nearly always does allow in this completely Southern atmosphere). Afterwards you may care to cross the road to the Renaissance town hall where you will also find the Tourist Office (04762 3420). See also: parish church, modernised in 1966, but original nave; houses in Hauptplatz—particularly Nos. 3, 4 and 5. **Hotel Ertl** (04762 2048) has very good food and pleasant rooms and so does **Alte Post** (04762 2217), both moderately priced. (Incidentally, I am also informed that the Colt revolver was invented at Spittal an der Drau—by one Leopold Gasser and duly patented as M70, trade mark being an apple pierced by an arrow!)

Leave Spittal (direction Millstättersee) on 99, turning right onto 98 as signposted which will bring you first to **SEEBODEN** (pop: 5,400), a busy lakeside resort from which it is only a few kilometres to Millstatt travelling on the lakeside road. A slightly longer, and much more attractive road leads via Treffling (take left turning at Seeboden centre) with fortress ruin **Sommereck** on the way—now a restaurant with glorious views. You may even be able to see the famous 'hole in the sky' from there: whenever clouds gather for a thunderstorm, the actual storm rarely reaches this region—there may be rain, but this will be confined to the hills around the lake, whilst the clouds will part over the lake—and the lake itself will be bathed in brilliant sunshine.

Turn right at Treffling, below Sommereck (sometimes spelled Sommeregg) to Tangern and **LAUBENDORF** (foundations of a fifth century church about 100 m from the road) and descend gradually to **MILLSTATT** (pop: 3,200), an immensely pleasing lakeside resort. Legend has it that a Prince Domitian lived on the other side of the lake and when crossing the lake one day with his son, the boy fell overboard and was drowned. Domitian drained the lake—at least partially—until the child's body was found beneath a heathen temple built on a thousand pillars on which rested a thousand heathen statues. Domitian destroyed the temple and built a church in its place—the thousand statues were thrown into the lake and it is from these statues (mille statuae) that Millstatt takes its name. Domitian was revered as the Patron Saint of Lake Millstatt—though never canonised (despite gallant efforts supported by the Empress Maria Theresia). Holy Mass was read for him every February and when a priest refused to do so one year, the church sank about 1 m

Millstatt

below ground, leaving the altar exactly where it was. (When you visit Domitian chapel you have to step down and the altar is sited higher up). It is now believed that Domitian—or rather a prince of that name—did not exist at all one just wonders who lies buried in his coffin ...

There's no such mystery about the former Benedictine abbey which was founded between 1086 and 1088 by two Bavarian noblemen and became a cultural centre in the twelfth-century. Parts of the abbey are only accessible with conducted tours, but see particularly: Romanesque cloisters; great Renaissance fresco (Weltgerichtsfresko) by Görtschacher on the southern wall.

Most old Linden trees are reputed to be 'over one thousand years old', but the one in the abbey courtyard looks as if this could be true (there is also a 'young one' of a mere 500 years)—it was struck by lightning, burnt out and yet it goes on flowering every year.

International music weeks are held at Millstatt Abbey from the beginning of July to the end of August as well as other musical festivals. Details from Tourist Office at the town hall (04766 2021).

Die Forelle (04766 2180 and 2050) directly on the lake and **Postillion am See** (04766 2552) are both excellent and so is **Alpenrose** (04766 2500) at Obermillstatt.

Leave Millstatt on 98 past **DÖBRIACH** with its sandy beach at the shallow end of the lake, to **RADENTHEIN**, now mostly known for its magnesit works. At one time garnets were found near Radenthein which were exported to Bohemia and sold as 'Bohemian garnets' all over the world. According to legend, garnets are the solidified blood of giants who fought and are buried in the neighbourhood—and garnets can still be found, albeit only occasionally, around Radenthein.

Continue on 98—which actually means keeping to the right immediately after Radenthein—to **FELD AM SEE**. Another lake, another legend (Carinthia has more legends to the square kilometre than any other part of Austria). According to this one the Feldsee (also known as Brennsee) and Lake Afritz on the other side of the road were one huge lake at one time. There was a pretty mermaid who loved a local fisherman and this infuriated a dragon who lived on the Mirnock mountain. One day—seething with jealousy—the dragon swished his tail so fiercely that it snapped off the top of the mountain which fell into the lake—and that accounts for there being two lakes now (and the bit missing off the top of the Mirnock!) **Lindenhof** (04246 2274) at Feld is a much favoured hotel with very good restaurant, but for real local cooking **Gasthof Hubmann-hof** (turn right at petrol station between Feldsee and Afritzer See—04246 2667) should not be missed—and there are also rooms.

Still on 98 (direction Villach) you pass Lake Afritz on the right and the village of **AFRITZ** a little further on (Gothic church; onion dome added later). You may also notice some unusually shaped wooden silos which have a wooden ledge running round the top—called 'mouse collars' and that is exactly what they are: a barrier against mice! Further on 98—between Innere Einöde and Aussere Einöde—officially at Winklern, but it is signposted on the road so that you cannot miss it—there is Elli Riehl's delightful **Doll Museum** with over 600 hand-made dolls. Continue on 98 through **TREFFEN** with its impressive seventeenth-century Schloss, after which join 94 for return to Villach.

Lake Ossiach, Gurk, Metnitz and Glan Valleys
2-3 days/about 190 km/from Villach

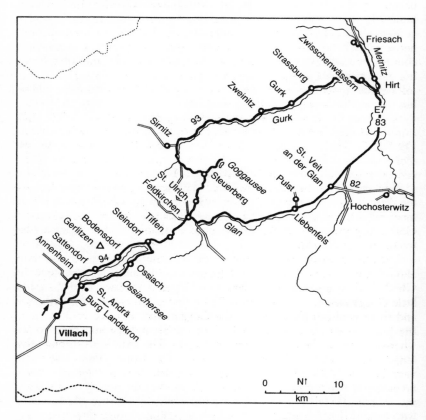

Some more Carinthian highlights, on a route that should be uncrowded on the whole even in July and August. It travels first along the northern shore of Lake Ossiach to the charming old town of Feldkirchen, then crosses over to the narrow valley of the river Gurk—having paid a visit to one of the lesser known little lakes, the Goggausee. It follows the twists of the river to the tiny market town of Gurk—famous for its cathedral—and Strassburg with its ancient castle. Zwischenwässern ('between waters') is the aptly named village between the rivers Gurk and Metnitz where the route turns to Friesach, Carinthia's oldest town. The return journey leads to St Veit, once the capital of Carinthia and then along the Glan Valley to the northern shores of Lake Ossiach, offering a chance to attend a performance of the 'Carinthischer Sommer', the annual music festival which takes place between the end of June and the end of August.

Leave **VILLACH** (for description see previous route) on 94 (direction Ossiacher See Nord). The road meets the lake at **ANNENHEIM** (from where a cable car leads up to the Kanzelhöhe) and continues to the lakeside resorts of **SATTENDORF** and **BODENSDORF**, where at the beginning of the village—on the left—a toll road starts for the Gerlitzen mountain. You may not care to go right to the top, about 12 km, but drive at least as far as **Gasthof Stoffl** (about 3 km, 04243 6920, closed Monday between October and May, otherwise open all week), a marvellous country inn with good food—and terrific views over lake and mountains. It's very reasonably priced, as are the pleasant rooms. (As you buy your toll ticket, say that you are only going to Gasthof Stoffl—the toll will be less and it will also be refunded at the inn.)

Return to 94, turn left and continue along the lake through **TIFFEN** (interesting fortified church on hill with painting by Thomas of Villach) to **FELDKIRCHEN**, a pretty little town surrounded by a series of small, secluded lakes. Particularly attractive main square with a seventeenth-century fountain and lots of Biedermeier houses.

Feldkirchen belonged to the bishopric of Bamberg until 1759, administered from the rather majestic sixteenth-century Amtshof (now a retirement home). There are some interesting thirteenth-century frescoes and a Gothic triptych altar at the parish church at the northern end of the town, and a charnel house.

Turn left at Feldkirchen onto 93 direction Sirnitz and Gurk and then almost immediately right for St Ulrich and Goggausee. Go through St Ulrich, Polling and Rennweg, direction Goggau—you will find the quiet little **Goggausee** on right (altitude 770 m and warm enough for bathing!) and there is also a pleasant inn, the **Goggauwirt**. Retrace your steps to the junction where take the right fork for Steuerberg and then to 93 where turn right (direction Sirnitz and Gurk). The road leads through the 'enge Gurk' (narrow Gurk) valley—more of a gorge than a valley and very beautiful—to **SIRNITZ** where turn left for the village. Much favoured as a holiday spot practically the whole year round, with ski-ing in winter and lovely walks at all other times, Sirnitz is a pretty little village with its sturdy old farmhouses, Gothic parish church (fourteenth-century frescoes, Baroque altar) and octagonal Romanesque charnel house. Follow directions at beginning of village for **Schloss Albeck** and five minutes later you will be in another world altogether—a world of ceramics and paintings, of hand-woven materials with 'on-the-spot' tailoring, of occasional candlelit concerts, and a pleasant small restaurant. Definitely worth the detour from Sirnitz and open daily from 8 am to 8 pm (04279 303).

Return to 93 and continue (direction Gurk) past Altenmarkt to **WEITENSFELD** where the ancient custom of 'Kranzelreiten' takes place on Whit Monday—followed and preceded by much celebration. (An outbreak of plague had wiped out almost the entire population of Weitensfeld and surrounding villages in the sixteenth-century—all except for three young men and a noble lady who lived at nearby Schloss Thurnhof. All three asked for her hand in marriage and, not wanting to offend any one of them, she suggested that they should compete in a race. History does not relate the outcome—or whether she really married the winner—but the custom of the race continues to this day. The winner arrives on horseback to kiss a statue of the noble lady—as well as the prettiest girl in the village—and a splendid time is had by all!)

You will see **Schloss Thurnhof** on the left as you continue on 93 to **ZWEINITZ** where a fifteenth-century fresco in the Romanesque parish church, depicting Holy Hemma with a model of Gurk Cathedral makes a suitable introduction to one of the most remarkable women in the history of Carinthia. Heiress to vast fortunes but with no heirs of her own (both her sons were murdered and her husband died soon afterwards), Hemma devoted the rest of her life (and her possessions) to a building programme of enormous proportions. She built eight churches as well as Gurk Convent (Admont Monastery was commenced after her death, but with her money and on her instructions) and of all those Gurk was probably closest to her heart. She supervised the work personally, paying out the wages every week—her little 'chair', made of green slate and known as the 'Hemma Stone', can still be seen in the crypt of Gurk Cathedral and miraculous healings were reported by those who touched it. (It was also said that if one of the workmen was not satisfied with his pay, Hemma would hold out her moneybag, inviting him to take whatever he felt was due to him, but no matter how deeply anyone delved into that bag, no-one ever managed to take out more than their fair pay.)

The convent was given over to the Benedictine nuns from the Nonnberg at Salzburg. Hemma joined the order and died at Gurk in 1045. The nuns did not stay long after her death—the Archbishop of Salzburg became owner of the convent and later on Gurk was created a bishopric in its own right. One of the earliest bishops—Roman I, a friend of Emperor Barbarossa's—was accorded the title of Prince and building of the cathedral started under his aegis, about a hundred years after Hemma's death. Thus all the pictures of Hemma (who was beatified in 1287 and canonised in 1938) with a model of Gurk Cathedral are allegorical only—though she is certainly considered the 'founder' of Gurk, cathedral and bishopric!

Approaching **GURK** (pop: 1,400) and seeing the twin towers in the distance one rather expects to find a modest deanery church, only to be confronted by a mighty cathedral, one of the most impressive Romanesque buildings in Europe. Apparently Roman I, when outlining his wishes, asked for a crypt for the foundress, a separate choir for the canons, a church for the people and a private chapel for himself—and it went without saying that the building was also to vie with Salzburg Cathedral! Guide books (in English) are available outside the cathedral and it is not a bad idea to repair to the **Kronenwirt** (04266 8237) opposite the entrance—exactly the type of comfortable country inn one would expect to find in a place like Gurk—for at least a cursory glance at the book before joining one of the guided tours (from Ash Wednesday to All Saints Day at 9.30 am, 11 am, 2.30 pm and 4.15 pm—also at 1 pm from 15 May to October. Sundays and holidays at 10.30 am, 11 am, 2.30 pm and 4.15 pm—otherwise by arrangement. Priest's office 04266 8236). See particularly: west porch in outer vestibule; Samson's tympanum, Romanesque sculpture on north side; high altar by Michael Hönel, one of the most important early-Baroque altars in Austria; rococo pulpit in central nave and cross altar with Pieta by Raphael Donner; crypt with 'forest' of a hundred white marble columns—also containing sarcophagus of St Hemma and the 'Hemma Stone'; Bishop's chapel in west gallery with famous frescoes of 1230 and 1263.

The bishops did not reside at Gurk but at the arcaded Bischofsburg high above the tiny town of **STRASSBURG** (pop: 2,830) a few kilometres further along 93. Originally built as a fortress by Roman I and later rebuilt into a small palace with its own theatre, it stayed the official residence until the end of the eighteenth-century when it transferred briefly to Pöckstein and then to Klagenfurt. The building was badly damaged—first by lightning and then by an earthquake—but restored and now houses a museum and a pleasant Schlossschenke. See also parish church—late-Gothic with superb Baroque organ—with graves of nine bishops and two cardinals, including that of Count Franz Salm-Reifferscheidt, bishop of Gurk who financed several expeditions to the hitherto unconquered Grossglockner mountain in the eighteenth-century and who died a pauper as a result!

LIEDING, to the west of Strassburg on a hill, was granted market and minting rights by Emperor Otto II (the rights were in fact granted to Countess Imma, an ancestor of St Hemma). It contains one of the churches built by St Hemma—worth seeing for it combines most happily the styles of three completely different periods, spanning five centuries (see particularly: early-Gothic choir and stained glass windows; magnificent Baroque altar).

Continue on 93 to Zwischenwässern and junction with 83 (E7) where turn left. **Schloss Pöckstein,** built at the end of the eighteenth-century and briefly the bishops' residence, stands rather impressively to the left of the junction. It is still the property of the Carinthian bishops, but visits are said to be 'occasionally' possible—worth exerting a little persuasive power!

Drive along 83 (direction Friesach). **Braukeller Hirt** (04262 2519), almost immediately on left (next to brewery which owns it), is probably the oldest tavern in Carinthia (Renaissance arcades). It's very busy, and sometimes noisy: a large country inn with (of course!) splendid beer.

Continue on 83 (E7)—practically the ancient route linking the Danube basin with the Adriatic—to **FRIESACH** (pop: 7,000), Carinthia's oldest town. Medieval and moated and an absolute joy—except for the many cars parked in the small main square, obscuring not only the square, but also the Renaissance fountain in the centre. Friesach belonged to the bishopric of Salzburg until 1803—in fact a much-favoured 'second' residence of the Prince archbishops—except for the earliest days when part of it belonged to the bishopric of Gurk (thanks to St Hemma who was born a Countess of Friesach) and the dividing line ran right through the centre of the church on the Petersberg! Immensely important in the Middle Ages—famous visitors included the Emperor Barbarossa and (unofficially) Richard Lionheart—with its own Mint ('Friesacher Pfennige' were a much coveted currency as far as the Levant), it was the scene of the greatest jousting tournament of all times in which 600 knights were said to have participated. Minnesänger Ulrich von Liechtenstein reported on the event, including that Hermann of Osterwitz fought so fiercely that he bashed in his opponents' helmets like 'rotten pears'.

Through the centuries Friesach was occupied in turn by the Bohemians, Hungarians, Turks and French, swept by thirteen fires and two plagues—yet most of the important buildings have remained intact and where there are ruins, they are highly decorative. See particularly: Fortress Petersberg (about 20 minutes' gentle walk from centre) with enormous keep, Ruperti Chapel (thirteenth-century frescoes) and Peterskirche; the Dominican church—the largest church in Carinthia—(early fourteenth-century Sandstone Madonna and crucifixion; late-Gothic St John's altar and tomb of one Balthasar Thannhäuser, a descendant of the 'real' Thannhäuser); Church of the Teutonic Order (twelfth-century frescoes and two sixteenth-century triptych altars); also the stained glass windows at St Barthlmä and the Heiligenblutkapelle. And there's much, much more if you have time. The Tourist Office at Hauptplatz 1 (04268 2213) is particularly helpful, and will also hand you a 'Schlemmerpass' in which you can have your meals in and around Friesach recorded—if you have consumed the requisite number you will be given a piece of nicely-cut glass as a souvenir. Not that one would need much persuading to stay on at Friesach (see the sights such as inside of churches in daytime and savour the marvellous old town in the evening when most of the day trippers will have departed) and there are a number of good little inns such as the **Metnitztalerhof** (04268 2510), the **Friesacherhof** (04268 2123) and **Zum lustigen Bauer** (04268 2232), but even if you do not stay overnight, don't leave Friesach without paying a visit to **Café Craigher** (04268 2295, open 7.00 to 20.00 except Sunday) Hauptplatz 3 where the selection may be small, but the pattisserie some of the best in Austria!

Retrace your steps onto 83 direction St Veit—past Pöckstein (and a sign for Gurktaler Museumsbahnen—narrow gauge railway which operates on Saturdays and Sundays during the summer) and at fork keep to right onto 94 for St Veit.

ST VEIT AN DER GLAN (pop: 12,000), former residence of the Dukes of Carinthia, was capital for 400 years. Then in 1518 the citizens of St Veit refused to accommodate troops sent to suppress a peasant revolt at nearby Althofen, whereupon the Emperor Maximilian I made the completely burned-out Klagenfurt capital in its place, on condition that it would not only be rebuilt, but fortified as well. St Veit remained prosperous though—and after a series of setbacks in the eighteenth-century

St Veit an der Glan, courtyard in the town hall

regained its prosperity, having spread well beyond the old city limits. The old town centre has remained virtually unchanged: the Hauptplatz (Oberer Platz) is one of the most beautiful squares in Austria with its splendid town hall (richly ornated façade and Renaissance courtyard), two fountains (one dedicated to Walther von der Vogelweide who was a frequent guest at the Ducal Court) and Baroque plague column. Tourist Office at town hall (04212 3193-13 and 2326-13). **Pukelsheim**, Erlgasse 11 (04212 2473, closed Tuesday) is an excellent little restaurant, and practically at the beginning of the route to **Schloss Frauenstein**— one of the twenty (or more) castles and fortresses surrounding St Veit. (There are also three lakes in the vicinity, but that is no more than one would expect in Carinthia!). The grandest of these—and one of the grandest in Austria—is **Burg Hochosterwitz**—about 10 km to the east on 82—where each of the fourteen towered gateways forms a little fortress of its own. And, if you think you have 'seen it all before', that is more than likely, for Hochosterwitz was Walt Disney's inspiration for the castle in Snow White!

Leave St Veit on 94 (direction Feldkirchen), joining the Glan river near **LIEBENFELS** with its fortress (and a possible short detour to the ancient and very rural **PULST** on the right). Keep to the right just before Feldkirchen—still on 94, direction Villach—then drive on to Steindorf (still on 94) where fork left for Ossiach and then right at junction, following direction for Ossiach, where turn right into the village.

OSSIACH (pop: about 500) derives its name from the Slovene 'osoje', those who live in the shade. Sitting closely and handsomely on the shores of the lake, and consisting of only a few houses, an imposing former monastery (the oldest Benedictine monastery in Carinthia) and a magnificent abbey, it is certainly not 'in the shade' from the end of June to the end of August when the '**Carinthischer Sommer**' takes place, one of the best (and least publicised) music festivals in Europe. Performances are held in the former abbey (now parish church), the old monastery as well as at the Kongresshaus at Villach. Programme details and tickets (from 29 May) at Stift Ossiach (04243 510 and 502), before that date from Carinthischer Sommer, A.1060 WIEN, Gumpendorfer Strasse 76 (0222 568198). At present the monastery which always offered (albeit somewhat 'basic') accommodation is in the process of being restored and will eventually house a comfortable hotel, including re-opening of the

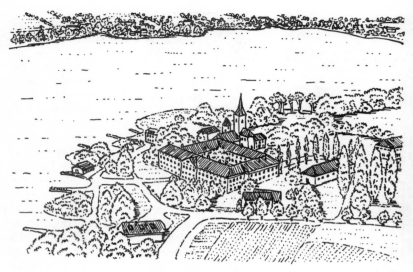

Ossiach, the monastery

'Stiftsrestaurant'. **Schlosswirt** (04243 347), next door (open May until October) is a typical Carinthian inn with good local food.

Return to the main road and follow directions for Villach along the southern shores of the lake—quite frankly the least attractive part where a few large apartment blocks and their 'dependants' raise their ugly heads, though some are mercifully submerged by the beautiful surroundings. At St Andrä you will find a sign pointing to 'Burgruine Landskron' and you would be well advised to take that turning—Landskron was one of the grand fortresses in Carinthia, grand enough for the Emperor Charles V to be entertained there in 1552 and for the Archdukes Ferdinand and Maximilian to stay in 1613. Landskron was later confiscated—the Khevenhüllers were Protestant and the rightful heir had joined Gustav of Sweden against the Imperial armies in the Thirty Years War—and later still was hit by lightning when decay had set in. It is still very impressive though, with splendid views over the countryside, and a restaurant has been built into the thick walls of the fortress ruins. **Burgruine Landskron** (04242 563) is open from 11am, but is really considered an evening restaurant, though light meals are served throughout the day.

Descending from Landskron return to main road and follow directions for Villach.

5 STYRIA
(Steiermark)

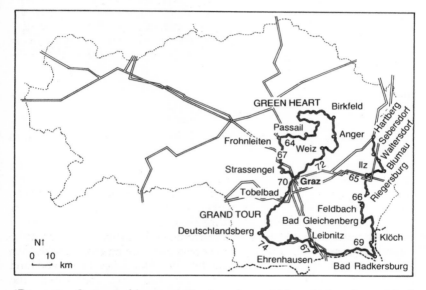

'Die grüne Steiermark'—green Styria—they said long before 'green' had anything to do with conservation and merely stood for a colour. And green it certainly is—9,700 of its 16,000km² are covered by forests and a further 25 per cent by meadows and pasture land. Green are the lakes and green it certainly is—9,700 of its 16,000km² are covered by forests and a meadows to reflect in them—and even the national emblem is a green shield on which stands a silver panther breathing fire (though not as fiercely as when it was first created in 1160—censure was applied when a woman deputy in the 1920s lodged an official complaint about the panther being—well, rather offensive to her sense of decency!)

Named after the Counts of Steyr to whom the country was entrusted in the eleventh century—Styria is Austria's second-largest province, stretching to the south-eastern tip where it borders Yugoslavia as well as Hungary. Sunny, with vineyards in the south and south-west which produce some excellent wines—though little known outside their own country—including pale to dark pink Schilcher from the Wildbach grape. It is also Austria's apple orchard—and was its plum orchard until those parts fell to Yugoslavia after the Second World War, but potent Sliwowitz is still being made, as well as some remarkably good apple brandy, sometimes sold as 'Apfelwurm' (sold only in apple country near Puch). It is deeply traditional country—from national costume which is probably worn more frequently in Styria than anywhere else in Austria (in more urban parts of Austria the term 'Steirergwand'—Styrian costume—is used to denote national costume as such) to the ancient 'Peasant calendar' still published today, containing an often astonishingly accurate weather forecast.

Styria is rural Austria at its best—there are less than half-a-dozen five-star hotels (of which two are in Graz) and certainly no fashionable resorts, but it is full of undiscovered treasures from ancient monasteries to imposing fortresses, good old-fashioned spas and vast stretches of country where the grass really is greener, the pines smell sweeter—and where you'll probably sleep more soundly than anywhere else in the world.

Styria's Grand Tour

4-5 days/about 225 km/from Hartberg to Graz

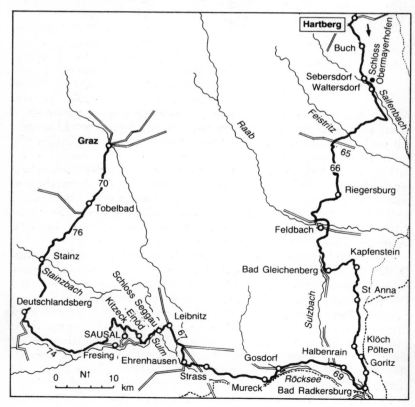

Charnel house at Hartberg

This is a route to 'show off' some of the best of Styria: gentle green hills and vineyards, ancient towns and imposing fortresses; the highest wine village in Europe and a small town with one foot in another country; a rather unusual spa (and a very old-fashioned one); meeting a Klapotetz (or a whole horde of them) and tasting 'Verhackerts'—and finishing up in Graz which Napoleon called 'Ville de grace' and—taking the play on words even further—'aux armes de l'amour' (la Mur being the river on which Graz is built).

HARTBERG could be called the classic small town in Styria: handsome twelfth-century Deanery church, duly baroquised (only quite recently, during restorations, they found a complete Roman building underneath), romantic medieval castle and—pride of Hartberg—Romanesque charnel house with remarkable frescoes. Add to this some sturdy old houses, a sixteenth-century parsonage, a pretty pilgrimage church—and you have (as any Styrian would casually tell you) a typical small town in Styria. Hartberg goes one further:'the town fortifications—some of which are still in existence—were paid for with the rather large ransom Duke Leopold shared with the German king for the release of Richard Lionheart. A very suitable place from which to start touring Styria and **'Zum alten Gerichtshof'** Herrengasse 4 (0332 3356), in Hartberg's oldest street, is a very suitable place in which to stay. Prices are more than moderate—but so is the whole of Styria. Nice little shops too. Tourist Office: Stadtamt, Hauptplatz (0332 3420)

Leave Hartberg direction Fürstenfeld, through *BUCH* and **SEBERS-DORF** where turn right, following signs for Ilz (and also—in green—Schloss Obermayerhofen) and then left, still marked Ilz and Obermayerhofen, through Neustift where you will find the drive to **Schloss Obermayerhofen** on the left. This is a beautifully restored Renaissance castle, with an eighteenth-century chapel (crucifix dated 1500), now run as a hotel (at prices well below those of other far less luxurious castle hotels). **Hofstüberl** (0333 2959) is a very good, reasonably priced restaurant in a former farmhouse building belonging to the castle.

Coming down from the castle, turn right and follow road to junction,

71

then turn right signposted Waltersdorf and follow signs for Waltersdorf throughout, being careful not to stray onto the motorway.

WALTERSDORF is just an ordinary little village which gained significance a few years ago when—during drilling for oil—a thermal spring was discovered. It is probably the most informal and most pleasurable spa to be found anywhere. To explore this, drive through Waltersdorf in the direction of Fürstenfeld and Heiltherme. About 3 km outside Waltersdorf there is a small sign pointing to the left, marked 'Heiltherme' which you follow and just when you think that I am leading you into a wilderness (after about 1 km) you will find the **'Heiltherme'** which is simply an indoor and an outdoor pool (open also in the evening and in winter when you can swim under a starlit sky, surrounded by snow-covered hills). Here you 'take the waters' by simply relaxing (maximum time recommended 30 minutes) in one of the pools (free), possibly interrupted by gentle underwater exercises. During the summer—usually on Fridays—there is a vast outdoor barbecue, complete with one-man band and even dancing on the lawn! There is now also a very modern hotel (Bio-Thermen Hotel, 03333 29810).

Return to the main road, turn left for Leitersdorf and Fürstenfeld, through Schwarzmannshofen, after which turn right for Riegersdorf and Lindegg. Drive through both villages, then follow directions for Ilz. At the beginning of Ilz turn right into 65, direction Gleisdorf, and then almost immediately left onto 66 direction Bad Gleichenberg and Riegersburg. This is an extremely pretty route—well worth taking, even if it were not for the mighty Riegersburg rising on the right (it is also by far the best approach since the road skirts round the fortress hill, giving a beautiful view). There are supposed to be a thousand paces between the road and

The Riegersburg

the village square of **RIEGERSBURG** (very interesting parish church) and a further thousand between the square and the fortress (care—do not attempt it after rain. The ascent is alright, but the descent can be precarious). The **Riegersburg** has been called the 'strongest fortress in Christendom' and it is certainly the most important fortress in Styria (which is not exactly devoid of fortresses). It was originally built in the twelfth and thirteenth centuries, but greatly enlarged in the seventeenth by Elisabeth Freifrau von Gallern, known as 'die Gallerin' or, more disrespectfully, 'wicked Liesl'. She was married three times, fought against all and sundry—mostly the clergy—and probably had trouble with her builders even in those days, as hinted by one of the inscriptions: 'Bauen ist ein schöner lust, was es mich kost ist mir bewusst' which can be freely translated as 'To build is a pleasurable hobby—I know what it is costing me.' And, in another spot, 'Was ich in 16 Jahren hier hab lassen bauen, das ist woll zu sehen und zu schauen. Kain Heller mich reuen thuet, ich mains dem Vaterland zu guett' meaning 'What I built here in 16 years is well worth seeing. I don't regret a penny of it—I did it for my country. So there.' Soon after building work had been completed it looked as if the fortress would be put to the test—enemy forces were lining up near Mogersdorf in what is now Burgenland and the fortress was crammed with refugees—but the enemy lost the decisive battle and no attempt was ever made on Riegersburg. Riegersburg may be viewed between 15 March and 15 November. (03153 213) See particularly: portals and courtyards, Rittersaal and Weissen Saal, 'Turkish' room, fifteenth-century chapel—and, of course, the beautiful view from the top.

Zur Riegersburg (03153 216; closed November to March) is a very good country inn with pleasant garden and own patisserie.

From Riegersburg continue on 66 direction Feldbach—Schloss Kornberg on right after about 5 km. **FELDBACH** is one of the oldest villages in Styria, with old 'Tabor' (fortification) still in existence and now housing a local museum (showing how oil is extracted from green pumpkin seeds—a Styrian speciality).

At the beginning of Feldbach—almost immediately after village sign—turn left, following signs for Bad Gleichenberg on 66 and at **BAD GLEICHENBERG** follow signs for Ortsmitte. The Romans considered the thermal springs around what is now Bad Gleichenberg beneficial to health. For a long time forgotten in favour of more fashionable spas, it was 'resurrected' during the last century, since when Bad Gleichenberg has developed as a centre for treatment of respiratory diseases. Bad Gleichenberg is a thriving and pleasant spa, the largest in Styria, and while the treatment centre certainly keeps up with all the latest developments, the little town has kept its Biedermeier character completely intact. Its climate is considered 'sub-Alpine' which means that a great many unusual trees flourish there—mostly in the Kurpark where, incidentally, smoking is not permitted. Tourist Office: Kurkommission (opposite cinema, 03159 2203). **Hotel Austria** (03159 2205) is a marvellous old family hotel, very reasonably priced, and ideal for longer stays.

From Gleichenberg there is a direct, albeit rather twisty, road to

Kapfenstein; alternatively get onto 66 (direction Bad Radkersburg) and then fork to left (direction St Anna), taking left fork again for **KAPFEN-STEIN**. Drive through Kapfenstein village and then up the hill, variously signposted Schloss Kapfenstein and Schlosswirt. **Schloss Kapfenstein** (03157 2202) built in the twelfth century and greatly enlarged over the centuries may look gaunt and forbidding, but in fact it is one of the most welcoming places in Styria. The view alone, reaching far into Hungary and Yugoslavia, would make the journey worthwhile. Add to that the delicious food (home-grown vegetables and salads), wine from their own vineyards, home-baked bread (and home-cured ham for breakfast)—and a Styrian buffet every Thursday during the season—and you will understand why it is essential to book, particularly if you want to stay (there are only eight rooms!). Closed mid-November until mid-March.

Coming from Schloss Kapfenstein follow directions for Bad Gleichenberg and Fehring and, at the bottom of the hill, for Bad Gleichenberg and St Anna. At the next fork in the road, follow directions for Yugoslavia, Bad Radkersburg and St Anna. The road winds its way through vineyards fairly close to the Yugoslav border, and from St Anna follow the direction signposted Yugoslavia, Radkersburg and Klöch. This is the Klöcher Weinstrasse and you will soon be completely engulfed by the vines—useless to look for a road sign. The only sign you are likely to find are those for so-called 'Buschenschenken' sometimes with the 'helpful' additional notice that you may also expect a 'Brettljausn'. This goes back for over two centuries when wine growers were granted the right to sell their home-made products on the spot—wine, cold meats, sausages and other pork products. Hence the Brettljausn—a wooden platter (Brettl) of sausages and meat, home-made bread and 'Verhackerts' which can best be described as a sort of highly-spiced rough pâté. All served out of doors amid the vineyards. Klöcher Traminer or Gewürztraminer, grown on volcanic ground, has a strong bouquet and fits perfectly into the landscape. About now you will probably also meet your first Klapotetz. This is a curious kind of spiked wheel which turns in the wind and is supposed to scare away the birds. (Some vintners think differently: they say that the birds come at the sound of the Klapotetz, like being called for a dinner of extra juicy grapes!) Klapotetz are certainly picturesque and a Styrian landmark even if other means are now being used for scaring away the birds.

At **Klöch** (seventeenth-century parish church, fourteenth-century fortress ruins) take the left fork—unmarked as are most of the others—for Pölten and Goritz (do not stray onto road for Halbenrain) and at Pölten follow directions for **BAD RADKERSBURG**, an enchanting town with pastel coloured houses, mostly Renaissance, where the river Mur changes into Mura and Radkersburg becomes Gornja Radgone—for on the other side of the river lies Yugoslavia. Radkersburg was founded by King Ottokar II of Bohemia as a fortified town against all invaders—but the fortress is now on the other side of the border. Radkersburg is surrounded by meadows and marshland in which storks stalk about and rare flowers grow and although it is a busy little spa, the large spa hotel has been wisely placed outside the town so that nothing disturbs the tranquillity (except shoppers coming over from Yugoslavia). To see particularly: old and 'new' town hall, fourteenth-century parish church; practically all the houses in Hauptplatz, Langgasse ('wicked Liesl' of the Riegersburg was born at No. 43), Emmenstrasse, Grazertorplatz and Murgasse. Tourist Office: Hauptplatz 1 (in town hall with octagonal tower—03476 2545).

Kurhotel Jauschowetz (03476 2571) is rather nicely situated (once you have managed to get past the Long Life mineral water depot), very comfortable, with excellent food and not too expensive. Indoor and outdoor swimming pool with thermal water (which incidentally emerges at 80°C: the water temperature in the outdoor pool is kept at 36°C irrespective of weather).

From Bad Radkersburg take 69, following directions for Strass to **HALBENRAIN**. This has a rather impressive Schloss (given to Witigo by Frederic 'the Quarrelsome' in the thirteenth-century, rebuilt during the sixteenth and seventeenth-centuries—03476 2205), an interesting parish church, and **Gasthof Simmerl** (03476 2207—on road to Klöch: particularly good for game specialities, but also for wine from their own vineyards where wine tastings can be arranged). You may have noticed that in addition to the usual 'Buschenschenken' signs there are now also those for 'Steirisches Kernöl'—this is the marvellous dark brown oil from green pumpkin seeds which are lightly roasted before the oil is extracted. On being mixed as a salad dressing it turns dark green and is absolutely delicious. Ask for it to be used the next time you order a salad and if you like the taste, buy some at the next farmhouse that displays the sign.

Stay on 69 following signs for Graz and Mureck and then take the left fork—still 69—for Mureck. (At Gosdorf there is a sign to the left for Röcksee—a very pleasant little bathing lake—some camp sites too, but well away from bathing—ideal for a quick swim on a hot day.)

MURECK (pop: 1,700) is a tiny town set in meadows near the river (you can cross into Yugoslavia—in fact the old fortress is on the other side). Like so many small towns in this part of the world, Mureck was almost totally destroyed by the Turks and rebuilt (with fortifications) at the initiative of a worthy citizen called by the apt name of Bartlmä Lorber (Laurel). To see: parish church St Bartholomäus and the St Patritius Chapel; town hall; lots of attractive old houses in centre. Tourist Office: Stadtamt (03472 2105).

Follow directions for Strass on 69. Go through **STRASS**, which is rather dominated by its sixteenth-century castle, now military barracks. See too the parish church with important altar painting by Weissenkircher (1680) and ceiling frescoes by Mölck (1776).

After Strass follow directions for Ehrenhausen which marks the beginning of the Sudsteirisches Weinland—the South Styrian vineyards, which really deserve a route all for themselves. **EHRENHAUSEN** is the sort of unexpected treasure one could only find in Styria: Renaissance castle (twelfth-century fortress rebuilt with original tower still in existence), mausoleum built by the Eggenbergs between 1609 and 1680, left unfinished and completed later, a fine eighteenth-century parish church and town hall, eighteenth-century Emma fountain and even earlier plague column, some charming old houses and the attractive Georgi Schlössl sitting high on a hill (nineteenth-century admittedly, but rather picturesque seen from below)—and all this is in a 'town' of 1,050 inhabitants!

Outside Ehrenhausen turn left for Ober-Vogau which will bring you onto 67 for Leibnitz.

LEIBNITZ (pop: 7,800) stands—almost—on the site of the old Roman Flavia Solva, founded by Vespasianus (details at Joanneum in Graz and some also at Schloss Seggau). It's now a pert little market town (centre of the South Styrian wine trade, but also known for tobacco, green pumpkin seed oil and chestnuts) with attractive old houses (No. 19 Hauptplatz: Renaissance portico).

Drive through Leibnitz and at the end turn right (direction Graz) and almost immediately afterwards left for Schloss Seggau. Drive up the Seggauberg for **Schloss Seggau** with consists of three separate castles, including **Schloss Polheim** (03452 2435 May to October). Note Roman reliefs in arcaded courtyard. Part of the castle, as well as a newly-built separate area, are now run as hotel and holiday flats respectively, complete with swimming pool and restaurant. This is not luxurious castle living, but comfortable accommodation and very reasonably priced (03452 2435). Vines were grown around Seggauberg well over 2,000 years ago, but commercially 'only' since Roman days and the wine cellar at Schloss Seggau is a mere stripling at just over 300 years old—well worth a visit! See also the pilgrimage church at Frauenberg (south of Schloss Seggau) where during restoration work in 1951 the foundation walls and apsis of a Roman temple dedicated to Isis Noreia were found.

Return to main road 74 and turn left (direction Eibiswald and Deutschlandsberg). The road runs along the river Sulm, with the particularly warm Sulmsee on the left. Drive as far as Heimschuh and at the end of the village—practically opposite the village sign—turn right (signposted Einöd, also marked Römerstrasse). Careful, this is easy to overlook! This particular road gets rather narrow and steep as it twists along, but it also leads through some particularly pretty scenery (if you are worried about winding road—or have missed the turning—take the next one on the right, at the beginning of the next village, Fresing). The road winds and twists, with magnificent views; at the junction (no signs, but it's the top of the road) turn right. (This is in fact the road that comes up from Fresing and you are now joining it.) Drive straight on. On the left is a seventeenth-century church (later additions, rococo altar), and the Styrian Wine Museum in an eighteenth-century vintners house (open from 1 April to 30 November; otherwise by arrangement, 03456 2243). This is **KITZECK**, at 564 m above sea-level, reputedly the highest wine village in Europe. As villages go, it's fairly widely spread, but charming. **Weinhaus Kappel** (03456 2347, closed Thursday open March to January) has excellent food, good accommodation and reasonable prices. **Steirerland** (03456 2328, closed Wednesday, open February to

Kitzeck im Sausal—the highest wine-growing region in Europe

December—farther along the road, follow directions for Steirerland) is
another excellent restaurant (where they wrap escalopes in ground hazel-
nuts instead of breadcrumbs) with pleasant accommodation. Plenty of
signs for Kernöl and Buschenschenken along this road. The latter would
certainly be worth trying were it not for those two excellent restaurants!
Tourist Office: at Gauitsch (03456 2243)

Wind your way down to main road 74, following signs—which admittedly are sparse—for Graz and Gleinstätten and even if you miss a turning
you should still come out on 74. On reaching 74 turn right through
Gleinstätten (direction Deutschlandsberg) and then right onto 76 for
Deutschlandsberg Zentrum. Archduke Johann (practically 'patron saint'
of Styria for he ruled not only wisely, but well and even—having finally
won round his brother, the emperor—married a postmaster's daughter
from Aussee) called **DEUTSCHLANDSBERG** the 'paradise' of Styria.
Far be it from me to quarrel with an archduke for whose judgement in
other matters I have the highest respect, but other places spring to mind
before Deutschlandsberg. It is a thoroughly nice little town, however,
centre of the Schilcher wine country, at the foot of the Koralpe, with a
twelfth-century (restored) **Burgruine Landsberg** (now good hotel and
restaurant 03462 2760), some good Baroque houses in main square and
particularly pleasant shops.

Continue on 76 direction Stainz, through **FRAUENTAL** (Renaissance Schloss Frauental on right), which has an excellent patisserie, to
STAINZ. The former Augustine monastery became the residence of Archduke Johann, who was also a Mayor of Stainz, and the building is now a
museum (April to October 034633 2772). See also collegiate church St
Katharina and nice old houses in main square. **Wolfbauer-Barbaeck**
(03463 2291 closed Wednesday) is a typical Styrian inn and so is **Messner**

(03463 2115) with its own butchery and said to make the best Sulmtaler Krainer sausages in Styria.

This is Schilcher country—wine which varies in colour from light to almost dark pink and made from the Wildbach grape. During August there is always a special Schilcher festival. There is also a narrow-gauge railway which operates during the summer between Stainz and Wohlsdorf, when every guest is given a free 250 g bottle of Schilcher which should make for a happy journey ... Tourist Office: town hall (03463 2211).

'From Graz to Stainz there are seven hills' it used to be said. They are not noticeable now: simply drive on 76, which changes to 70 for no reason at all, through so-called Höllental (Hell's valley—very tame now, but in the old days travellers were often waylaid there) and **TOBELBAD**. See the Festsaal by Josef Carlone (1731-1732), also the sixteenth-century parsonage, formerly an Imperial hunting lodge. Then on to Graz (see next route).

The Green Heart

2-3 days/about 175 km/from Graz

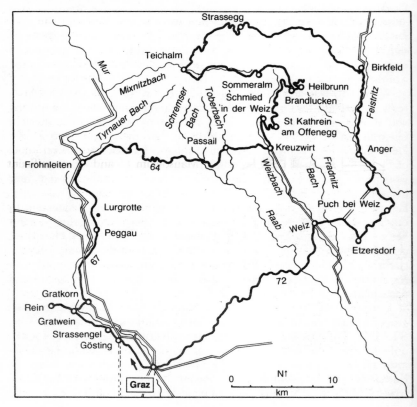

A route that leads to the heart of Styria—starting from Graz along the river Mur valley, with brief excursions to the oldest Cistercian monastery in Austria and a stalactite grotto, then to Frohnleiten which looks like a toy town—particularly if seen from across the river. From there it goes on to St Kathrein, voted the prettiest village in Styria and to the lush meadows of the Teichalm—the largest cultivated Alpine pasture area in Europe, stretching out at about 1,400 m above sea-level. The journey back to Graz delves deeply into 'apple country' with some very pretty rural towns on the way.

GRAZ (pop: 243,000) is the capital of Styria, the second-largest city in Austria and a ravishing beauty. And well she knows it! Sometimes compared to Salzburg—probably because of the 'fortress on a hill' aspect—except that the Schlossberg in Graz has not got a Schloss any more: it was pulled down as a condition of the peace treaty after the Napoleonic Wars and there is now a beautiful park instead. Only the clock and bell towers were left standing (Graz citizens paid 2,987 Gulden and 11 Kreuzer for that privilege! And when Napoleon came to Graz and expected due respect to be paid to him, the eldermen of Graz made it quite clear that he was NOT there by invitation . . .)

At night the way up—stone steps subtly lit—is magical, but it is more comfortable to take the 'elevated train' for a splendid view of the town before starting to explore it. The Tourist Office at Kaiserfeldgasse 25 (0316 76591) will provide maps, information and a guide if wanted, as

The glockenspiel in Graz, which plays every day at 11am and 6pm

well as details of conducted walks through the city. 'See the sights' by all means, such as the sixteenth-century Landhaus and the arsenal, the fifteenth-century cathedral, the marvellous arts collection at the Joaenneum, the castle, the famous Mausoleum and magnificent Baroque Schloss Eggenberg, and lots more besides. But above all, gently *explore* Graz, on foot: steeply rising little Sporgasse; the 'farmers market' on Kaiser-Josef Platz; look into the courtyards and passage-ways and up at the façades of ancient houses . . . Buy some bread from the 400-year-old Imperial bakers Edegger-Tax (and admire the shop front); and even getting an aspirin stops being a chore when it is done at the ancient pharmacist in the Herrengasse . . .

Schlossberghotel (0316 702557) is a charming small *hotel garni*, built against the fortress hill (with terraces and even a tiny swimming pool hewn into the rock); **Erzherzog Johann** (0316 76551) is another good, stately hotel—both with restaurants. Good restaurants—and patisseries—abound in Graz, such as the excellent **Hofkeller** (0316 702439), traditional **Goldene Pastete** (0316 73416) and **Stainzerbauer** (0316 71106). Outside Graz there is the elegant **Plabutscherschlössl** (0316 571055) and **Schloss Planken-warth** (03123 2838), priced accordingly, though by no means exorbitant. (Plankenwarth is also run as a hotel.)

Leave Graz on 67 which leads onto a short stretch of motorway. Exit after about 2km at Graz Nord for **STRASSENGEL** which, with its Gothic pilgrimage church and Provost house and sixteenth-century former tavern for pilgrims, looks like a huge fortress on a hill. The church tower was a sort of 'trial' run 'for St Stephen's in Vienna', but see particu-larly the fourteenth-century painted glass windows, pulpit and paintings by Kremser Schmidt.

From Strassengel follow directions for **GRATWEIN**, a pretty village set against a background of mountains (impressive fifteenth-century church, but its fifteenth-century painted glass windows are now at Joanneum in Graz), where turn left for **REIN**. **Stift Rein**, founded in 1129 by Margrave Leopold I, is the oldest Cistercian monastery in Austria. In its present form it dates back to the eighteenth century. (Guided visits on Sundays at 3pm, otherwise by arrangement 03124 516210.) See particularly: Deanery church with frescoes by Josef Mölck; Tumba of Archduke Ernst; library.

Retrace your steps to Gratwein and cross river, direction Gratkorn which will bring you onto 67 where turn left (direction Peggau. If you have strayed onto the S35 motorway by mistake, exit at Peggau.) Entrance to **Lurgrotte** is signposted just outside Peggau. This is one of the most beautiful stalactite grottos in Europe, 7km long, well-lit and with conducted tours lasting 1, 2 and 3 hours (open 1 April to 31 October, 03127 2580).

Continue on 67 which turns into an unnumbered road (it is in fact 121, but does not say so on any map) and after Ungersdorf follow direc-tions for **FROHNLEITEN**.

Frohnleiten sits prettily on the Mur river, framed by gentle hills and the best place from which to admire it, before crossing over on the old bridge to explore it, is from the terrace of **Gasthof Weissenbacher** (03126 2334). Seen from across the river it looks like a toy town set down very carefully by a giant's hands, and it is every bit as enchanting on closer inspection. Frohnleiten was founded in 1300, but severely damaged by fire and rebuilt, which explains the attractive rococo interior of the parish church (and also the missing church tower). See also: old fortifi-cations, former St Katherine's church (now apartments) and tower; old monastery garden, houses round market square, and lots more.

Return to unnumbered 121 and first follow directions for Bruck and Weiz and, shortly afterwards, for Region Teichalm, Passail which will bring you onto 64, later signposted Weiz, Rechberg. This is a lovely panoramic road with plenty of wide parking spots for viewing at leisure and even for having a picnic. Continue on 64 for about 17 km until you come to a road fork with garage and farmhouse on left; take the right fork, signposted Weiz (still 64), to **PASSAIL** which was founded by the Stubengergs in the thirteenth century. Here you can see two types of farmhouses—cluster-type and three-sided. Also interesting are the seventeenth-century church, some sixteenth-century houses (including parsonage with Roman stone dated AD 1) and little seventeenth-century St Anna's Church, north of the village on a hill.

Still on 64 drive for about another 4 km (still signposted Weiz and St Kathrein, also Sommeralm and Brandlucken) until you reach an inn called Kreuzwirt, where turn left (signposted Birkfeld, St Kathrein). Stay on this road for about 4 km to Schmied in der Weiz where turn right following directions for St Kathrein. **ST KATHREIN AM OFFENEGG** was voted the prettiest village in Styria and the reason for this is apparent as you approach: an absolute picture-book village, wreathed in flowers, sitting on top of a hill. It is 972 m above sea-level with sturdy little inns like **Gasthof Schwaiger** (03179 8234 and 8383), **Gasthof Eder** (03179 8235) and **Gasthof Pieber** (03179 9236), all with comfortable rooms, food in enormous quantities and at almost ridiculously low prices—Styrian hospitality at its best.

When—and if—you want to leave St Kathrein, leave from the main square (school on right) and take the road marked Sommeralm, Brandlucken to T-junction and what will now almost appear to be a main road (compared to the one you have travelled on). Turn right for Brandlucken. (A 4 km detour along a twisty road to the right leads to Heilbrunn, 1,032 m above sea-level, a place of pilgrimage with a pretty eighteenth-century church built on earlier foundations and recently restored. Legend tells of a blind Dutchman who regained his sight at the 'Heilin Brunn' well. There's an eighteenth-century chapel in front of well).

St Kathrein am Offenegg

Turn left at Brandlucken (or take right fork if returning from Heilbrunn) for **SOMMERALM** which lies 1,400 m above sea-level. There are lovely walks from there across the Teichalm region, the largest cultivated Alpine pasture area in Europe. Sommeralm is the highest point. From there the road meanders along the little Mixnitxbach. At Angerwirt turn right, signposted Bruck 34 km. There is a pretty little lake at **TEICHALM**—which despite the 'top of the world' location can get a bit crowded during the season—but **Zum Teichwirt** (03179 23260) is well equipped to cope. It is large, sprawling and comfortable, with good food, own patisserie and very reasonable prices. **Teichalmhaus Pierer** is a fraction farther from the lake and seems more exclusive and a little quieter, an old family hotel with the cosy **Latschenhütte** directly on the lake (03179 23272).

Skirt the lake, past Hotel Pierer on left and follow signs to Bruck. This is a fairly narrow road, joining a larger road where turn right (signposted Birkfeld 23 km) after which the road narrows again and gets rather bumpy with many twists and turns. (Drive carefully along this comparatively short stretch which has a 19 to 22 per cent gradient and don't curse me too much. I have done all I can to encourage the authorities to improve the road—and for all I know it has had some effect by now—it is only for a few kilometres and as soon as you arrive at Strassegg it is all plain sailing.) Drive on this road (direction Birkfeld) through Gasen. Just before Birkfeld, at Haslau, you will see a sign pointing to the right saying '**Forellenwirt Restaurant Kulmer**' and if it happens to be the right time of day (and not a Monday or Tuesday when they are closed) it is a sign which you would do well to follow. A very simple inn, with trout a speciality as the name implies. Resist the temptation to have one of their puddings—wait for Birkfeld!

Return to the main road and on to **BIRKFELD** where you can visit the delicious patisserie **Heschl** (03174 4565—excellent bread too) next to the church. Birkfeld is a pretty little market town with attractions other than the patisserie (remarkable though it is for a town with a population of 1,600). There's the Deanery church (originally thirteenth-century, but pulled down as it was too small and newly built in the eighteenth century, with particularly good Baroque interior); formerly Gothic charnel house transformed into an eighteenth-century chapel; some delightful old houses; and, just outside Birkfeld, the sixteenth-century Schloss Birkenstein sitting above the river, with dreamy arcaded courtyard; and, just north of town, thirteenth-century gallows. Birkfeld is also where you can board the old Feistritztalbahn—a narrow-gauge steam railway which runs between Weiz and Birkfeld, along a line with many bridges, tunnels and viaducts, using the original coaches which date from around 1900 (open in July and August).

Leave Birkfeld on 72 (direction Weiz) along the Feistritz river through Koglhof (Schloss Frondsberg on right on hill, surrounded by Feistritz river on three sides. Perfect example of medieval fortress turned into Renaissance castle, remarkable Rittersaal; seventeenth-century chapel) to **ANGER** where the little train from Birkfeld can also be boarded. This is a pretty village with an impressive church (Gothic frescoes, beautiful altar), also a former pilgrimage church at the cemetery, and some attractive old houses and sturdy inns.

Continue on 72. Drive slowly as you will want to take a left fork about 3 km outside Anger (signposted Hartberg, Stubenberg and Puch 5 km) which is easy to overlook. Follow signs for Puch. There are several routes and if you miss one turning, there is bound to be another, as eventually 'all roads lead to Puch'. You are now deep into 'apple country'. It is a lovely route, through orchards and past farmhouses with signs offering fruit (strawberries as well as apples), honey and some pretty potent apple brandy. None is better in the region than the one sold at **Ettljörg-Scholz 'Zum Bäck'** at Puch, a marvellous thick-walled country inn where they bake their own bread, offer delectable Brettljausn (all kinds of home-cured meats and sausages, several kinds of bread, good Styrian wine and of course, their apple brandy which they call 'Apfelwurm'). Full meals as well, of course, and very comfortable rooms (large public swimming-pool right behind hotel). They are particularly welcoming to children who are given their own apple trees. Full board for a week (for adults) costs about as much as a night's bed and breakfast in a luxury hotel in a big town. Indeed, that goes for most of rural Styria. **PUCH** is considered 'the' apple village, and most endearing it is too, with its fifteenth-century church, and eighteenth-century parsonage, all surrounded by orchards.

Leave Puch via Schrankenhof and Lingstätten to Etzersdorf, where turn right for Weiz—past Schloss Münichhofen—which will bring you onto 72, from where follow directions for Weiz, then for Weiz Zentrum. This should bring you into the centre via the suburb of **Weizberg** and the beautiful Deanery and pilgrimage church on the hill (see particularly frescoes by **Mölck**, High Altar and 'Rosary' altar, pulpit).

WEIZ (pop: 9,500) is really a small industrial town—though mercifully all the industry is outside the town centre (and the late nineteenth-century 'Elin-Union' buildings are certainly worth a glance in passing). The centre of Weiz has many charming Renaissance and rococo houses as well as a twelfth-century fortified church (St Thomas of Canterbury), Tabor (fortified tower) and sixteenth-century Schloss Ratmannsdorf (now the County Court). **Modersnhof** (03172 3747), a Romantik hotel, just outside the town at Buchl is rather special: good, if rather pricey restaurant, charming rooms and blissfully quiet. Tourist Office: Südtiroler Platz 3 (03172 231925)

From Weiz take 72 for Graz—a good, if sometimes rather winding route, which leads past Schloss Dornhofen on the little Rabnitz river to **MARIA TROST** with its important pilgrimage church set on a hill (see particularly marble altars and fifteenth-century painting). Maria Trost, like all places of pilgrimage, abounds in good inns and restaurants; such as the **Kirchenwirt** (0316 391112) and **Ohnime** (0316 391143) both of which also have good accommodation. Also at Maria Trost: a seventeenth-century chapel Maria Grün and a tram museum.

From Maria Trost return to Graz on 72.

6 UPPER AUSTRIA
(Oberösterreich)

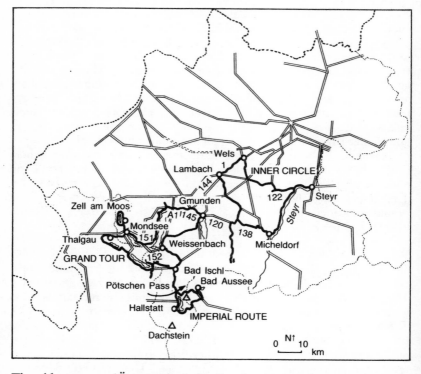

The old name was 'Österreich ob der Enns'—Austria above the Enns, the river which forms the border between Upper and Lower Austria. Not an important border now, but from the end of the Second World War until 1955 it was the demarcation line before entering the Russian zone.

Upper Austria is a province of many different aspects and many changes of scenery: the dark forests of the Muhlviertel, which is really an extension of Bohemia; wide farmlands where 'Vierkanthöfe' ('four-square' buildings) sit like farmers' castles in the middle of vast fields, rich and dominating; the Danube valley. Above all, the Salzkammergut, Austria's lake district, the largest part of which is in Upper Austria, has some of the loveliest landscape in Europe (and where for all its popularity there are still stretches of 'undeveloped' beauty.)

Linz is the capital, but the charming old market town of Wels with its Baroque town hall is the geographical centre. Anton Bruckner and Adalbert Stifter were natives of Upper Austria and, according to Austrian writer, Hans Weigel, it also holds the key to 'why Kafka had to be Austrian and why the Austrians did not consider him in the least sensational': the railway station of Selztal with no exit or entrance, where you cannot alight or board, but merely change trains!

The Inner Circle

2-3 days/about 210 km/from Wels

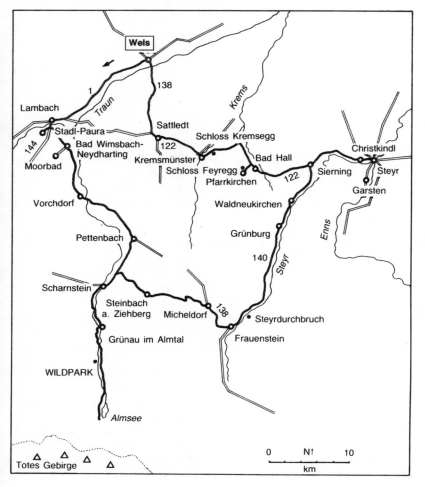

A truly rural route picked as much for the scenic beauty as for the places of interest on the way. There are some exceptional buildings, such as the Stadl-Paura church or the observatory at Kremsmünster (the first high-rise building in Europe, constructed in the eighteenth century), as well as some unusual towns, like ancient Steyr, all well away from the usual tourist routes. Allow time to appreciate it all, to absorb the atmosphere and pause on the way—and also to enjoy some good meals whilst you are about it.

WELS (pop: 55,000) sitting solidly on the river Traun is the town where the Muses kissed Hans Sachs in 1513 (whereupon he resolved to become a poet), where the Emperor Maximilian I died in 1519 (having left Innsbruck in a flurry of unpaid bills on his way back from Augsburg, when Innsbruck hostelries refused to put up his retinue unless they were paid), and Austria's top town for shopping as the posters acclaim. It is certainly very old—the name probably stems from the pre-Celtic Vilesos, 'on the curves'—obviously those of the river Traun. The Romans called it Ovilavis and it was nominated 'Colonia'—which was more or less the equivalent of being given town status—by Emperor Caracalla. The importance of Ovilavis waned during the following centuries, to rise again as Castrum Uueles in the eighth century. It became a market town in 1056 and was declared a city by the Babenbergs in 1222, after which it remained a prosperous trade centre until well into the seventeenth, and again from the nineteenth century onwards. No wonder Wels' main square (Stadtplatz) is a multi-splendoured thing, with its may Baroque facades, but also Gothic and Renaissance features such as arcaded court-yards and alcoves. Tourist Office: Stadtplatz 55 (07242 3495) in a sixteenth-century building with arcaded courtyard, will provide 'Walkman sightseeing' with tape (in English) for a very small fee. If you want to strike out on your own, make a point of seeing Burg Wels, Altstadt 13, where Maximilian I resided and died—now a museum (07242 4171; open Tuesday to Sunday, closed Monday. There are in fact several museums housed in this building, including an agricultural one and the Austrian Bakery museum); thirteenth-century Schloss Pollheim; town fortification with Ledererturm (Tanners' tower); parish church (originally Gothic basilica—see particularly the fourteenth-century stained glass windows); and Minoritenkirche (one of the earliest Gothic churches in Austria). Practically all the houses in Stadtplatz deserve to be seen, especially the Baroque town hall, No. 18, with arcaded courtyard; No. 24 known as 'Salome Alt's house'—she was married to Wolf Dietrich, Prince Archbishop of Salzburg and after his fall retired to Wels; and No. 39, a particularly imposing sixteenth-century house. There are many more interesting houses in the square and in Kaiser Josefplatz.

Wels really is a splendid town for shopping (the centre is a pedestrian zone) and there is a great market every Wednesday and Saturday from 6 am until noon at the Marktgelände, as well as a Flea Market at Stadt-platz on Saturday morning. **Hotel Rosenberger** (07242 82236) is a good modern hotel, supremely comfortable and reasonably priced, with a very good restaurant. If you want to sample good—if occasionally robust—local cooking, try **Restaurant zur Linde** (07242 6023, closed Sunday and holidays, Saturday from 3 pm).

Leave Wels on road marked 1—this is the old Vienna/Salzburg road—for **LAMBACH** (pop: 3,100), a tiny market town, completely dominated by the Benedictine monastery. Founded in 1056 by St Adalbero, Count of Wels and Lambach, Bishop of Würzburg—who turned the family castle into a monastery—both church and monastery were partially destroyed in the thirteenth century and gradually rebuilt in the seventeenth and eighteenth centuries. About thirty years ago some Romanesque frescoes were uncovered in the choir of the original church which probably date back to 1080 (the church was consecrated in 1089). These late Ottonian frescoes show a marked Byzantine influence and are considered to be among the best north of the Alps. Lambach Monastery also has its own theatre (where Marie Antoinette attended a performance on her way to France), but see particularly Refectorium and 'Ambulatorium' in North Wing (stucco by Diego Francesco Carlone), library, Kaiserzimmer, Romanesque Adalbero chalice kept in the 'Treasure Chamber'. (Open 9 am to 11 am and 2.30 pm to 5 pm, or by arrangement. 07245 2351).

From Lambach centre (with monastery on left), take a left turn onto 144 (direction Gmunden) and then almost immediately turn right for **STADL-PAURA** where follow directions for Zentrum. Drive through the so-called centre (just a few houses, though—surprisingly—Stadl-Paura has a slightly larger population than Lambach) until you come to a small turning on the right marked 'Stadl-Paura Kirche'. Follow this road which will bring you to the slight hill on which stands the parish and pilgrimage church—one of the most extraordinary churches in Austria. Built between 1714 and 1724 by J.M. Prunner, the church is dedicated to the Holy Trinity and the basis of the ground plan is an equilateral triangle—the usual symbol for Trinity—within and itself containing a circle (for eternity). There are three towers and three porches—yet the church gives the impression of having a twin-towered facade on each of its three sides. The concept of Trinity is carried throughout—there are three altars, three organs—and even the marble glows in three colours—red, white and black. Three artists (Carlo Carlone, Martino Altimonte and Domenico Parodi) were responsible for the altar paintings which the indirect lighting makes appear like stage sets. One might wonder how this church with its great Baroque splendour came to be built in tiny Stadl-Paura: it was commissioned by Johannes Pagl who had risen from rather humble beginnings at Stadl-Paura to become abbott at Lambach—and who had vowed that he would have a very special church built if Lambach and surroundings were spared from the plague. They were and he did.

The very fine Baroque building (also by Prunner) opposite the church used to be an orphanage (founded by Abbot Pagl) for children of fishermen drowned in the Traun and is now the parsonage.

Retrace your steps to the main road and go across (direction Neydharting). You will get a rather splendid view of Lambach on the left. Take the right fork for **BAD WIMSBACH-NEYHARTING**, a sleepy little village with a good Baroque church (remarkable high altar), eighteenth-century castle (with Gothic core) and at nearby 'Totenhölzl' excavations of a Roman villa. The actual 'Moorbad'—practically adjoining the place from which the moor is lifted—with tiny spa centre, circular swimming pool (with moor suspended in water) and pleasant parkland—is about 2 km away and well signposted. Not an elegant spa, but they take the treatments—on the National Health in Austria—very seriously.

From Bad Wimsbach-Neydharting continue to **VORCHDORF** with former Schloss Hochhaus (built around 1600, attractive rococo tower added mid-eighteenth century) and interesting parish church (very good high altar and statuary) and **PETTENBACH** which has a small Gothic Hallenkirche with Baroque interior. In Pettenbach follow directions for Gmunden—and later Aussee—to the right on 120 which will bring you to **SCHARNSTEIN** where the Police and Criminology Museum is housed in Schloss Scharnstein (May to October, closed Monday, 07615 550 and 600).

Leave 120 after Scharnstein, taking the road to the left for **GRÜNAU IM ALMTAL** along the little Alm river, an extremely attractive river valley which is really considered part of the Salzkammergut. Grünau is an idyllic little village set against a background of high mountains. There's an exceptional Baroque altar at the local parish church; it was transferred from Kremsmünster Abbey and it had to be whittled down in size, but is still impressive. **Hotel Almtalhof** (Romantikhotel, 07616 82040, closed 10 October to 20 December and 10 March to 30 April), looking rustic as befits the setting, is in fact rather elegant, beautifully run and not too expensive. **Forellenhof** (Wieselmühle) on the main road is good and solid and moderate in price—ideal for a family holiday (07616 8250). A 14km drive from Grüau will bring you to the romantic **Almsee**—with a huge Game Park *en route*.

Double back to Scharnstein, then follow directions to Pettenbach on 120 for about 4km after which turn right for Steinbach am Ziehberg. Continue through Steinbach (direction Kirchberg) to Micheldorf.

MICHELDORF was known for its scythemakers, particularly in the sixteenth century and there is now a rather unusual Scythe Museum at the old 'Gradn' Forge which also includes some room settings (07582 3407, 1 May to 31 October daily, except Monday. Visit too the Calvary church (Gothic and Baroque on earlier foundations) on Georgenberg where remains of a Gallo-Roman temple were found. As you meet the main road, 138, at Micheldorf turn right, direction Graz (you will find that in doing this you drive out of Micheldorf and then back into it again). Continue direction Graz on 138 for about 6km (signs for 'Sensenschmiedmuseum'—Scythe Museum—on left and you will also see the church on top of Georgenberg), then turn left onto 140 for Steyr and Molln at **FRAUENSTEIN** (Gothic pilgrimage church on hill with particularly fine fifteenth-century carving of 'Madonna with cloak'.)

The drive through the Steyr Valley is exceptionally attractive and when—after about 3 km—you come to a sign on the right marked 'Steyrdurchbruch', pull in at the parking place and go to the observation platform to watch the river crashing through the gorge in a spectacular fashion. Continue through the Steyr Valley at a leisurely pace, passing Leonstein and **GRÜNBURG** where you can meet the longest narrow-gauge railway in Austria, called 'Museum Railway' (built 1889) which runs between Steyr and Grünburg (mid-June to end September, Sundays only). Continue on 140 through Waldneukirchen until you come to road junction at Sierning where turn right into 122 for **CHRISTKINDL**, a tiny hamlet about 2 km outside Steyr. (Christkindl, literally Christ Child, is not only a typically Austrian and Southern German term of endearment for Baby Jesus, but also for Christmas itself and there are Christkindl markets in many towns, including Vienna. Austrian children address their wishes to the Christkindl rather than to Father Christmas—who really does his duty as St Nickolaus on 6 December.)

The story of the hamlet Christkindl starts in 1695 with an organist at Steyr called Sertl who suffered from epilepsy. He was given a small waxen figure of the infant Jesus—a Christkindl in fact—by the local nuns. He took the figurine into nearby woods, setting it into a hollow he had cut into a fir tree—to return time and again to pray at this self-made shrine. He was cured of epilepsy and as the word of his 'miraculous' cure spread, pilgrims came to pray to the 'Christkindl under the skies'. By 1697 a small chapel had been built, but a year later the Abbot of Garsten reported to his bishop that a much larger church was necessary as pilgrims were now coming from far and wide. Building started in 1708 under Carlo Antonio Carlone, but the church was completed by the great Prandtauer whose principal work is Melk Abbey. Consecrated 'Zum göttlichen Christkind', the church is one large central room, formed by five circles arranged as a cross and the very unusual high altar, probably designed by Prandtauer, is a formation of angels and clouds, incorporating the original fir tree. The hamlet—which takes its name from the church—has its own special post office where about 2 million letters get their Christkindl stamp every year.

From Christkindl follow directions for Steyr and Zentrum—the first easy, the latter tricky since Steyr has a rather quixotic little ring road and one-way system which means that you could be going round the town three times before finding the right turn to the centre (the last time this happened to me, a kindly policeman all but took my hand to guide me there). **STEYR** (pop: 43,000) sits at the confluence of rivers Enns and Steyr and any other town possessing merely one or two of its attractions would be gathering visitors from all around the globe. Not so Steyr, where it is all taken for granted—the Stadtplatz with its magnificent old houses which has been described as 'a festive hall under a clear sky', the castles and courtyards, Medieval towers and Renaissance arcades—there is so much that it is almost impossible to decide where to start. Standing on the bridge below the castle perhaps, at the confluence of the two rivers, when on a good day, with the light falling in the right direction, the changing colours of the water as the two rivers mingle mark it as a very special spot. Or should one perhaps first go to Lamberg Castle, towering above—the old Styrapurg, first mentioned in 980 and the very beginning of Steyr? Perhaps best make the Tourist Office the first call, at Stadtplatz 27 (07252 23229) a handsome eighteenth-century building—only to be diverted by Steyr's pride and joy, the '**Bummerlhaus**' facing across the square—a late-Gothic gem with three colonnaded courtyards and a spiral staircase (during recent restoration work a Gothic chapel and precious wooden ceiling were uncovered). The name, incidentally, stems from the time when the house was an inn called Löwenwirtshaus. The old inn sign is still in place—displaying a lion—which everybody agreed at the time looked exactly like the landlord's dog called Bummerl! (Open Monday to Friday, or by arrangement with the Tourist Office). According to a worthy citizen of Steyr there are at least fourteen absolutely essential sights to be seen in and around Steyr and about as many again which it would be a pity to miss. They include the parish church, late-Gothic and begun by Puchsbaum who was architect for St Stephen's in Vienna (Bruckner was a frequent guest at the sacristan's house where the staircase now bears his name—as does the square in which the church stands); Dunklhof, Kirchengasse 16—with one of the most attractive arcaded courtyards in Steyr where serenades are held during the summer; Innerberger Stadel, Grünmarkt 26—a double-gabled Renaissance building once a granary and now the Municipal Museum; Schnallentor—former city toll gate, built 1613; St Michael's Church on the left river bank—

Bummerlhaus at Steyr

built as a Jesuit church in 1635, with excellent frescoes; and Schloss Engelhof, Haratzmüllerstrasse 66—the most beautiful Renaissance building in Steyr. The former watch tower, known as Tabor, standing above St Michael's Church is now **Hotel/Restaurant Minichmayr** (07252 23410) with good views from the terrace. **Gasthof Mader**, Stadtplatz 36 (07252 23358) is a lovely old-fashioned inn with good food and pleasant rooms and **Rahofer** (07252 24606) a charming coffee house/patisserie as well as a restaurant.

The former Benedictine monastery at **GARSTEN**, about 2 km south of Steyr, is now a prison, but there are guided tours at the monastery museum and both parish church (former abbey) and monastery are rated as supreme examples of Austrian Baroque.

Leave Steyr direction Bad Hall which means getting back onto 122 for Sierning and then continue on this road to **BAD HALL**. The local iodine/salt springs—said to be the most powerful in Europe—were probably known to the Celts. Present-day Bad Hall is a rather quiet, well-run spa with an exceptionally large and beautiful park and even its own little 'Spa orchestra' (conducted at one time by Gustav Mahler!) **Schloss Feyregg** (07258 2591), an imposing Baroque castle just outside Bad Hall, is now run as a Schlosshotel. Guest rooms are on the ground floor, but if you stay there you will almost certainly be given a chance to view the rest of the castle. Not exactly cheap, but extremely comfortable to the point of being luxurious. (To get there from Bad Hall follow directions for Schloss Feyregg which lead through Pfarrkirchen, where the parish church has an exceptionally fine rococo interior.)

Take 122 out of Bad Hall (direction Kremsmünster). Just outside Bad Hall—in the suburb of **Hehenberg** and well signposted—you will find the excellent **Hofwirt Schröck** (07258 2274, closed Monday), with good fixed-price menus (as well as *à la carte* of course) and nice rooms, all reasonably priced.

Stay on 122 which after about 1km turns left rather sharply for Kremsmünster. **Schloss Kremsegg**—solidly rebuilt in the seventeenth century, probably by Carlo Carlone—now houses a splendid Old Timer Museum of about 70 cars and motorcycles from 1891 onwards (on main road, 07583 361, closed Monday). Continue on 122—you will get an excellent view of Kremsmünster Monastery on approach—and in **KREMSMÜNSTER** follow directions for 'Stift'.

Kremsmünster Monastery, the largest in Austria, looks like a college housed in a huge Vierkanthof, the 'four-square' form of building much favoured in Upper Austria. And, in a sense, this is perfectly correct—Kremsmünster Benedictine Abbey school has existed for over 400 years (Adalbert Stifter was a pupil) and the building consists of no fewer than six Vierkanthöfe—or rather, buildings the design and dimensions of which were clearly based on that of a typical Vierkanthof.

Kremsmünster was founded in 777 by Tassilo III, son of Duke Udilo of Bavaria and a cousin of Charlemagne, with whom he fell out in later years (Tassilo was accused of desertion twenty years after the event and banished to Jumieges monastery near Rouen). The Tassilo Chalice—one of the oldest in the Christian world (copper inlaid with silver and gilded)—was probably made for Tassilo's wedding, but it is not quite certain whether he presented the chalice to the monastery or whether this was done by his wife Liutpurga after he was imprisoned, to keep it safe from Charlemagne's clutches!

In its present form Kremsmünster is mainly the work of that well-known 'successive' team of Carlo Carlone followed by Prandtauer, though others took part in it as well. Since a 'minimum' description of Kremsmünster and its treasures runs to about ten closely-set pages, with each item listed as an absolute 'essential', it would be futile to attempt this here—but there are sections which deserve special attention: the ornamental fish tanks—started by Carlone and enlarged by Prandtauer—colonnaded and embellished with statuary, where 'the fish live in richer surroundings than many a bishop' (how long before somebody copies the design for a swimming pool at some grand hotel?); and ask to see the Kaisersaal—absolutely magnificent with a huge fresco by Melchior Seidl; the library, 65 m long and divided by wide arched doorways, is stunningly beautiful, with valuable manuscripts, 630 books produced before 1500 (before Gutenberg invented the printing press) and about 140,000 later works; the 'treasury' which holds two Gospels over 1,000 years old; the observatory—begun in 1748, but only completed in 1759 (part of the top floors had collapsed as builders were unfamiliar with this type of construction) looks almost modern; the first high-rise building in Europe, it is 50 m high.

There is also a shop selling books and, above all, Prälatenwein—and you may heed the legend on one of the fountains 'Guett Watter—Wein better'!

Kremsmünster is open to visitors from Easter until the end of October, 9 am to 10.30 am and 2 pm to 3.30 pm (07583 2750).

From Kremsmünster follow 122 to Sattledt, thence on 138 back to Wels.

Salzkammergut—The Grand Tour

3-4 days/about 190 km/from Bad Ischl

'Go and complain to the Salzamt' one says in Austria if one wants to imply that a complaint is either unjustified or unlikely to succeed—for there is no such place. Yet the Salzamt (Salt Office) did exist, though by various names and the naming of the region known as Salzkammergut stems from it (in a sense it still exists, for salt—like tobacco—is a State monopoly). The people administering and working the salt mines in that area were the 'Hallingers' ('Hall' denoting salt—as in Hallein, Hallstadt, Hall in Tirol) and in 1500 there were about sixteen Hallinger families. In the fifteenth century the Crown took over the Hallingers' interests, compensation—if any—being none too generous, for when Khalss, one of the Hallingers, was enobled in 1612 the citation read: 'As there was a great shortage of salt, the Emperor Friedrich III took away the salt mines and administration from the Hallingers and appointed Khalss as master of mines—who thereafter found great sources of salt.' It also confirmed that the family Khalss had been 'for four hundred years *in continuo* and at this hour ... working the salt mines at Ischl, Aussee ...' all of which sounds much like belated honours rather than cash on the spot at the time of take-over!

The actual administration of the mines passed from the Hallingers to the Hofkammer (Court Chamber) and the estate thus administered became Kammergut (Chamber Estate) the revenue for which went to the

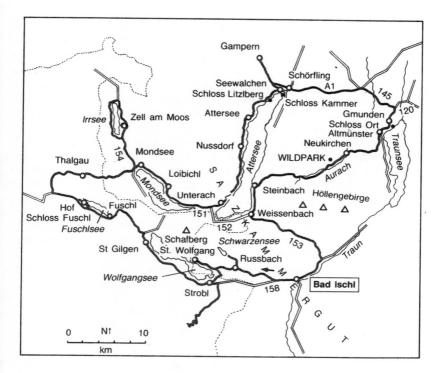

State and it is from this 'Kammergut' that the name Salzkammergut (literally Salt Chamber Estate) came to be applied to the whole area. Anyone disagreeing with that might as well complain to the Salzamt!

The region now known as Salzkammergut has no definite borders and there are occasional discussions as to what is or is not still part of the Salzkammergut (mostly a question of various tourist boards coming to terms with each other). No official map defines the region—the word 'Salzkammergut' is simply spaced over an area that stretches into three provinces—Salzburg, Styria and Upper Austria, the latter having the principal share of land and lakes—and the unofficial 'capital' Bad Ischl. The area around Aussee is known as the Steirische Salzkammergut—as far as Styria is concerned this is the 'real' Salzkammergut and if they could, they would dearly love to add Ischl to it as well. (When the Germans occupied Austria in 1938, they added the whole of the Steirische Salzkammergut to Upper Austria and Styria had to put up a good case to get it back after the Second World War.)

Whatever its borders, the lakes and mountains of the Salzkammergut make it one of the loveliest areas in Austria and although it is so very easily accessible (and close to Salzburg), wide stretches of it have remained completely unspoiled. And will remain so forever, one hopes. Until 1957 a narrow-gauge railway ran from Salzburg to Bad Ischl, skirting the lakes and occasionally pausing in the middle of a meadow—all at a very leisurely pace (it was said that one could get out to pick flowers and still not be left behind). Its official name was the Salzkammergutlokal-bahn—also known as Ischler Bahn or, more fondly, 'Fiery Elias' after the engine about which an operetta of the same name was written (what else?) and duly performed at Bad Ischl (where else?). It now stands proudly on a grass verge along the 158 between Bad Ischl and Strobl, doing its duty as an extra Tourist Office during the season—faithful to the last!

Even the grandest of Grand Tours could not hope to take in all that is most beautiful in the Salzkammergut in one route—I am only too aware of how much had to be left out—but I have included certain vantage points (and also suggested some optional excursions) which I hope will encourage you to explore still further.

Leave **Bad Ischl** (for description see the following (Salzkammergut Imperial) route) on 158, direction Salzburg. After about 5 km, at Pfandl, leave 158 to right, direction St Wolfgang über Russbach. Drive for approximately 5 km until you come to a crossroads, where turn right for Russbach and 'Schwarzensee 2.5 km'. The road up to the **Schwarzensee** has a 17 per cent gradient, but it is fairly short and well worth taking for the lovely seclusion of the lake. A complete circle of the lake on foot takes about one hour, but if you just want to relax at leisure, there is a pleasant restaurant **Zur Lore** on the shores.

Double back from Schwarzensee to the crossroads and 'Stop' sign, and turn right, following directions for St Wolfgang where—unless right out of season—it is prudent to park at the beginning of the village. **ST WOLFGANG** (pop: 2,500) really is as pretty as legend has it, though arriving by car or on foot is not really the best way—ideally it should be approached by boat and if you are taking this route at a leisurely pace, there should be time to take a steamer from just outside the famous **White Horse Inn (Im Weissen Rössl)** for a trip around the lake and returning to St Wolfgang to find it looking exactly as it has done in hundreds of operetta productions. Surprisingly, the **White Horse Inn** (06138 2306) which one might expect to be noisy, touristy and having all the other disadvantages of a living legend, is a superb family-run hotel. Somehow they have managed to keep the two sides of the business—day trippers and permanent visitors (many of whom come back season after season) entirely separate without offending either. It is a Romantik hotel, prices are very reasonable, the food is excellent (marvellous breakfasts, too) and although there have been additions and extensions over the years, service throughout has remained admirable and personal. St Wolfgang—which has immense charm—does not owe its popularity entirely to the operetta though: in the fifteenth, and the early sixteenth century it was one of the most visited places of pilgrimage, ranking in popularity only after Rome, Aachen and Einsiedeln. The local parish church holds one of the great Gothic masterpieces—the triptych altar by Michael Pacher which alone would warrant a journey to St Wolfgang (except for Lent, the altar is now permanently opened). There are also other treasures—in 1675, 200 years after the Pacher altar had been completed, a 'replacement' was ordered from Thomas Schwanthaler (fortunately he could persuade the abbott to leave Pacher's altar in place) and his double altar—considered Schwanthaler's chief masterpiece—stands in the nave. Three beautiful side altars are by Guggenbichler who was also responsible for the pulpit and Ecce Homo statue. See also sixteenth-century pilgrimage fountain (1 May to 31 October) and former parsonage, now 'Schloss'. Tourist Office: 06138 2239.

A little train runs from St Wolfgang to the top of the **Schafberg** mountain with a hotel/restaurant at an altitude of 1,783 m (9 May to 11 October, 06138 2232) and magnificent views, but if you'd just like a brief escape from the crowds at St Wolfgang, there is no better place than the **Hupfmühle** (06138 2579) about ten minutes walk north of the village (you can even drive up to within 100 m of the house). It is set deep in the woods on a little stream—with fresh trout, delectable Strudel (baked by grandmother) and simple, but good rooms—all very reasonably priced.

Return along the way you came—signposted Salzburg and Strobl and then follow signs for Strobl. You are now entering the province of Salzburg. **STROBL**, named after a family who owned the local tavern hundreds of years ago, is a scattered little village with sturdy farmhouses, slightly faded turn-of-the-century villas, eighteenth-century church and a shallow bay for bathing which makes it a 'family favourite'. The **Schlosshotel** (06137 310) though not on the beach, is practically a world on its own (and a fairly luxurious one at that) set in a beautiful park, with good restaurant, coffee house and even a 'Heurigen'—as well as a medically supervised treatment centre for rheumatism (moor baths, underwater therapy). Reasonably priced and very comfortable.

From Strobl follow signs for Salzburg which will bring you back onto 158. (You will see posters for the Postalm which is a 12km drive south from the 158 and, if it is a fine day, you could do worse than allow yourself to be tempted to take it. A perfectly easy drive (a toll road) leading up to an altitude of 1,284 m with beautiful walks along the plateau on top— or just relax at an inn and admire the view.)

Back on the 158 follow directions for Salzburg, past Abersee (which is also the old name for Lake Wolfgang) to **ST GILGEN**, named after St Giles (St Agydius) and one of the most popular resorts on the lake. St Gilgen is still pleasantly old-fashioned—it had one of the earliest lakeside restaurants (complete with terrace) and the hotel on top of the Schafberg was the first mountain hotel in Austria (the railway up to the Schafberg runs from St Wolfgang, but the hotel perched precariously on top belongs to St Gilgen). Mozart's mother was born at Ischlerstrasse 15 and his sister also lived there at one time (now the county court), but one of the most attractive houses is the seventeenth-century **Gasthof zur Post** (06227 239), a very comfortable old inn. See also: parish church with Baroque interior; eighteenth-century chapel in cemetery and some rather attractive old villas. **Hotel Billroth** (06227 217, closed 1 October until 10 May) Billrothstrasse 2, is one of these—though grander than most—set in a lovely park with its own beach. Reasonably priced.

Continue on 158, leaving Lake Wolfgang and travelling towards Lake

Fuschl. **FUSCHL** (pop: 830) snuggles comfortably round the eastern end of the lake—at one time a truly rural retreat with good sturdy hotels like the **Schlick** (06226 237). It is still rural and still a retreat, but there are now more—and more luxurious—hotels, like the excellent **Parkhotel Waldhof** (a Silence hotel; 06226 342, open April/January) though prices are kept within reason and still below those of more fashionable resorts.

Continue in the direction of Salzburg. **Schloss Fuschl** will come into view on the right, set below on the edge of the lake; one of the loveliest and most luxurious hotels in Austria (Relais et Chateaux). It's expensive, but not excessively so. Once the property of the Prince Archbishops of Salzburg (fish were bred in the lake exclusively for the archbishop's table), the former hunting lodge passed into private hands at the end of the last century (in more recent years it was briefly owned by Ribbentrop) and was transformed into a hotel in the 1950s. The view from the dining rooms and terrace is breathtakingly beautiful. It is worth a visit for this alone, even if the food were not as excellent as it is, with many genuine Austrian specialities. (Closed 16 January until 12 February, 06229 22530.) There is now an additional restaurant, the Imperial, which promises to be even better. **Jagdhof am Fuschlsee** (directly on 158, 06229 23720) is under the same management, far more modestly priced—staying there and dining at the Schlosshotel could well provide the best of both worlds. (The road to the Schlosshotel leads down by the side of the Jagdhof. Incidentally, should you ever have occasion to look up either hotel in a telephone directory—they are listed under Hof bei Salzburg, not Fuschl.)

Still on 158, drive through **HOF BEI SALZBURG** (interesting parish church) and about 2 km after Hof turn right, leaving 158 for Thalgau—a lovely peaceful drive through meadows and farmland framed by high mountains—and after about 7 km turn right for Unterdorf and Thalgau. Continue on this road through **THALGAU** (Baroque Deanery church built on earlier foundations) and small villages like Voglhub which will bring you onto 154 at the beginning of Mondsee (town of same name as the lake) and follow directions for Zentrum. Back in Upper Austria once more, **MONDSEE** (pop: 2,500) is a charming small market town on the northern shores of the lake, with particularly attractive sixteenth and eighteenth century houses in the main square (Marktplatz)—only the size of the parish church seems slightly out of proportion. It is in fact the former abbey church of the Benedictine monastery founded in 748, rebuilt in the fifteenth century and considerably altered in the seventeenth and eighteenth centuries (possibly planned by Munggenast). It has an interior of great Baroque splendour (if the church seems familiar to you, your memory is probably not deceiving you—it has featured on countless brochures and in more recent years achieved practically star status on television). Note the Baroque side altars, pulpit and statuary by Guggenbichler; the Gothic sacristy portal and statuary; and the high altar by Hans Waldburger.

The former monastery, mostly rebuilt after a fire in 1774, is now partly a museum (Neolithic Lake dwellings of the area, open 1 May to 18 October, 06232 2270), but see also the fifteenth-century cloister.

Patisserie Frauenschuh (06232 2312) Marktplatz is one of the best in Austria (also light snacks and hot puddings) and **Hotel Weisses Kreuz** (06232 2254) not only a very pleasant hotel, but the food—which has always been excellent—seems to get even better with every visit. (Closed 1 December to 15 December and 15 January to 30 January, restaurant closed Wednesday.)

You could now continue to Unterach on 151, but I would suggest first taking the 154 out of Mondsee for about 5 km—as far as Kasten, where turn left for Irrsee Westufer. It is a somewhat bumpy road, winding its way through meadows and past farmhouses, skirting the **Irrsee**—completely rural and utterly delightful and likely to remain so, for building is severely restricted—until you come to a T-junction at the top of the lake, where turn right and continue to Laiter, then turn right onto 154 for Zell am Moos. This is the more 'fashionable' side of the lake which means that there are a few houses, set well back from the road and mostly hidden by trees. **ZELL AM MOOS** will seem almost large after the seclusion of the western shore—there is a marvellously solid inn called **Gasthof zum Seewirt**, also known as Enzinger, right on the lake; good simple cooking and huge portions.

The 154 will bring you back to Mondsee where turn left onto 151 (direction Unterach and Attersee). At times the road all but touches the water and there are nice grassy patches—like miniature beaches—ideal for a quick swim (the Mondsee is one of the warmest lakes in the Salz-kammergut). **Hotel Seehof** on right at Loibichl (06232 2550, closed mid-September until mid-May) is set most beautifully on the lake, but unfortunately I have no first-hand experience of either hotel or restaurant as they were always closed when I have been there. Continue on 151 (direction Unterach). Rather confusingly the village sign is placed well before the actual village of Unterach—in fact whilst still on the road along the Mondsee (Unterach is on the next lake, Attersee). Just con-tinue on 151 and you will eventually get to **UNTERACH** and when you do, turn right (or right and then immediately left if you missed the first turning) which should bring you onto the road running along the lake (it re-joins 151 at end of village). This is one of the prettiest spots—houses practically built into the water and stately villas, some with a slightly faded grandeur redolent of a past when Unterach was one of the 'in' places (and remembered tales of a famous opera singer who had twenty Dirndl dresses made—of identical cut, but in different colours and materials—'to wear at my villa at Unterach'.)

Rejoin 151 and continue along the lake through small villages (direc-tion Seewalchen). The Attersee is the largest of the Salzkammergut lakes, stretching over 21 km, never very crowded and dotted with small resorts which are ideal for family holidays. Drive through Zell and Nussdorf to **ATTERSEE** where the parish and pilgrimage church above the village is well worth a visit (splendid Baroque altar and pulpit, also statuary by Guggenbichler). Continue on 151 (direction Seewalchen)—you will see Schloss Litzlberg practically standing in the lake on your right and, on the other side of the lake, Schloss Kammer. This is when you will have to make a decision: **Schloss Kammer**—first mentioned in 1249 and lavishly rebuilt in the eighteenth century—is an absolute beauty set on an island in the lake and connected to the mainland by an avenue of Linden trees, subject of a famous painting by Klimt. The castle is privately owned and not open to the public but 'During the weekly concerts in summer all the great rooms may be visited.' Dates for the concerts are not specified and obviously vary, but there is usually a musical festival during the last week in July (and details can be ascertained from 07662 2578 nearer the summer).

You will now have to make up your mind whether to chance your luck—there may after all be a concert at the time or some kindly soul might ask you in (among other things, the castle is being used as a holiday centre by a chemical firm!) and in any case you will certainly be able to look at the outside and the famous Linden trees—in which case follow directions for 152 and Schörfling at the top of the lake which will bring you straight to Schloss Kammer. If, on the other hand, you have decided that Schloss Kammer is best admired from afar, stay on 151 for Seewalchen and make for Zentrum.

SEEWALCHEN is a perfectly pleasant lakeside resort with one of the best restaurants in the Salzkammergut, **Gasthof Häupl** (07662 8300), rather inappropriately called 'Gasthof,' ie Inn, although it is also a fairly luxuriously appointed Silence hotel. Not exactly cheap, but to sit on the terrace overlooking lake and mountains, enjoying Mrs Häupl's superb food (she is one of Austria's star cooks) and possibly spend the night in one of the comfortable bedrooms, is a special treat.

(You may think you have seen enough church interiors by now, but **GAMPERN**, about 5 km north-west of Seewalchen has a beautiful late-Gothic parish church with one of the most important Gothic triptych altars in the country. Worth a detour if it can be fitted in.)

From Seewalchen follow directions for the motorway (not only the best, but in this case the only way) and then direction Gmunden, Wien for about 10 km to exit Regau from where follow signs for Gmunden onto 145.

Gmunden (pop: 13,000) sits very comfortably on yet another Salzkammergut lake—the Traunsee—its main square open to the lake on one side. A town grown rich on salt, Gmunden was the administrative centre of the old Salzkammergut and the principal gateway to the 'outer world', the road leading south from Traunkirchen not being built until 1872 so that everything had to be transported across the lake. There is an abundance of richly-embellished houses such as the sixteenth-century Hotel Schwan with marble portal, arcaded courtyards (Theatergasse 4 and Traungasse 4 and 12) and towered and turreted buildings (Kirchengasse 6 and Kurzmühlgasse 6). The town hall—the third in the town's existence—looks like a Renaissance palace (which in a sense it is) except for the carillon bells which are made of sound Gmunden ceramic. The Kammerhof from which the Chamber Estates were administered—including the famous Salzamt—a splendid building, Gothic at the core—

The town hall, Gmunden

now holds the town's museum (07612 3381 241). The first East/West treaty was signed there in 1514 between Tsar Vassilij Ivanovitsch III and the Emperor Maximilian I (who had also signed and sealed his marriage contract with Bianca Maria Sforza in the same building). See also Gmunden parish church with beautiful Baroque altar by Schwanthaler.

During the last century Gmunden became a favourite retreat for exiled crowned heads—including George V of Hanover who fought on the Austrian side in 1866, lost his all to Prussia and settled at Gmunden where a Protestant church was hastily built for him and his retinue. Only the names now remind of these royal retreats—Schloss Cumberland is now a hospital and Schloss Würtemberg a school, Villa Toscana is attached to a modern congress centre—but Gmunden's 'own' castle and landmark is **Schloss Ort**, sitting majestically on an island in the lake. It consists of two castles—the Landschloss on the shore, basically a 'Vierkanter' ('four-square' building) typical of Upper Austria. Originally seventeenth-century, but much altered in the nineteenth and this century, it is now a school, but can be visited—note the superb casement ceiling in the main hall and wrought-iron 'caged' fountain in courtyard.

A wooden bridge—first mentioned in 1110—runs to the castle in the lake (Seeschloss) which, according to legend, was built on Roman foundations and first mentioned as 'Veste Ort' in 909. Some of the old Gothic structure has remained, but there was massive rebuilding and restoration after a fire in 1634. The chapel—now parish church—was a late Gothic structure with later additions (particularly fine fifteenth-century statue of Virgin Mary and Renaissance frescoes).

Like all the best romantic castles, Schloss Ort—or rather its last owner—is surrounded by mystery. Archduke Johann Salvator, a nephew of Emperor Franz Josef, renounced his titles, married an actress called Milly Stubel and adopted the name of Johann Ort. He sailed from Chatham on the St Margaretha, bound for Buenos Aires—the ship was last sighted in July 1890 and then lost without trace. The fact that he renounced his titles shortly after the Mayerling tragedy in 1889 was thought to be an indication that he might have been involved in some way—and so the mystery remains.

Apart from mysteries such as this particular one, Gmunden has some more tangible treasures like the lakeside promenade and **Patisserie Grellinger**—and **Gmunden Keramik** which has been famous for over 200 years. The factory has existed since the last century at Keramikstrasse 24 (on top of town—07612 5441) known for the so-called 'Grüngeflammte' (smudged stripes of green), but also many other more recent patterns. The factory showroom is an absolute treasure trove for bargains. **Schlosshotel Roith** (07612 4905 and 66081) is a splendid, reasonably priced hotel (open April to October). Tourist Office: Am Graben 2 07612 4305.

Leave Gmunden on 120 (past Schloss Ort) which leads onto 145 for **ALTMÜNSTER** (pop: 8,900) the oldest settlement on the Traunsee. It is a charming lakeside village with rather remarkable Gothic church (note sixteenth-century altar in chapel, also statuary). At the end of Altmünster take small turning on right marked Steinbach am Attersee and Zentrum and then turn left almost immediately for Steinbach. This is one of the most rewarding drives—through the Höllengebirge and following the little Aurach stream. There is a Game Park well-signposted near Neukirchen (07618 205—April to October) if you would like to meet a Mufflon!

Continue on this road, signposted Steinbach, and you will arrive virtually on top of the Attersee. Take the left fork for Steinbach—the road winds down to the lake very gently until you meet the 152 on the shores at **STEINBACH**. Gustav Mahler had a little retreat nearby—call at **Gasthof Föttinger** (07663 3420 and 4930) if you want to visit it—or call at Föttinger in any case, since it is a good, reasonably-priced family inn on the lake.

From Steinbach follow 152 (direction Weissenbach) along the lake—and at times all but in the lake. **WEISSENBACH** has the only slightly 'grand' hotel on the lake—**Hotel Post** (07663 240 and 208), recently rebuilt, very comfortable and not too expensive. Also **Villa Langer** (07663 242) which is lovely and secluded—and an absolute joy.

At Weissenbach take 153 to left for Bad Ischl. You will notice a small jeweller's shop at the corner, **Trucker** (07663 234), with a parking place placed conveniently opposite. It's worth a look-in—all the work is done on the premises and most reasonably priced. (Closed Saturday.)

The 153 leads along the little Weissenbach (pause to admire the green, crystal-clear water—there are practically no houses for about 10km and it is one of the most attractive stretches in the Salzkammergut) to Mitterweissenbach, onto 145 and back to Bad Ischl.

Salzkammergut—The Imperial Route

1 day/about 70 km/from Alt Aussee (80 km from Salzburg)

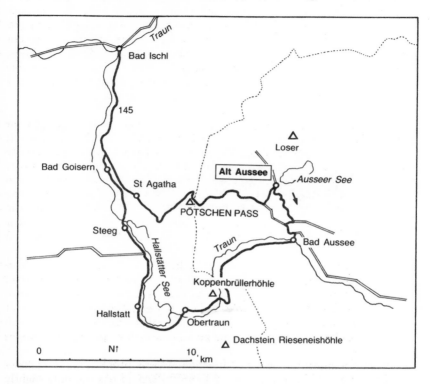

The area around Alt Aussee and Bad Aussee is known as 'Steirisches Salzkammergut' and although part of the old Kammergut it likes to be looked upon as a world on its own—which it is. Deeply traditional—there are strong associations with the legendary Archduke Johann (practically the Patron Saint of Styria), whose wife was the daughter of an Aussee postmaster—it links far more naturally with Bad Ischl in Upper Austria than with the more popular holiday resorts of the Salzkammergut. Bad Ischl is of course forever associated with the Emperor Franz Josef—it was his summer residence and even his very birth is attributed to the beneficial effects of the saline spa: his parents 'took the waters' at Bad Ischl for several seasons before his birth and Franz Josef and his brothers were known as the Salt Princes.

The route leads from Alt Aussee and Bad Aussee past the foot of the Dachstein mountain to Hallstatt—deep, dark and mysterious—and on to Bad Ischl with a return journey across the panoramic (but very easily negotiated) Pötschen Pass back to Alt Aussee.

ALT AUSSEE (pop: 2,000) is scattered round the lake like confetti: few

101

Alt Aussee

houses (except for the very centre) stand next to each other, and even then only in small groups, sitting on the edge of a meadow or on a hill rising towards the mountains, wreathed in flowers and looking like the Imperial posy set in precious stones which is kept at the Hofburg in Vienna. Aussee has been a favourite holiday resort of poets and writers from the nineteenth century onwards and the lake—dark green shading into blue on a fine day—was once called 'the inkpot into which we all dip our pens'. Certainly the grass seems to smell sweeter, the scent of sun-warmed pines is headier and the mountains mirrored in the lake appear to stand out more clearly than anywhere else—and Alt Aussee has remained completely unchanged. No-one has thought about building a high-rise hotel on the lake—and if they had, it would have to stop with the thought, for even the building of private houses is severely restricted. This makes for one of the loveliest walks around the lake, the paths strewn with pine needles, thickly carpeted with wild strawberries and sweet-smelling cyclamen. In spring the meadows sloping to the lake are covered so densely with narcissi that it looks as if winter had come back overnight and snow had fallen once more, while at the beginning of June there is the famous Narcissi Festival with 'sculptures' of narcissi everywhere. (On Shrove Tuesday there is a huge Carnival procession at which the 'Flinserl' play a prominent part—'Flinserl' being worthy Aussee citizens allowed to wear robes entirely covered with sequins—not unlike those worn by London's Pearly Kings and Queens, except that they glitter with every movement.)

Salt is still being mined at the nearby Sandling mountain as it has been since the twelfth-century (at the end of the Second World War art treasures were stored in the mine which came close to being blown up on Hitler's orders). The salt mine is open to visitors (note particularly St Barbara Chapel underground) from 18 May until 12 September (Monday to Saturday, closed Sunday and holidays. 06152 71332). Alt Aussee has a very pleasant spa centre and an unusual 'inhalation room' on the edge of the woods which is open day and night—completely free of charge—where the natural saline solution drips down the walls in a steady trickle and evaporates. You just walk in whenever you like to inhale the salty air—supposed to be beneficial for all sorts of respiratory diseases (I found it brought great relief during an attack of sinusitis) and certainly very relaxing—a great aid to sound sleep if visited fairly late in the evening.

From Alt Aussee a splendid road leads up to an altitude of 1,600 m on the Loser mountain from where a comfortable 15 minutes walk will bring you to a small mountain lake. Alt Aussee has some good hotels and inns—it is just a question of choosing the one most suited to one's own preference. **Seevilla** (06152 71302) right on the lake is the grandest (though not at all 'grand' in a pompous way—it is owner-run by a nice music-loving family who are rather proud of the fact that Brahms stayed at a house previously on that site).

Hubertushof (06152 71280) sits beautifully above the village with marvellous views—a former princely hunting lodge now run as a hotel garni (though light snacks are often willingly provided). **Zum Loser** (06152 71373) is a good solid inn with very good food (home-smoked fish) particularly if they will curb their flirtation with nouvelle cuisine. **Schneiderwirt** is where the locals go to eat (and probably have done since it was built in 1550). Tourist Office: Kurhaus (06152 71643).

Leave Alt Aussee (direction Bad Aussee), following the river most of the way. **BAD AUSSEE** (pop: 5,000), though a market town since 1295, is much younger than Alt Aussee (hence the 'Alt' for the original settlement). The administration of the salt mines was transferred to Bad Aussee in the thirteenth century, even before they became Kammergut (Chamber Estates)—witness the magnificent Kammerhof at Chlumecky-platz (now a museum), which remained administrative centre until 1924, with window and door frames in red marble, built probably round 1400 and greatly embellished in the seventeenth century. There are many fine old houses, though it means a steady climb to locate some of them (Bad Aussee was originally made up of a Lower and Upper market) such as the Hoferhaus at Chlumeckyplatz 2 (sixteenth-century frescoes), Herzheimer-haus at Hauptstrasse 156, fifteenth-century town hall (Hauptstrasse 48) and many more. Meranplatz 37 was the birthplace of Anna Plochl, wife of Archduke Johann whose era brought forth a spate of building and there are some lovely old villas dating back to that time. See also the parish church (Romanesque nave, remarkable fifteenth-century Madonna) and fourteenth-century Spitalskirche (two fifteenth-century triptych altars—one bearing Friedrich III's 'Hallmark' AEIOU which he used to affix everywhere—there are about 300 conflicting interpretations for those initials).

Aussee has been a spa since the end of the nineteenth century and been allowed to carry the official 'Bad' before its name since 1911. There are in fact several 'spas' for drinking as well as for bathing, plus packs with saline mud—as well as a very modern spa centre. Tourist Office: Kurhausplatz (06152 2323). **Villa Kristina** (06152 2017) is a charming hotel set in a beautiful park, **Blaue Traube** (06152 4471) a good sturdy inn and **Hotel Wasnerin** (06152 2108) has been appreciated by whole generations of families (outside town). **Lewandofsky** is a superb patisserie (marvellous honeycakes which can also be bought at the shop across the road) where, as someone once remarked, even the waitresses look as if they had been modelled in marzipan. And, if you have ever hankered after a typical Styrian hat complete with chamois brush (getting rarer and rarer), **Leithner** is the place—'since 1532' as they proudly proclaim.

From Bad Aussee follow directions for Obertraun and Hallstatt—the road which runs along and above the river Traun has an upward gradient of 16 per cent and a downward one of 23 per cent—passing into Upper Austria. You will notice Gasthof Koppenrast on the way—it is about 20 minutes walk from there to the **Koppenbrüllerhöhle** (open daily 1 May to 30 September, 06131 362), one of the Dachstein caves with a river passing through it. (For the great and magnificent **Dachstein Höhlen**— giant ice caves, Mammoth cave with a 40km labyrinth, cave museum, etc., follow signs for 'Dachsteinseilbahn' from Obertraun to cable car station. Guided tours from 1 May to 15 October. Worth a separate trip, but take warm, weatherproof clothing.)

At the end of Obertraun take left fork, badly signposted for Hallstatt and Bad Ischl. You will get a splendid 'advance view' of Hallstatt as you drive along—the road runs close by the lake which looks rather inviting at this point—and there are plenty of convenient spots for having a quick dip. The picture changes completely as you approach Hallstatt—the lake turning almost black and the whole of Hallstatt seems remote and unreal, as if it had risen from the lake by some dark mysterious force. Houses cling to the hillside, and you fear that they might slip back into the lake and disappear forever.

Salt has been mined at **Hallstatt** for 2,800 years, and probably long before that time. It is certainly the oldest known salt mine in the world, but Hallstatt's most important period was between 800 and 500 BC giving the name of Hallstatt to a whole epoch (Hallstatt Period). There are about 2,000 Illyrian graves of which nearly 1,000 were opened (the most valuable finds of that and previous eras are at the natural history museum in Vienna, but much can still be seen at the two local museums). In the seventeenth century a wooden pipeline using some 13,000 trees was constructed to run between Ebensee and Hallstatt, a distance of approximately 40km, to transport the saline solution. Entrance to the Salt Mine (open 1 May to 15 October) is about 500m above Hallstatt (prehistoric graves on the hill) and is reached by cable car.

The Corpus Christi procession across the lake is 'the' great event of the year, but at whatever time you visit Hallstatt, park your car and explore the tiny town on foot. Don't miss the sixteenth-century houses, eighteenth-century Calvary chapel, parish church with late-Gothic altar

Hallstatt

and one of Hallstatt's most famous—if somewhat gruesome—sights, the Charnel house: because the cemetery is so tiny, bodies are disinterred after 10 to 14 years, the bones bleached in the sun and—a Hallstatt tradition for over 400 years—the skulls are painted (ivy and oakleaves for the men, wreaths of Alpine flowers for the women), fully inscribed with their names (and titles, of course!) after which they are neatly piled up in the charnel house where they are photographed so much that the colours have started to fade ... All part of a new Hallstatt culture, one might say ... Tourist Office: Verkehrsamt 06134 208.

Hotel Grüner Baum (06134 263) is a particularly pleasant family hotel with a lakeside terrace, and known for its fish specialities.

Leave Hallstatt (direction Bad Ischl)—there is only one road which leads through a tunnel—and stop where you can for a backward glance at Hallstatt. At the fork bear right for Goisern and Ischl to Steeg where the road crosses river and lake—and suddenly everything is light and clear again, the water looks like a bathing lake once more. You begin to wonder whether it is even the same lake and whether Hallstatt was not a Fata Morgana!

Keep on this road which leads through **BAD GOISERN** (pop: 6,500), a rather sedate spa. It is not at all fashionable, but has an excellent **Kur-hotel** (06135 8305) and is the type of spa where Austrian doctors go if they want to 'take the waters'. Other attractions include some quite interesting museums such as a woodcutters' museum, an open-air museum and a cobblers' museum. The latter is linked to Goisern's fame for its heavy mountaineering boots known as 'Goiserer' all over Austria and in mountaineering circles well beyond the borders.

At the end of Goisern the road joins 145, where turn left for Bad Ischl, then follow signs for Zentrum/Stadtmitte (watch out for these, otherwise you could be driving out of Bad Ischl again).

BAD ISCHL (pop: 13,000), the very heart of the Salzkammergut, has been an Imperial spa since 1820. After Franz Josef made it his summer residence in 1854, 'everybody' went to Bad Ischl. There must have been so many famous faces there at one time that one wonders just how ordinary mortals managed to fit in—yet they did, leaving their mark on many a beauty spot—you will still find 'Sterzens Abendsitz' (named after a doctor who liked to rest there in the evening) or 'Ernestine's choice' (whoever she was) along with more famous names such as 'Sophiens Doppelblick' (Franz Josef's mother 'looking both ways') and 'Batthany's Ermunterung', leaving one to guess precisely who or what he found encouraging! Brucker and Brahms, Franz Lehar (who wrote 'The Merry Widow' there—his villa is now a museum) and Emmerich Kalman, Johann Strauss and Oscar Straus—they all spent long periods of time at Bad Ischl and while Johann Strauss also favoured the spa of Baden bei Wien, his villa was at Bad Ischl where he took up summer residence, exactly like his ruling monarch.

Even today, Bad Ischl is still steeped in that tradition. The emperor's birthday is duly celebrated on 18 August, and so is the Glöcklerlauf on the 5 January (where the runners traditionally wear enormous headgear up to 3 m wide and weighing up to 15 kg, lit with candles, ringing bells to drive out evil spirits), and the Lichtbratlmontag in October (a huge and colourful procession ending with a celebratory 'Braten', roast). The Emperor's Villa (Kaiservilla), where Franz Josef signed the Ultimatum that resulted in the First World War, is open to visitors from Easter (or 15 April) until 15 October (06132 3241) and you could possibly be met by Franz Josef's great grandson who is in residence there. (See also the Marmorschlössl in the grounds, built for beautiful Empress Elizabeth. It is now a photographic museum; 06132 4422.)

Patisserie Zauner (06132 3310) Pfarrgasse, is also practically a museum—after Demel in Vienna it's the most famous patisserie in Austria (in fact their selection is infinitely larger than Demel's), but it tends to get crowded and you may have difficulty in getting a table. (If this happens, duly admire the display at Zauner and either buy some pastries to take away or go to **Pracher**, in Kreuzplatz, where the locals go).

Attwenger (06132 3327, closed Monday) next to Lehar's villa on the river Traun is Ischl's best restaurant and absolutely delightful (Brahms stayed there when it was just a little inn and had rooms to let), but the restaurant at **Zum Goldenen Schiff** (06132 4241) directly across the river, though not as elaborate, has much to commend it and they have some very pleasant rooms, many overlooking the river, all reasonably priced. The **Kurhotel** (06132 4271) is large and modern, connected with the up-to-date spa centre by underground passage. During the summer months there is an operetta festival which is getting increasingly popular. Tourist Office: Bahnhofstrasse 6 (06132 3520) who also have detailed information about visiting times for nearby salt mines.

From Ischl take road signposted Graz and Bad Aussee which means doubling back on the 145 as far as Bad Goisern. Alternatively, there is another, very romantic road back to Alt Aussee, leading through dense woods along the Rettenbach river. Beautiful as a walk, but a bit precarious to drive at times.

At Bad Goisern do not go into the town, but continue on 145 through **ST AGATHA** (interesting late-Gothic church—also Gasthaus Petter, an enormous Renaissance building). Cross the Pötschen Pass from which you will get another view of Hallstatt in the distance. The road sweeps down to Lupitsch where dwarves were said to reside (there is a road called Waukerlweg, meaning 'dwarves path' in Aussee), but since they clearly would not want to be disturbed, stop at the **Alpengarten** on the right instead—it is a lovely, tranquil place with a fine display of Alpine plants—a constant source of inspiration (and some frustration) to anyone trying to build an Alpine garden!

Continue on 145 (direction Bad Aussee). There is now a fairly new road (not yet marked on maps) turning off to the left, signposted Alt Aussee—it is signposted well in advance. Take this left turning and turn left again at the next junction, which will bring you straight to Alt Aussee (if you have missed the first left turning you have to return via Bad Aussee).

7 LOWER AUSTRIA AND VIENNA
(Niederösterreich and Wien)

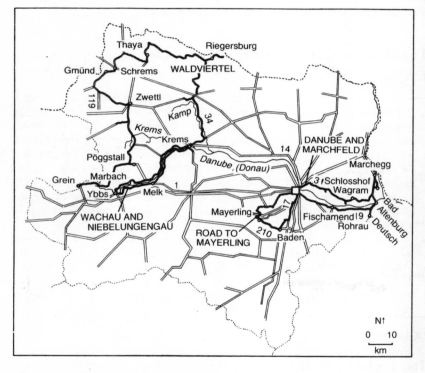

'Regione vulgari vocabulo ostarrichi'—in a region commonly known as Ostarrichi—said a document dated April 998, referring to a piece of land and naming the region in which it is situated, and for the first time mentioning the name Ostarrichi which was later to become Österreich. The actual place was in what is now known as Niederösterreich (Lower Austria), the country east of, i.e. 'below', the Enns river.

Lower Austria is the largest of all Austrian provinces, the Danube making a natural division between north and south. The north is further divided—by a small mountain this time—into the Waldviertel ('forest quarter'), deep, dark and mysterious with fortresses and fortified towns—

and the Weinviertel (the 'wine quarter', although vines also grow in great profusion along the banks of the Danube and in the south). Both stretch towards the Czechoslovak border, as does the Marchfeld in the east, with its almost forgotten (and, at long last, slowly awakening) Baroque castles.

Until a few years ago Lower Austria had no capital, eventually electing Baroque St Pölten—when all the odds had been on Wiener Neustadt in the south, known as 'die allzeit getreue' (forever faithful). Vienna, sitting about halfway between north and south in Lower Austria, is 'merely' the capital of Austria . . . and of Vienna, a province in its own right—and a very rural one at that, as a visit to one of the villages like Neustift am Wald or Pötzleinsdorf will prove, to say nothing of Heilgenstadt where you can still follow Beethoven's path on the Sommerheidenweg.

The Danube East of Vienna and the Marchfeld

1-2 days/about 150km/from Vienna (eastern sector of map)

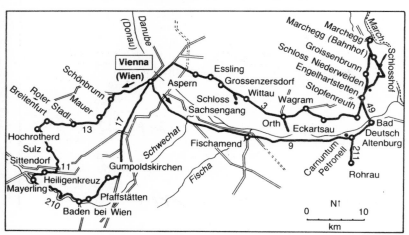

'Asia', Metternich is reputed to have said, 'starts at Erdberg.'

Erdberg was a suburb of Vienna, now part of the city's Third District. This is where, centuries before, Richard Lionheart was arrested when attempting to pay with foreign currency. Perhaps Metternich may have felt that this was not the correct way to treat travellers, royal or otherwise. Or perhaps he was just trying to convey that anything further east than Erdberg belonged to another world. Certainly visitors to Austria do not automatically make for the land east of Vienna and the wild, untamed beauty of the meadows and marshes along the eastern Danube. Asia may not start at Erdberg, but Rome certainly does within a few kilometres of it. The road due east from Vienna is the old Via Principalis which ran along the Limes, the Roman frontier fortification, and leads to Carnuntum, ancient Roman garrison and town. Unlike Pompei, it was abandoned gradually until it all but disappeared underground—to be excavated, mostly during the last century.

Cross the Danube near Deutsch–Altenburg just after Carnuntum and there is another world again: the Marchfeld, granary of Vienna. Great distances of cornfields, small clearings bordered by robinias (planted by the Empress Maria Theresia to stop the sand blowing across the plains), lilac hedges and the occasional vineyard. And asparagus fields—Marchfeld asparagus is considered the best in Central Europe. Granary of Vienna—and battleground of old: Ottokar II, King of Bohemia defeated the Magyars there in the battle of Kroissenbrunn in 1260, when 14,000 Magyars were said to have drowned in the river March that now forms the border between Austria and Czechoslovakia. Then Rudolf I fought Ottokar in 1278 at nearby Dürnkrut, in one of the largest battles ever fought in Europe, with 30,000 men on either side. Ottokar lost the battle—and his life—and thus began the Habsburg rule of Austria which was to last for over 600 years. (At the St Cyr academy in Coetquidon, near Beignon a parade ground is named Marchfeld, 'after one of the principal battlefields in Europe.')

In the sixteenth and seventeenth centuries the Marchfeld was overrun by the Turks, but when they were finally beaten back after the siege of Vienna in 1683, the Marchfeld 'relaxed' and a spate of sumptuous building followed. The defenders of Vienna led the way—there was fierce competition between Kinsky at Eckartsau, Prince Eugene of Savoy at Schlosshof (Starhemberg had got in first with Niederweiden which he sold later to Prince Eugene), and the Palffys at Marchegg. Fortified castles were turned into magnificent palaces and some of the finest examples of Baroque architecture are to be found in the Marchfeld.

Only once (or to be precise, twice) more was the Marchfeld the scene of battle: in 1809 when Napoleon suffered his first defeat on land at Aspern, to be reversed soon afterwards at nearby Wagram. (The Austrians are inordinately proud of being the first people to win a battle against Napoleon, but it is best not to mention the second. Legend has it that although their first victory was complete, they did not realise this until Napoleon had struck back. As they are so fond of saying, 'a typically Austrian fate'.)

The suggested route thus passes from ancient Rome through medieval relics to Baroque splendour. The distance in kilometres could certainly be covered in a day, but the distance in time may well suggest an overnight stop. The area is not as yet particularly blessed with restaurants and the best ones are near Vienna, but there are one or two good country inns.

Leave **VIENNA**, direction due east via Rennweg which leads into Simmeringer Hauptstrasse. Continue on this road, passing Vienna's huge municipal cemetery (Zentralfriedhof) on the right. At the fork keep left, signposted 'Hainburger Bundesstrasse 9' and later 'Hainburg/Fischamend'. Keep on 9 throughout—oil refinery on left, airport on right—until you come to **FISCHAMEND**, an attractive small place built on the site of the Roman Aecquinoctum. Worth seeing here are the medieval tower (topped by a fish) which houses a small museum, and the parish church with an altar painting of the Last Supper by Maulpertsch. **Merzendorfer** (02232 2401) is a splendid old restaurant, a great favourite with the Viennese since well before the First World War and famous for its fish specialities and Esterhazy slices. Fischamend does not take its name from fish however, but from the river Fischa which used to flow into the Danube at this point, i.e. it 'came to an end'.

Continue on 9, direction Hainburg, Bratislava/Pressburg (same town—two languages, the border is but a few kilometres away) coming after about 1 km to **MARIA ELLEND** with its Baroque pilgrimage church (the church dates back to 1770, but the mosaics are of this century) and carry straight on through Haslau, Regelsbrunn and Widmungsmauer to Carnuntum and Petronell. There is no town sign for Carnuntum, only for Petronell, but there are road signs pointing to both. Arriving at Carnuntum it is best to make straight for the small kiosk—to left on the main road—from which guided tours are arranged (April-Oct.).

Carnuntum was built at the junction of the old Amber road (running from Jutland to the south) and the Danube and it occupied an area of about 12 km^2, stretching from west of Petronell right to Bad Deutsch Altenburg. It was first mentioned in AD 6 when Tiberius led his legions against Marbod and the Marcomanni from there. In its heyday the civilian population was around 20,000 to 30,000 and at one time it surpassed Vienna in importance. Marcus Aurelius though he is believed to have died in Vienna of the plague, made Carnuntum his headquarters and wrote one volume of his meditations there. In 307 Carnuntum was the scene of a summit meeting between Galarius, Maximian and Diocletian who had been hauled back from his retirement at Salona (now Split in Yugoslavia). After hours of debate Diocletian declared that everyone concerned would be much healthier and happier if—like him—they grew cabbages at Salona!

Excavations in Carnuntum have been going on since the sixteenth century, with interruptions such as those caused by the invading Turks. In the eighteenth century most of the digging was done with varying degrees of expertise by a colonel from Bologna, some British tourists (!) and a Prussian colonel held prisoner during the Seven Year War. At the end of the last century the original garrison was excavated, duly measured, photographed, registered and then covered up again and where once the men of the XIV Legion were stationed and proclaimed Lucius Septimus Severus as their ruler, independent of Rome, potatoes, wheat and maize grow. This 'covering up' applies to quite a few excavations where maintenance was just not feasible, but photographs taken from the air in recent years clearly show 'soil marks' defining the foundations through the growing wheat. See: two amphitheatres (one for the population seating 13,000 and one for the garrison seating 8,000); Heidentor—which may be a memorial or a Pagan arch; palace ruins (in the grounds of Traun Castle at Petronell) the largest in Austria—originally thermal baths, later converted into a palace worthy of receiving Diocletian.

Heidentor, near Petronell

PETRONELL, early medieval and built practically on top of Carnuntum, seems almost contemporary after that. The splendid seventeenth-century Traun Castle may be visited (02163 2231—prior call advisable as Traun family in residence). See particularly: Sala terrena and enormous ceiling fresco celebrating victory over the Turks. See also Romanesque chapel by the roadside which is now burial vault of Traun family. The stones used for the chapel are Roman, as are those in some of the roadside walls: for about 1,000 years Carnuntum was the cheapest—i.e. free—quarry.

Take 211 from Petronell for a short excursion into yet another world; to **ROHRAU**, birthplace of Joseph Haydn. Drive slowly through the one and only main street or you will miss the small and pretty thatched house (No. 60) on the left. 'In this humble dwelling ... a great man was born' says the inscription—by Beethoven. There is a small museum, open all year (closed Monday.) (When the Turks overran nearby Hainburg in the seventeenth century, everybody made for a small door in the town wall, leading to the Danube. Somehow the door could not be opened and the entire population of Hainburg, numbering over 8,000 people was trapped and subsequently massacred. All, that is, except for eight who had hidden in the chimney of a deserted house. One of these was a young coachbuilder called Thomas Haydn—grandfather of Joseph).

Continue through Rohrau and at the end of the village you will find the entrance to **Schloss Harrach**, a rather imposing seventeenth-eighteenth-century castle which houses the largest private picture collection in Austria. This was held, until 1969, at the Palais Harrach in Vienna. It consists mostly of Neapolitan, Spanish and Netherland masters. See also Rohrau altar in the private chapel and a bust of Haydn by Grassi. (Open from Easter until 1 November, closed Monday.) Nice sidelight: Haydn's mother was cook at Schloss Harrach and Count Harrach became one of his earliest benefactors.

Return to Petronell on 211 and at junction with 9 turn right for **BAD DEUTSCH ALTENBURG**. The health-giving sulphur/iodine springs were known to the Romans and although Bad Deutsch Altenburg can hardly be termed a fashionable spa, it is pleasant enough and the spa waters are certainly powerful. **Hotel Kaiserbad** (02165 2335) is a typically comfortable spa hotel and by far the best place to stay if you wish to break your journey. See: thirteenth-century parish church on hill (Romanesque with Gothic choir and early Gothic tower); thirteenth-century charnel house; eighteenth-century Schloss Ludwigstorff with Africa museum.

Museum Carnuntinum with its splendid collection of Roman finds, including over 12,000 coins and other treasures is at present undergoing renovations, but should be open again later during the year (02165 2480). Tourist Office: Badgasse 26 (02165 2459). (Also recommended: **Golden Krone** (02165 2105) at **Hainburg**, about 4 km further east on 9. Good country inn with comfortable rooms.)

Still on 9 drive through Bad Deutsch Altenburg and at the end of town turn left onto 49 for Marchegg, crossing on the rather grand bridge that spans the Danube, with marvellous views of meadows and marshes bordering the river. Much fought over in every way—the conservationists staged demonstrations and held all-night vigils during the coldest time of the year as a protest against any development destroying this wild and wonderful countryside.

After about 8 km on 49 you will find **Schloss Niederweiden** on the right, the only one of the Marchfeld castles originally built as a hunting lodge. All the others were fortresses or fortified castles. Johann Bernhard Fischer von Erlach was Count Starhemberg's architect—Prince Eugene of Savoy greatly embellished the interior and engaged Lukas von Hildebrandt to design the gardens—after which Empress Maria Theresia added another storey without disturbing the beauty of it all. Severely damaged at the end of the Second World War, looted and nearly destroyed by fire, it has now been restored to its former glory (except for the gardens). Niederweiden is usually only open during the summer months (dates variable) when special exhibitions are staged and concerts held. At other times you may find Niederweiden with its shutters tightly closed and asleep like the proverbial princess in a fairytale, but it can be visited by prior arrangement (02285 6580 which is the telephone number of neighbouring Schlosshof). See also Baroque kitchens in garden with separate fireplace for each guest. (Still in the gardens and a few hundred metres towards the river is the forgotten and vanished fortress and village of Grafenweiden of which nothing remains except some ruins, an avenue of lime trees—and tales of a wicked Robber Knight called Leonhard Arberger who together with his equally wicked wife did some terrible deeds and came to a sticky end.)

Leave 49 at Schloss Niederweiden and turn right for **Schlosshof** (castle and village of the same name). This is the old avenue linking the two castles and will bring you out at the entrance of Schlosshof. Prince Eugene of Savoy bought it before he bought Niederweiden and Lukas von Hildebrandt, who had previously built Belvedere Palace in Vienna for him, transformed what had been the rather gaunt 'Veste Hof' into one of the grandest of all castles. (Three Canalettos at the Kunsthistorische Museum in Vienna show Schlosshof in all its glory). The greatest triumph was the gardens sloping gently down to the river; 800 workers were used for these alone. Prince Eugene loved Schlosshof as much as, if not more than, the Belvedere, sometimes arriving by river for his lengthy sojurns. After his death his heirs—grand-niece Victoria (dubbed 'ugly Victoria' by the Viennese) and her much younger husband of whom she was rapidly tiring (!)—staged one of the biggest sales presentations of the century, in 1754: a fête that lasted for a week to impress the most important person in the land, the Empress Maria Theresia. It must have been a splendid occasion for not only do the people of Schlosshof still talk about it as if it had happened last week, but the empress bought Schlosshof as well as Niederweiden as a present for her husband. Later on Maria Theresia held the wedding reception of her favourite daughter at Schlosshof and after the death of her husband even contemplated retiring there. After she died Schlosshof was neglected—her son Joseph II thought it extravagant—and eventually it ended up as a cavalry institute before the Russians, at the end of the Second World War, took it over and all but destroyed it. Now it is all beautifully restored (except for the gardens where work is still going on), and open during the summer months (tel. 02285 6580). At present there are negotiations about turning Schlosshof into a hotel which would of course be very grand indeed: enjoy the splendour while you can!

Drive through Schlosshof village and at the end turn right for Markthof. Drive just for a few hundred metres and then stop for a view of the gardens and stairs sloping down. Double back and carry straight on for Marchegg. This is a typical country road with fields on either side, leading through a viaduct and through **MARCHEGG BAHNHOF** (the citizens of Marchegg would not allow a railway to be built close to the town, so that the railway station stood lonely in a field, until a small settlement grew around it—this too, is typical of the Marchfeld) rejoining 49 for **MARCHEGG**. Marchegg was founded as a town by Ottokar II after his successful battle against the Magyars—but never lived up to that promise. The Turks burnt it down completely in 1529, but did not storm the castle or destroy the church, which were both built by Ottokar.

The church was consecrated to St Margaret, patron saint of Ottokar's first wife whom he had divorced by the time the church was completed. See Baroque altar and pulpit. Altar painting by Leopold Kupelwieser (Franz Schubert's great friend). Marchegg castle was rebuilt several times, finally in 1733 (there is a sundial dated 1628 in the grounds) and, like all Marchfeld castles, was severely damaged and looted after the Second World War. When the last of the Palffys died (they had owned Marchegg since 1621) it looked as if the castle would be lost, but the citizens of Marchegg rallied round and saved it—it is now a hunting museum. (Open 15 March to 30 November, 02285 224.)

Marchegg, Ungartor

114

Parts of the old town walls are still in existence and so is one of the gates, the Ungartor. Meadows and forests near the March river hold the largest white stork colony in Europe, nesting in oak trees, and there are also cormorants and asiatic plants (perhaps Metternich was right after all!). The World Wildlife Fund and Marchegg municipality have acquired land near the river and guided tours can be arranged (02285 291).

Double back from Marchegg on 49, and (staying on 49) take the right fork about 1 km after Marchegg for **GROISSENBRUNN**. This is the Kroissenbrunn of 1260 battle fame—having changed the K to a G (the name means 'Cress in a well' and watercress still grows there in abundance). You will see three small lakes, perhaps better described as ponds, on the left: these are the lakes which used to feed the fountains at Schlosshof, and the great feast for Maria Theresia extended to them as well.

Stay on 49, passing Schloss Niederweiden again on the left and about 3 km later turn right for Stopfenreuth and Eckartsau which leads to the beginning of Engelhartstetten. Here turn left, following signs for Stopfenreuth and Eckartsau. (If you have missed the turning, there is one a little further down the 49 which also leads to Stopfenreuth.) Drive through Stopfenreuth (where Amber road crossed the Danube) to **Eckartsau**, then follow directions for 'Schloss'. **Schloss Eckartsau** was a medieval fortified castle, lavishly rebuilt by Count Kinsky in the eighteenth-century. Its architect is not known, supposedly 'after plans by Fischer von Erlach', though the staircase suggests Lukas von Hildebrandt. Kinsky overspent and eventually had to sell—to Maria Theresia's husband Franz Stephan who had conveniently inherited 600,000 gold ducats from his aunt in Lorraine. It remained Habsburg property: Franz Ferdinand, whose death at Sarajevo triggered off the First World War, used it mainly as a hunting lodge (looking after the gardens personally). The last Austrian emperor, Karl I, lived at Eckartsau at the end of the First World War (where he is supposed to have signed a document renouncing his rights which has never been found) and it was from Eckartsau that he went into exile—not so very far from the battlefield on which his ancestor Rudolf I had won the victory which established Habsburg rule for over 600 years.

Though badly looted after the Second World War (valuable paintings were used to make a de-lousing tent), Eckartsau is still well worth seeing and makes a particularly suitable setting for the chamber music concerts which are held there during the summer. (Open 15 May to 15 November, Saturday, Sunday and holidays, 02214 2240). See particularly: ceiling fresco by Daniel Gran; Gold Cabinet and Chinese Cabinet; chandeliers; statuary.

From Eckartsau take a left fork for Wagram (not to be confused with nearby Deutsch Wagram of Napoleonic battle fame) and at Wagram turn left into 3 for **ORTH** which leads straight to the castle. **Schloss Orth** looks pretty fierce—though in June a centuries old tulip tree in full flower lends a certain magic. There are three museums in the castle, the Bee's Museum, Fishing Museum and the Danube Museum. (Open 2 March to 11 November, closed Monday, 02212 2555.) See also the chapel St Peter and St Nikolaus, where on 6 December a special 'fisherman's mass' is held; the parish church; and the pillory. Napoleon's sister Caroline Murat lived for a short time at Schloss Orth and, later on, the ill-fated Crown Prince Rudolf was a frequent visitor with his wife, for whom local musicians composed 'The Rose of Orth'. Rudolf also stayed there with his mistress Mary Vetsera (at least, according to local legend). **Uferhaus** is a good, reliable restaurant, specialising in fish dishes, where portions are enormous, pleasantly situated directly on the Danube (follow directions from castle). No telephone.

The last castle in the Marchfeld, **Sachsengang**, is private property and there is a stern 'No Entry' sign, but on occasion it has been possible to visit. It is worth trying your luck as it stands almost on the direct route back to Vienna.

Continue on 3 towards Vienna, through Probstdorf and Wittau. Immediately after Wittau turn left marked 'Oberhausen 1 km' and at a T-junction in Oberhausen turn left marked only 'Mühlleiten'. **Schloss Sachsengang** is immediately on the left. It is probably the oldest, and one of the most interesting, castles in the Marchfeld, built in the eleventh century. ('Gang' meant 'arm'—in this case of the Danube—and 'Sachsen' referred to the old colony of Saxons settled there by Charlemagne). It is surrounded by legends, mostly concerning the two tumuli which are supposedly the graves of Attila the Hun and Charlemagne (this has been thoroughly disproved of course—but it lives on in the manner of all good legends).

Return to 3 and continue in the direction of Vienna. Almost immediately—at the next crossroads—there is the **Taverne am Sachsengang** (02249 29010) an excellent, if somewhat pricey, restaurant with comfortable hotel. It is set near the old Donau-Oder Kanal, which was originally intended for transport of coal from Silesia to Vienna and never completed and is now bordered with holiday bungalows.

Continue on 3 through **GROSSENZERSDORF** where some of the town walls are still standing and where **Gasthof zur Sonne** (02249 2344) is a highly-recommended inn—same ownership as Am Sachsengang, but prices more 'rural'.

Return to Vienna on 3 via Essling and Aspern, following directions for Zentrum.

The Road to Mayerling

1-2 days/about 75 km/from Vienna (western sector of map)

A hundred years and countless books, plays, films, a ballet (and talk of a proposed musical) as well as literally thousands of newspaper articles and 'revelations' after what is always described as the 'tragedy of Mayerling', the real truth will probably never be known—or made public. And perhaps just as well. Only one detail remains unchallenged—the route which the Crown Prince took on that last journey to Mayerling on the 28

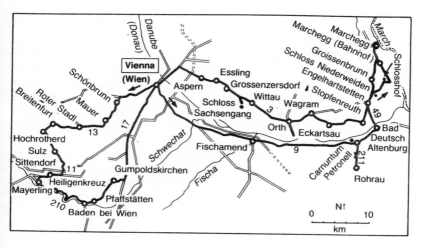

January 1889, starting at the Hofburg in Vienna—though there have been speculations as to why he took that particular route. (Lovely though it is, the route is not a good one in winter, even today; he probably chose it because it enabled him to arrange for Mary Vetsera to join him when he changed carriages at the Roter Stadl and for her to come to Mayerling unobserved. The Crown Prince walked the last bit of the journey to detract attention.)

Mayerling is now on the regular 'list of excursions' from Vienna, but hardly any of them use the original route which leads through some of the most attractive parts of the Vienna woods, through Heiligenkreuz where Mary Vetsera was buried somewhat hastily a few days after the shooting.

Mayerling is still lovely and remote, if sad and even slightly eerie at times, but the journey back to Vienna through beautiful Helenental and strictly nineteenth-century Baden bei Wien (to return slowly to the present) followed by the charming wine villages of Pfaffstätten and Gumpoldskirchen should more than lift your spirits.

To follow the Crown Prince's route as closely as possible—allowances being made for one-way streets—leave from Vienna centre along Linke Wienzeile (now a one-way street) leading eventually into Hadikgasse, to Schönbrunn where turn left, crossing Kennedy Bridge. After this take right fork into Lainzerstrasse which leads into Speisingerstrasse. Go through Mauer—turn right at the main square (Maurer Hauptplatz) into Endresgasse and then left into Valentingasse. At end of Valentingasse turn right into Maurer Langegasse and almost immediately left into Rodaunerstrasse. Drive to the end of Rodaunerstrasse where turn right onto 13 (Breitenfurter Strasse). Continue on this road—direction Breitenfurt—with Roter Stadl on left (now a retirement home, but still painted red) where the Crown Prince changed carriages and was joined by Mary Vetsera. After Roter Stadl take the left fork, leaving 13, to Breitenfurt.

BREITENFURT is a dusty little village best known for creamy pastry called Millirahmstrudel (or Milchrahmstrudel) which is served warm and can be found all over Austria, usually described as 'Breitenfurter Millirahmstrudel'. Its fame appears to have spread much further than that of the rather splendid Breitenfurt Baroque church with its very opulent interior!

From Breitenfurt follow directions to Hochrotherd, where fork left for Sulz. Drive through Stangau to **SULZ** where **Postschaenke** (02238 335) is an excellent restaurant, albeit open only for dinner. (Lunch on Saturdays, Sundays and holidays only. Closed Mondays and Tuesdays.) Continue to Sittendorf, where turn right, following sign 'Heiligenkreuz 4 km'.

HEILIGENKREUZ (pop: 1,100—not to be confused with Heiligenkreuz-Gutenbrunn, also in Lower Austria and Heiligenkreuz in Burgenland) is a deceptively small village within which the **Cistercian monastery** sits like a small fortified town. Founded in the twelfth-century by Margrave Leopold III, Abbot Gottschalk and his twelve brethren built the monastery and worked the land—Zwettl and Lilienfeld (also in Lower Austria) followed on the same pattern and so did the cultivation of vineyards in Burgenland's Seewinkel near Mönchhof. Heiligenkreuz was severely damaged by Turkish invaders, ravaged by fire and rebuilt several times. Sculptor Giuliani and painter Altomonte worked as 'familiares' at the monastery and are buried there. See particularly: fourteenth-century stained glass windows; paintings by Rottmayr and Altomonte; lead crucifix in vestry by Raphael Donner; Mausoleum of the Babenberg dukes including tomb of Frederic II (Babenberg, not Prussia); library, cloisters; enclosed courtyard with plane trees; trinity column and fountain; collection of more than 150 'bozetti'—clay models by Giuliani—and much more besides. Also recommended: visits to **Stiftstaverne** for good food and excellent wines from the Heiligenkreuz vineyards.

(A simple tombstone—the original was destroyed by marauders at the end of the Second World War—marks the grave of Mary Vetsera at the local cemetery, even now attracting visitors.)

At Heiligenkreuz turn into 11, direction Alland (you will note that Mayerling is rarely signposted and certainly never in Heiligenkreuz), then after about 2 km turn left for **Mayerling** (signposted for once). **Hotel Marienhof** (02258 2379) just before you arrive at Mayerling has a good restaurant, if somewhat irreverently named after the Crown Prince, and is pleasantly sited on a hill. Drive slowly down the hill—you could easily miss the former Jageschloss at the end on right, except for the parked cars and occasional coaches and the steady trickle of visitors. A chapel was built soon after the shooting around the room in which the Crown Prince died and the hunting lodge converted into a convent. (The Nazis dissolved the convent, gave the nuns 24 hours to leave, then put in refugees from Bessarabia. The convent was severely damaged at the end of the Second World War. When the nuns returned they restored it as best they could.) There are some relics of the Crown Prince in the very sparse exhibition scarcely worth seeing—scraps of carpet from his bedroom, some cups from which he may or may not have drunk—but there is no denying the fact that the atmosphere is definitely strange, not to say eerie. (I was taken there when I was about six years old and fled screaming from the place—not knowing anything about the background.) It is however possible to stay at the hunting lodge. One of the outhouses has been converted into a modest little hotel, meticulously run by Carmelite nuns.

Turn left into 210 marked Helenental and Baden and then follow directions for Baden. Helenental is a particularly lovely valley along the river Schwechat, with fortress ruins of Rauhenstein and Rauhenck on cliffs on either side. St Helena chapel at foot of Rauhenstein on left, late-Gothic with Baroque additions. See: pottery altar given to St Stephens in Vienna in 1500 by the potters' guild, but banned by the Council of Trento so that it was hastily removed to St Helena! Continue on 210 to Baden bei Wien.

BADEN BEI WIEN (pop: 23,000) is an enchanting spa town, though it smells strongly of sulphur at times. The sulphur springs—fifteen of them and beneficial to sufferers of rheumatism—were known to the Romans,

Baden bei Wien, the casino and flower clock in the Kurpark

but Baden became fashionable only in the nineteenth century when the Emperor Franz I (father-in-law of Napoleon) spent 31 successive summers there. The town was severely ravaged by fire in 1812 and rebuilt, which accounts for the almost uniformly Biedermeier character. Practically every house can boast of a famous visitor: Beethoven wrote part of his 9th Symphony and 'Missa Solemnis' at Rathausgasse 10, but also lived at Frauengasse 10, whilst Johann Strauss favoured Frauengasse 8 and Rathausgasse 11! Mozart wrote his 'Ave Verum' at Renngasse 4 (first performed at Baden parish church), Schubert was a frequent visitor, as were composers Diabelli, Ziehrer and Komzak, painters Waldmüller, Daffinger and Kriehuber—the list could go on. Especially worth seeing: St Stephar's Church, thirteenth and fifteenth century, with altar painting by Paul Troger; Kaiserhaus (the official Imperial summer residence at Hauptplatz 7); town hall by Kornhäusl (who was responsible for many of the Baden buildings); Trinity column.

Some of the beautiful old buildings are now hotels, such as the **Sauerhof** (02252 41251) built by Kornhäusl in 1820 and the thirteenth-century **Schloss Weikersdorf** (02252 48301) which has Baroque additions and was restored in the nineteenth century. There is a splendid park with casino and arena theatre with sliding roof where operetta is performed during the summer, also elegant **Park Hotel** (02252 44386). **Frauenhof** (02252 80666) is a more modest hotel, but has a restaurant in a charming courtyard and excellent food at reasonable prices. As befits a spa town, Baden has a very pretty theatre (lots of operetta) and—unlike most spa towns—excellent wines. Tourist Office: Hauptplatz 1 (02252 86800).

Gumpolsdskirchen, famous for its fine wines

Leave Baden via Kaiser Franz Ring, then follow signs variously marked Weinstrasse and Weinbergstrasse (left at church and right into Germergasse) which leads through vineyards first to **PFAFFSTÄTTEN** (interesting thirteenth/fourteenth-century chapel at the Lilienfelder Hof) known, like Baden and the surrounding villages, for its fine wines, then on to Gumpoldskirchen.

GUMPOLDSKIRCHEN, named, according to Cuspinian, after Gumpold, brother of Margrave Leopold I (his other brothers were responsible for neighbouring Guntramsdorf and Perchtoldsdorf) is a wine village *par excellence* and one to be taken seriously: nearly half its wines are classified as 'Prädikatsweine'. Add to that the charm of the place with its Renaissance town hall and the numerous fine houses ranging from Gothic to eighteenth century, many of which sport the green fir branch indicating that the new wine is ready for sampling. See also: fifteenth-century St Michael's Church; the castle; fountain in main square built from a Roman sarcophagus; sixteenth-century pillory.

From Gumpoldskirchen follow signs for 'Wien' which lead onto 17 and straight back to Vienna.

Wachau and Nibelungengau

2 days/about 135 km/from Krems

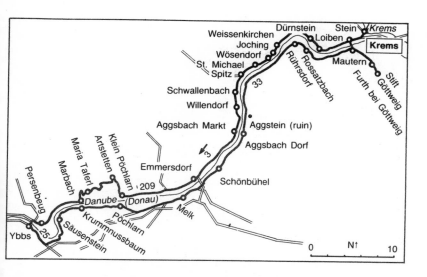

The Wachau, the Danube Valley between Krems and Melk, is the loveliest stretch of the river. There are few regions which can equal it for beauty and romantic treasures—where you will find a castle (or at least a castle ruin) atop almost every hill—and quite a few spread out below between ancient villages. At its best when the fruit trees are in blossom, or in summer when you can barely see the leaves for golden apricots. The Wachau region produces some beautiful wines—and there are plenty of excellent restaurants on this route in which to sample them—as well as the splendid Eau de Vie made from local apricots.

The Nibelungengau which adjoins the Wachau may be a little more austere, though hardly less interesting, and both regions are best explored by driving along the banks of the Danube on either side—once for close inspection and then for admiring from afar.

KREMS is small and old and beautiful, the oldest town in Lower Austria, first named as Urbs Chremisa in 995 and now joined with neighbouring **STEIN** (combined pop: 24,000) which dates back to the eleventh century (there were settlements in the area 30,000 years ago). A local saying 'Krems und Stein are three towns' has some justification: on the river there was a village between the two towns, and now linking them called 'Und' (and), being derived from '*ad undas*' (on the waters). At one time Krems surpassed Vienna in importance and it can claim many 'firsts': the first mint of the Babenbergs; the first landing stage for a Danube steamship; even the first pruning shears—invented in Krems in 1849, duly patented and in the following year 10,000 of these shears (forged by hand) were exported all over Europe. In the Middle Ages 75 per cent of the population made their living from wine and Krems is still an important wine

town. Buildings range from Gothic via Renaissance to Baroque and Biedermeier. There are about 750 houses in the old part of the two towns, of which about 400 are over 200 years old. All are beautifully restored, and Krems has twice been nominated by Europa Nostra as a model town for preservation.

Call at the Krems Tourist Office, Undstrasse 6 (02732 2676) to get a map and guidance. If needed, they will also arrange for a guided tour (in English). You might start at the Steiner Tor (fifteenth-century with octagonal Baroque Tower) and walk through Obere Landstrasse to No. 32, **Gasthof Alte Post**, a Renaissance building with beautiful arcaded courtyard, still run as an inn; pass on to No. 22 where sculptor Matthias Schwanthaler was born in the seventeenth century, or call in at No. 2, the Mohrenapotheke

Stein an der Donau: Frauenbergkirche seen from the Rebentor

(rebuilt after a fire in 1532) with ceiling fresco by Martin Johann Schmidt—and there are at least eight more notable buildings in that road alone! See also: sixteenth/eighteenth-century town hall; Trinity column; Göglhaus (founded twelfth century); Pelikan Haus (Untere Landstrasse 4) and other houses in the same road, notably Nos. 7 and 9 with Gothic arcades; Gozzo Burg on Hoher Markt; Piaristenkirche: Bürgespitalkirche and much, much more besides. The thirteenth-century Dominican monastery and church, its cloister only recently discovered, was varyingly used as button factory, fire station, theatre and cinema and now houses the only wine museum in Austria. (Open April to November, closed Monday, 02732 4927.)

Stein too is rich in ancient buildings, like the parish church St Nikolaus founded in 1263 (with former charnel house) from which rather steep steps lead to the fourteenth-century Frauenbergkirche (now a war memorial); Grosser and Kleiner Passauer Hof (twelfth and sixteenth century) and the eighteenth-century Mazzettihaus, birthplace of Ludwig Ritter von Köchel who catalogued Mozart's works; the seventeenth/eighteenth-century town hall; and much else.

(Note: apart from Schwanthaler and Köchel, the eighteenth-century painter Martin Johann Schmidt is the favourite local celebrity and his works will be encountered all along the Wachau and Nibelungengau. He is known as 'Kremser Schmidt'—to differentiate him from all other Schmidts, but notably from Johann Georg, known as 'Wiener Schmidt'.)

Am Förthof, Donaulände 8 (02732 3345) is an excellent restaurant and comfortable hotel (particularly delectable breakfasts) right on the Danube, and next to the ancient Förthof, foundations of which go back to the time of Charlemagne.

From Krems/Stein take 3 to **UNTERLOIBEN**, where the interesting parish church is made up of two Gothic churches (Baroque and rococo additions). **Loibnerhof** (02732 2890) is a good family restaurant with its own vineyards. Continue on 3 to **DÜRNSTEIN**, one of the smallest towns in Austria (pop: 1,000, town rights granted in 1462). It is closed to traffic except for access to hotels. There's an underground passage to the other side of town, with parking at either end. Richard Lionheart was kept prisoner at Dürnstein fortress in the twelfth century (only the ruins of the ruins remain) to be freed for about 4 tons of silver. On receiving the ransom, which he had to share with German Emperor Henry VI, Duke Leopold transferred Krems Mint to Vienna, melted down the silver and turned it into Viennese coins with which he paid for fortifications to be built in various vulnerable spots in Austria.

Dürnstein is delightful—crowds in the narrow streets notwithstanding—and there is a plethora of excellent hotels from which to choose. My own favourite is **Schloss Dürnstein** (02711 222), a Relais et Chateaux and Schlosshotel, which is splendid in every way: an early-Baroque castle with a terrace above the Danube (nothing like lording it once in a while, particularly if the cost is as reasonable as it is here) and a swimming pool into which a giant Linden tree sheds its blossoms. **Richard Löwenherz**

(02711 212) is no less splendid, built in the grounds of a former convent—the thirteenth-century former church is now used for exhibitions—also with swimming pool and terrace restaurant. **Sänger Blondel** (02711 253) is a typically Austrian inn, with wine from their own vineyards and home-made apricot jam for breakfast. To see: fifteenth-century former Augustine monastery (baroquised in the eighteenth by Prandtauer and Munggenast), and parish (former Deanery) church (paintings by Kremser Schmidt, statuary by his father)—a favourite church for weddings; ruins of St Kunigunde Church and charnel house; 'Kellerschlösl' (wine chateau) outside town walls—built as summer residence for Abbot Ubelbacher in the eighteenth century—stands over extensive wine cellars which now house the best Wachau wines; many interesting old houses in main street. A 30 minute walk up to Starhemberg Warte rewards with good views over the Danube.

From Dürnstein continue on 3 to **WEISSENKIRCHEN**, an extremely pretty village and inspiration to many painters, with fortified fifteenth-century church (baroquised in due course) which is reached by covered stairway. See the sixteenth-century Teisenerhof (Marktplatz 22) built into fortification walls, with Wachau Museum, many paintings by Kremser Schmidt. (Open 1 April to 31 October, closed Monday, 02715 2268.) See also: medieval square 'Auf der Burg' and many fine old houses ranging from late-Gothic to Biedermeier. **Kirchenwirt** (02715 2332) is a very good, very Austrian inn, modestly priced. **JOCHING**, about 3 km further on 3, has the rather special—if more expensive—**Prandtauerhof** (02715 2310) in the Baroque St Pöltener Hof, one of the earlier works of Prandtauer. **Jamek** (02715 2235) are known for their wines as well as for their superb food, making choice of restaurant an almost impossible task, particularly as there is also the **Florianihof** (02715 2212) at neighbouring **WÖSENDORF**, in another good Baroque building, offering excellent food and some of the best Wachau wines. See also: eighteenth century St Florian church, with paintings by Kremser Schmidt.

ST MICHAEL further along the 3 is one of the oldest parishes in the Danube Valley. It has a very interesting parish church; the building and interior are far more interesting than the much-described roof which depicts a number of animals clambering over the roof (original models at Krems Museum). The story varies as to whether the animals are the 'signature' of the builder called Siebenhaas (seven hares), which seems most unlikely as there are other animals as well, or whether it was to mark a winter so severe with snowdrifts so high that animals really were seen to be walking across the church roof! A charnel house next to the church has a macabre altar of piled-up skulls and also two models of Emperor Josef II's 'economy coffins'. Quite unlike his sister Marie Antoinette, the good emperor could not bear to see anything wasted, not even a used coffin: the 'economy' coffin would be lowered into the ground, the body released by pressing a lever and the coffin be taken away to be used again. Not at all a popular idea with the Austrians who, above all, love what they call 'a good funeral'. (Key to church at No. 7.)

Still on 3, continue to **SPITZ** which is the centre of the Wachau and a much-favoured holiday resort. Spitz is built around a gentle hill, called Tausend Eimer Berg (Hill of 1,000 buckets) and it is said that in a good year the vines growing on the hill yield a thousand buckets of wine! There's an interesting parish church, with the choir veering gently north (fourteenth and fifteenth century). See also: Gothic town hall; ruins of fortress Hinterhaus with Romanesque keep; Niederes Schloss, mostly seventeenth century, with ruins of Protestant chapel which burned down in 1620; (Spitz was a Protestant stronghold of which the so-called 'Pastor's Tower' in former Protestant cemetery bears witness); seventeenth century Erlahof (in Ottenschlägerstrasse) with nautical museum (02713 246, open 1 April to 31 October).

Further west on 3 and driving towards Schwallenbach you will encounter an enormously steep rockface coming right up to the road. This is known as the 'Teufelsmauer' (Devil's Wall) and according to legend the devil was so infuriated by the excellent attendance at St Johann's on the other side of the Danube that he decided to build a river dam and drown the church. Like all the devil's works it had to be completed before dawn—so the devil bought up all the cockerels in the neighbourhood, heralders of dawn. All except one, which belonged to an old lady who refused to part with it. Came dawn, the lone cockerel crowed and the devil had to abandon his evil work and flee—but not before he shot the offending cockerel. If you do not believe me—witness the unfinished Teufelsmauer and, above all, see the cockerel on top of St Johann's Church (we shall be passing it presently on the other side of the river) with an arrow shot through his body!

SCHWALLENBACH, further on 3, is another attractive Wachau village with fifteenth century parish church (rococo interior and exceptionally good painting by Kremser Schmidt), Gothic houses and the Rannahof, mostly sixteenth century dominating from its hill. A seventeenth-century former castle opposite the church is known as 'Glöckerl von Schwallenbach' which may sound like the name of an operetta, but in fact links up with another legend, this time concerning wicked Robber Baron of Aggstein across the river.

Continuing on 3, drive through tiny **WILLENDORF**, known for the 'Venus of Willendorf', two early Stone Age figures found at the beginning of this century (they are actually numbered Venus I and Venus II, both now at the Natural History Museum in Vienna). Still on 3, continue through **AGGSBACH MARKT** (main street runs parallel to 3) with typical sixteenth-century Wachau houses, attractive parish church (late-Romanesque) and Baroque parsonage. Carry on to Emmersdorf. (Melk Abbey should now be coming into view on the other side of the river.)

EMMERSDORF is really two separate places—the former Hofamt, sitting prettily high above the village with lovely views across the Danube (fifteenth-century parish church with an eighteenth-century interior and Baroque parsonage) and the old village of Emmersdorf (there was a comparatively large settlement in the twelfth century). Emmersdorf is immensely pleasing. Its old castle has been more or less ruined by restoration, but there are many attractive old houses to make up for this, quite a few of them in the main street. Next to No. 11 a small passageway leads up steps to a statue of St Koloman, and good views over the village. No. 31 is a Renaissance building and No. 7 not only a rather attractive old house, but also one of the nicest family inns in the Wachau, **Gasthof zum Schwarzen Bären** (02752 7249) with good food and pleasant rooms.

Drive further west on 3, with ruins of fortress Weitenegg towering on the right, to **KLEIN PÖCHLARN** (interesting sixteenth-century parish church) where you enter the Nibelungengau. Leave 3 (and river) at Klein Pöchlarn and follow directions to right for **ARTSTETTEN** which is the name of the imposing Renaissance castle as well as that of the small village. The first two names on the war memorial listing the victims of the First World War are those of the Archduke Franz Ferdinand and his wife who were assassinated at Sarajevo. Schloss Artstetten was their home and they are buried in the vaults of the chapel (now parish church). Franz Ferdinand Museum and permanent exhibition 'From Mayerling to Sarajevo' at the castle. (Open daily 1 April to 2 November, otherwise by arrangement; 07413 8302.)

From Artstetten follow directions to **MARIA TAFERL** one of the most popular places of pilgrimage in Austria and certainly one of the most beautifully situated, perched high above the Danube with breathtaking views. In the seventeenth-century there was a mighty oak (roughly where the altar now stands) with a miraculous image, and processions were led there every Easter Monday. After increasing reports of miracle healings, visitations, visions, etc., a church commission was called to investigate—without conclusion, but clearly the findings were convincing enough for a splendid church to be built which took over fifty years to complete. (Prandtauer was one of the architects—crossing and inner dome—paintings are by Wiener as well as Kremser Schmidt, statuary by Peter Widerin.) The name of the village is a curious amalgam, 'Maria' obviously being taken from the church (Schmerzhafte Muttergottes), but 'Taferl' either refers to the miraculous image (Tafel = tablet) or—and this is considered to be much more likely—the much older stone table (Tafel also means table) outside the church which was used for pagan rites, possibly as a sacrificial altar. (After the church was completed, a balustrade was built around the table, probably to be in keeping with the Baroque style). Rather endearingly the typically Austrian diminitive 'r' has been inserted in Tafel, as if to emphasise the genuine popularity of the place, making Maria Taferl 'Maria of the little table (or tablet)'. It is certainly a very popular place—at the centenary in 1760 there were 700 processions and 326,000 people had taken Holy Communion and it still attracts streams of pilgrims. Naturally everything centres around the church (Basilica since 1947) and whilst at times the atmosphere may be more that of a country fair than a place of pilgrimage (booths selling not only candles and rosaries, but honeycake hearts inscribed 'Forever yours') the charm of the place is undeniable—and most of the booths are genuine Biedermeier! **Hotel Krone** (07413 6355) is marvellously sited with wide views over the Danube (and swimming pool on top) whilst **Hotel Kaiser-**

hof (same telephone number) has a pleasant garden (also with swimming pool). Excellent restaurant.

Descend from Maria Taferl, following directions for **MARBACH** (elegant church, many picturesque old houses, notably sixteenth-century Herrenhaus, now school) rejoining 3 and the Danube. Continue on 3 which after a few kilometres veers away from the river for a short stretch, meeting up with it again at **PERSENBEUG**. The name is derived from the ancient Piugun = Biegung = Bend, referring to the loop made by the Danube—in fact the full name means 'wicked bend'. Persenbeug Castle dominates the site (you will get another good view after you have crossed the river). It was built in 950 on Roman foundations as a fortress against the Magyars and barely a hundred years later was the scene of a disaster: in 1045 the German Emperor Henry II stayed at the castle and during the resulting festivities the floor caved in, depositing the emperor in the 'bath chamber' below—'bath chamber' probably being a euphemism for lavatory, but it saved his life, as well as that of many important guests, including the Bishop of Würzburg and that of the hostess! Schloss Persenbeug was rebuilt in the fifteenth and sixteenth centuries, then again extensively in the seventeenth century. It was eventually bought by Emperor Franz I who acquired quite a few castles in the area. The last Austrian Emperor Charles I was born there and it has remained Habsburg property to this day. After the Second World War (a condition of the St Germain peace treaty, but it had to wait for nearly forty years as there were no funds) a huge dam and electric power station was built on the Danube—one of the largest in Europe—turning the 20 km stretch of Danube between Persenbeug and Grein into a gently flowing lake. See also: parish church, and the Linden tree in Kirchenplatz, supposedly planted in 1300.

Turn left in Persenbeug, leaving 3 and crossing bridge to Ybbs. **YBBS** was built in the eighth century (called Ipusa and later Yparesburg) on the site of the former Roman settlement Adiuvense, founded by Vespasianus. It was granted town rights by Friedrich III in 1309 (present population about 6,000). There were also two huge fires—the first one is supposed to have left only seven houses standing—yet Ybbs has retained much of its ancient appearance. Built in a half-circle on a rock above the Danube, one side of the town faces the river, the remaining half-circle is surrounded by the old moat and some of the fortification walls. Ybbs might strike one as a rather gaunt little town at first, but it gains greatly on closer acquaintance and there are some sturdy old houses: sixteenth-century Salzamt (Kirchengasse 6), Alte Weinmaut (Kirchengasse 14) and many more, mostly in Kirchengasse, Brauhausgasse, Herrengasse, Wienerstrasse and Obere Donaulände. See also: Renaissance fountain and town hall, Schloss at Hauptplatz and parish church with terrace over the Danube. **Villa Nowotni**, Trewaldstrasse 3 (07412 2620) is a superb restaurant—no accommodation as yet, but accommodation can be arranged nearby and guests ferried to and fro if necessary.

From Ybbs take direction Wieselburg on 25 and after about 4 km (having just crossed river Ybbs) follow sign to left for Krummnussbaum (if you have inadvertently strayed onto 1, take next turning to left for Krummnussbaum). The road closely follows the Danube bend, past **SÄUSENSTEIN** (parish church with beautiful interior) and **KRUMMNUSSBAUM** (rather confusingly there is another Krummnussbaum near Marbach on the other side of the river—though one or the other sometimes obligingly drops an 'm' to 'avoid confusion'!) to **PÖCHLARN** at the confluence of Erlauf and Danube. Built around the Roman Arelape, Pöchlarn is mentioned in the fifteenth song of the Nibelungenlied as 'Bechelarn', residence of Ulrich von Bechelarn who accompanied Kriemhild down the Danube. (Ulrich von Bechelarn is about the only one in that grisly tale who emerges with any honour!) See: old fortifications and towers; parish church with paintings by Kremser Schmidt and Schletterer statuary; castle; pretty houses along Donaulände. Oskar Kokoschka was born at Pöchlarn and there is now a small museum at his birthplace, Regensburger Strasse 29. (Open mid-June to mid-September (02757 310.)

From Pöchlarn follow directions for Melk and Wien, joining 1 where turn left for **MELK.** You will of course have seen Melk Abbey and Monastery from across the river, towering high on a rock, the grandest Baroque monument of all. An Austrian writer once said that the best, indeed the only way to visit Melk would be accompanying royalty on a State visit, arriving by river and eventually being carried up the great staircase like the Empress Maria Theresia when she visited Melk. Just

Melk Abbey

128

driving up from the little town of Melk on the east side of the abbey entrance may be a less spectacular approach, but still impressive. When Abbot Dietmayr, who was 30 at the time, gave the contract for building Melk (or rather to take a series of buildings which had 'just grown' over seven hundred years and create a unified structure) to Prandtauer in 1702, not a few eyebrows must have been raised. Prandtauer was known, but by no means famous (it is said that Dietmayr was so impressed by a bridge which Prandtauer had built across the Erlauf river that this tipped the scales in his favour.) Neither Dietmayr or Prandtauer lived to see Melk completed. It was finished by Prandtauer's pupil Munggenast, and remains one of the greatest works of Baroque art. There are daily conducted tours (every half-hour; 02732 2312) to show the grandiose stairway, the Marmorsaal with ceiling fresco by Paul Troger, the Library with about 80,000 volumes including valuable manuscripts, the Kaiser-zimmer—a series of magnificent rooms which now house a museum, the paintings by Troger, Lukas Cranach, Rottmayr—and much more, including the statue of St Koloman, an Irish or Scottish prince on a pilgrimage who was mistaken for a spy and executed in 1012. The mistake was soon discovered and he was promptly canonised and declared Patron Saint of Lower Austria; he remained so until 1663, when Babenberg Duke Leopold 'took over' as Patron Saint!

(Napoleon made Melk Monastery his headquarters when his army are supposed to have drunk 50,000 pints of wine in four days. They are still talking about it in the Wachau—not so much about the quantity, but that Napoleon was rather scathing about the quality of the wine!)

Melk itself is also worth a second glance. See its Posthaus (Baroque), sixteenth-century Schiffmeisterhaus and seventeenth-century St Koloman fountain at Rathausplatz.

Leaving Melk, follow dirctions for St Pölten on 1, then turn left and almost immediately right onto 33 direction Schönbühel. The road closely follows the river practically all the way. Drive through **SCHÖNBÜHEL**, what has an imposing castle on the river (private property—admire from afar), and continue on 33 to **AGGSBACH DORF**, where there is a fourteenth-century former monastery and church (see also Baroque facade at Gasthof zur Post). After about 3 km more, still on 33, you will Leaving Melk, follow directions for St Pölten on 1, then turn left and find fortress ruins **Aggstein** towering 300 m above the Danube on a rock. This is certainly one of the most spectacular fortress ruins, with deep dungeons and 5 m thick walls, and a somewhat chequered history. Built in the twelfth-century it was first of all the property of the powerful Kuenringer—Robber Knights turned respectable who seemed to be permanently at odds first with the Babenbergs and then with the Habsburgs. It was conquered and partly destroyed, first by Duke Friedrich II and then by Albrecht I, after which it became the property of one Jörg Scheck vom Wald, soon to be nicknamed 'Schreckenwalder' (terror of the woods). He rebuilt the partially destroyed fortress, but, it is said, would kidnap prosperous travellers and if a ransom was not forthcoming, would have his victims lowered onto a small platform high above the Danube—quaintly named the 'Rose Garden'—leaving them a choice of either starving or jumping to death. According to the legend, one prisoner survived the jump and lived to tell the tale, after which Jörg vom Wald was hastily removed, though his successor proved to be no better: one of his prisoners begged to be allowed to say his prayers before jumping to his death for as long as the church bells were ringing. This was granted and the bells—from across the Danube at Schwallenbach—never stopped, since when they are fondly known as 'Glöckerl von Schwallenbach' (little bells of Schwallenbach). Turkish invaders destroyed the fortress which was rebuilt in the seventeenth century and was a refuge for many during the Thirty Years War. It has been allowed to decay since the end of the seventeenth century (some of the stones were used to build Langegg Monastery) but certainly remains worthy of inspection. There are marvellous views from the top of course, and also **Burgtaverne** restaurant (open March to November).

Back on 33 drive along Danube through **ST JOHANN**—note cockerel on top of parish church (see Teufelsmauer on other side for story).

Follow the Danube on 33 through St Lorenz after which the road leaves the river for a short stretch, to **ROSSATZ** which was a Slav settlement in the eighth century and a Protestant stronghold in the sixteenth. It has many lovely old houses, but is principally known for its picturesque 'Heurigen' set in old wine cellars (at the eastern end of the village).

Further on the same road, go through sleepy **RÜHRSDORF** (pretty vintners houses, some Baroque) and **ROSSATZBACH** where a river of the same name flows into the Danube. Marvellous views from Rossatzbach across the river to Dürnstein. Still on 33, once more closely following the Danube, you will see Schloss Baumgarten on a hill, but much more important the imposing Benedictine monastery Göttweig will come into view. More often than not it is surrounded by slight mists, so that it looks like a castle floating on clouds. Continue on 33 to **MAUTERN** which celebrated its millenium in 1980, but it is much older than that: Roman Favianis stood in the same place in the first century and some of the Roman walls are still in existence (thought to be medieval for a long time, but now definitely proved to be Roman). St Severinus founded a monastery and died there in the fifth century. Later called Mutaren (from Maut = toll), it was mentioned in the Nibelungenlied. Often the scene of severe fighting (and much damaged in the Second World War) Mautern managed to retain many of the beautiful old buildings and art treasures. See especially: the fourteenth-century parish church St Stephan (on earlier foundations); former St Margaret's chapel with fourteenth-century frescoes (now a museum with archaeological finds: open Saturday, Sunday and holidays; 02732 3151); Schloss Mautern; Nikolaihof—probably in place of the tenth-century St Agapit; Roman tower (with an eighteenth-century folly on top); and Janaburg, a former Renaissance castle.

Mautern is also the oldest documented wine village in Austria, which seems fitting for the place that now has one of Austria's best restaurants:

for **Bacher** (02732 2937) is nothing short of superb, the very best of good Austrian cooking with a great touch of elegance. Charming guest rooms too and their half-board terms must be one of the best bargains in Austria.

[From Mautern it is only a 6km drive to **Stift Gottweig** which you will have seen from a distance. It is a short journey well worth taking, if only to see the Kaiserstiege—the grandiose staircase by Lukas von Hildebrandt. If you make this excursion, **Schickh** at Klein Wien (02736 218) is an excellent restaurant with pleasant rooms, and the chef is the sister of the presiding genius at Bacher.]

From Mautern cross the Danube to return to Krems/Stein.

Waldviertel

5 days/about 315 km/from Krems to Grein (in Oberösterreich)

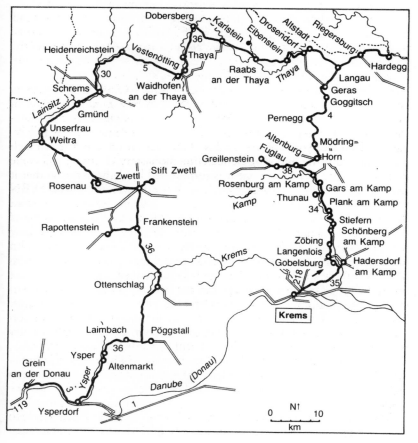

The Waldviertel (forest quarter) is the area north of the Danube in Lower Austria, bordered by the Manhartsberg in the east, which reaches right up to the Czechoslovak frontier. Ravaged by wars and torn by rebellions through the centuries, it is now an immensely peaceful and romantic area with attractive villages and an amazing number of castles and fortresses, beautiful churches ranging from Romanesque to Baroque, splendid monasteries and picturesque fortress ruins condensed into a comparatively small area. Driving through it you may well think that the 400 fortified castles claimed by Lower Austria are all contained in the Waldviertel!

It is almost impossible to give exact descriptions of all the places of interest—or even to list all of them: all I could hope to do is to point out the most important ones, giving a little of their history now and then—and hope that further investigation on the spot will become an enjoyable part of this route.

The Waldviertel is not a tourist area. You will encounter deep dark forests, lakes and a Waldviertel curiosity, the 'Wackelstein' (literally, 'wobbly stone'—huge slabs of granite so delicately poised on top of each other that gently rock at a touch). Roads are excellent, and while there are no large hotels, there are time-honoured old inns (more often than not in a historic building) or sturdy small new ones, built to last and to become time-honoured in due course, all at very moderate—and at times, downright ridiculously low prices!

From **KREMS** (for details see Wachau route) take 35 to **HADERS- DORF AM KAMP** which has one of the prettiest main squares in Austria. There is a little park in the centre and the houses, though by no means all of the same period, are an absolute joy. See particularly No. 6, No. 12 with large central doorway, Baroque No. 33 as well as Renaissance town hall, parish church, charnel house and many others.

Double back from main square onto 35 the way you came and just after crossing Kamp river outside Hadersdorf take a small turning to the right for **GOBELSBURG**, making straight for Schloss Gobelsburg. The castle was built during the fourteenth and fifteenth centuries, but was transformed so extensively in the eighteenth (probably by Munggenast) that it all but ruined the owner financially and eventually went to Zwettl Monastery. It is now a museum well worth stopping for (1 April to 31 October 02734 2422—see also chapel with paintings by Kremser Schmidt) as are the wines which may be sampled at the castle as well. Note too the parish church (with statuary attributed to Schletterer) and the seventeenth-century Trinity column, formerly at Spittelberg in Vienna. **Rebstockgrill** (02734 2356) serves good food, wines from its own vineyards and home-brewed Schnapps, but is open only from 21 October to 13 December and then again from 15 January to 15 April, from Friday until Sunday and from 5pm only—telephone first in case times have changed once more!

From Gobelsburg follow directions for Langenlois where you meet 218.

LANGENLOIS (pop: 6,500) formerly called Liubisa (the lovely one) is the largest 'wine town' in Austria. Together with the surrounding villages 12 million litres of wine are produced annually—and wine of historic quality at that! The birth of Empress Maria Theresia was toasted in Langenlois wine, Beethoven was partial to it (though to be fair, to other Austrian wines as well—but his brother owned nearby Schloss Gnexiendorf) and it is almost invariably served on State occasions. Before tasting the Langenlois wines—and opportunities are many—take a stroll through the small town which can easily be explored on foot. Langenlois originally consists of two separate villages which were joined in the fifteenth century: Obere Aigen where most of the vintners lived and Untere Aigen where prosperous merchants built their houses. Hauptplatz is an exceptionally appealing square with mostly sixteenth-century houses, albeit some over-restored. No. 2 **Langenloiser Hof** (02734 2475—very good inn) has a Baroque facade and impressive arcades; but walk too through Bahnstrasse, Rathausstrasse (fine town hall, museum at No. 13), Rudolfstrasse and up to Am Rosenhügel (eighteenth/nineteenth-century wine cellars, beautiful views of Langenlois) See also: parish church St Lorenz; St Nikolaus Church—and lots more.

Bründlmayer, Walterstrasse 14 (02734 2883) are famous for their wines which they also sell in bottles to take away. Excellent hot and cold buffet. (Open 1 March to 31 December, Thursday to Sunday, from 3 pm.) **Weinschlössl**, Dimmelgraben 1 (02734 3154) is a 'proper' restaurant with an extensive menu—what the Austrians would call 'gehobene' Küche—uplifted *cuisine*. (Open Saturday, Sunday from 3pm, Tuesday to Friday from 5 pm. Closed Monday and from 15 November until 31 March.) For a complete list of wine cellars, wine tastings, cellar visits, special events at local restaurants, etc., call at the Tourist Office in the town hall (02734 2101).

Take 34 out of Langenlois, direction Kamptal, through **ZÖBING** which has been called the 'Grinzing of the Kamp Valley' because of its many wine cellars (parish church with fifteenth-century tempera paintings; seventeenth-century pillory; eighteenth-century Saints columns) to **SCHÖNBERG AM KAMP**. From now onwards the road follows the river closely, twisting and turning almost as if to point out the various spots of interest on the way, such as the two towers and bastions which are all that remains of Schönberg Fortress (note the interesting parish church with painting by Kremser Schmidt) or the Calvary Hill on the way to **STIEFERN**, a small hamlet built around the sixteenth-century fortified church (particularly good altar painting by Kremser Schmidt, rococo side altar, seventeenth-century christening font in red marble).

Still on 34, drive through **PLANK AM KAMP**; here the river twists conveniently to point out a church set on a rock on the left, and again, after Plank, to show off Schloss Buchberg, also on the left.

Stay on 34 for **GARS AM KAMP**, a favourite holiday resort of the Viennese ever since the Kamp Valley railway was opened in 1889. Franz von Suppe had his country retreat there at Kremserstrasse 40 (now a small museum), but prior to that he stayed at Haangasse 27 which could easily be mistaken for a stage set from one of his operettas.

Cross the river to **THUNAU** for the impressive fortress ruins on the hill (an exhibition in two rooms, open during weekends in summer), St Gertrud Church (fourteenth-century painted glass windows in choir, fifteenth-century pieta) and charnel house.

Return to 34, driving north, passing fortress ruins Kamegg on right, to **ROSENBURG AM KAMP**. 'Es steht ein Schloss in Österreich, das ist gar wohl erbauet' ('a castle stands in Austria that has been built well') runs an ancient ballad and it has always been accepted that this refers to the Rosenburg. The words of the ballad tally not only with a description of the castle ('von Silber und von rotem Gold, mit Marmelstein gemauert'—'of silver and red gold, built in marble'), but refer to actual happenings there: the Rosenburg was a Protestant stronghold in the sixteenth and early seventeenth century, at one time known as the 'Austrian Wartburg' and its owner, Christoph Reuter, as the 'German Pope', a place of assembly for the Horner Bund, the Protestant Federation of Horn. It was later the property of Cardinal Franz von Dietrichstein, a loyal supporter of the Emperor and, in 1620, during the Thirty Years War, the Hussites took the castle 'und zu Rosenburg sein, gestorben gross und klein ... 300 Mann und Weiber, wie ander Kinder klein' ('and at Rosenburg there died 300 men and women, as well as small children'—who had sought refuge there). A column in the courtyard commemorates this terrible event.

After the Thirty Years War the castle was lavishly rebuilt with 13 towers 'so that it can now be counted among the four most noble castles in Austria', it was recorded at the time. It is indeed a lavish building, and lavishly restored during the last century after a fire had all but destroyed it. The tournament court (mis-named as time for tournaments had passed when it was built) is particularly beautiful with its galleries for spectators. (Open March to November, 02982 2911). **Gasthof-Hotel Josef Mann** (02982 2915) is a charming modern inn, reasonably priced, with very comfortable rooms.

Entrance to the Rosenburg

Turn left out of Rosenburg, direction Altenburg (leaving 34). Stift Altenburg is hardly signposted. In **ALTENBURG** follow directions for Fuglau on 38 and you will find the entrance to Stift Altenburg almost immediately on the left. A Benedictine monastery founded in the twelfth century and repeatedly overrun (Magyars, Hussites, Swedes, etc.), it was damaged so badly that it had to be practically pulled down completely before being rebuilt. There was some rebuilding in the seventeenth-century, but most of the work was done in the eighteenth.

Altenburg is one of the Baroque treasures of Austria (even if the authorities can barely be bothered to put up a few signposts!). See particularly: eastern facade above Kamp Valley; Library; Crypt (beneath library); Kaisertrakt (Imperial suite) with magnificent stairway; Deanery church. (Open Easter to 1 November, otherwise by appointment; 02982 3451. There are also special exhibitions and concerts).

You may think that you have seen enough castles by now, and indeed there are many more to come on this route. Nonetheless I feel duty bound to point out that Greillenstein, a superb Renaissance castle with Baroque gardens, is but 5 km away. To get there, turn left coming from Stift Altenburg onto 38 for Fuglau and then follow directions for **Greillenstein** to the right. (Open 1 April to 31 October, 02989 8321.)

Get back onto 38 direction Horn, following signs for Horn Zentrum.

HORN (pop: 8,000) is a very old town, sitting prettily above the Taffa river. It gained great importance at the beginning of the seventeenth century when the Horner Bund was formed and it was known as the 'Protestant Rome in the Waldviertel'. Prosperity was short-lived however: at the end of the Thirty Years War only 75 houses were habitable and much rebuilding up to the present has resulted in a not very united picture. Much still deserves to be seen though, such as the fortification walls with medieval towers, St George's (built as a Protestant church in 1593, now Catholic), parish church St Stephan (built 1046), Schloss Horn (originally Renaissance, Baroque additions), many old houses at Kirchenplatz—No. 3 with sgraffito, Hauptplatz and Thurnhofgasse, and also the Floriani fountain at Kirchenplatz. Höbarth Museum, Wiener Strasse 4 (02982 2372, Easter to 1 November) contains all you could ever want to know (and probably more) about Horn and surroundings; it is all the collection of one man who made it his life's work. The sixteenth-century hotel **Zum weissen Rössel** Hauptplatz 16 (02982 2398) is a cosy inn with a resplendent past. (About 4 km south-east of Horn is the pilgrimage church of Maria Dreieichen. Worth a detour for the superb interior and fresco by Paul Troger.)

Take 4 north out of town, direction Geras (careful—at one point there are signs for 4 pointing in all directions, the one you want runs alongside the town wall for a bit). Passing through little **MÖDRING** (interesting church) and woods known as Himmelreich (heaven), you may notice a drop in temperature: Horn has a particularly mild climate and is rather sheltered.

Ulrich von Pernegg—probably a relation of the Babenbergs—lived in great style at his fortress in the twelfth century, but when visited by the Abbot of Garsten the good abbot was shocked to find widowed Ulrich surrounded by a small harem of twelve women. Whatever the abbot said had immediate effect: Ulrich sent away eleven of the women and married the twelfth (history does not relate how the choice was made) and founded a monastery and a convent at Geras and **PERNEGG** respectively. It did not bring him much luck for the last of the Perneggs died 'an idiot and a fool, not worthy of possessions' and the fortress went to the Crown, was severely damaged by the Hussites and finally pulled down in the fifteenth century. The convent (later a monastery) was secularised in 1783 and the buildings ravaged in various wars (including by Russian soldiers at the end of the Second World War), but there have been extensive restorations (some still in progress).

Pernegg is still an impressive sight, sitting to the left of the road and surrounded by the old fortification walls. See: former convent/monastery with remains of Renaissance cloister; late-Gothic abbey (now parish church) with Renaissance pulpit; charnel house (now chapel) with Renaissance christening font and impressive twentieth-century stained glass windows.

Continue on 4, through Hötzelsdorf and **GOGGITSCH** (former sixteenth/seventeenth-century castle) to **GERAS** an idyllic little village, centred around the Premonstratensian monastery. The original monastery, founded in 1149, was almost completely destroyed and rebuilt; first in the seventeenth century, with additions by Munggenast in the eighteenth. See particularly: Deanery church (its facade looks like that of an Italian palazzo) with paintings by Maulpertsch, Altomonte, beautiful pulpit; monastery with grand staircase, Marmorsaal (where concerts are sometimes held) with two Troger paintings, also Troger fresco. Guided tours only, 1 May to 31 October except Mondays (02912 345). Since 1970 hobby courses have been held at Stift Geras (painting, grisaille, gilding, restoration of furniture and much more) which have proved so popular that a 'branch' had to be started some 200 km away at Feistrit. **Alter Schüttkasten** (02912 332), a seventeenth-century silo superbly converted into a hotel offers very good food and accommodation at very reasonable prices. Accommodation is also available at the monastery; meals are taken at the Schüttkasten and there is a delightful college atmosphere. (Enquiries for **Hobby Courses**—02912 34589. Language is no problem as participants come from all over the world.) Geras has some pretty old houses, a pleasant lake for swimming, and a huge nature reserve nearby.

From Geras drive in the direction of Langau where the T-junction turn left and then almost immediately right onto 30 for **RIEGERSBURG**. Schloss Riegersburg is one of the finest of all Baroque residences in Lower Austria, meticulously restored and refurnished after it had been all but destroyed during the Russian occupation following the Second World War. (It lasted for over ten years and the grand hall was used as a driving school, the chapel varyingly as dining-room, a prison and a potato cellar!) (Open 1 April to 15 October, Tuesday to Sunday, or by arrangement; 02916 400.)

Follow directions for Felling and **HARDEGG** (pop: 200), the smallest town in Austria (town rights granted 1383). Rather romantically situated in the narrow Thaya Valley amidst deep, dark forests and guarded by the mighty Burg Hardegg, the town was once known as a town of weavers and mother-of-pearl polishers, it is now 'the end of the world': the river Thaya forms the border between Austria and Czechoslovakia, but there is no bridge and no way of crossing. I have not dragged you to the end of the world for nothing though—a visit to the fortress should more than compensate for the short detour from Riegersburg! (Open April to end of November, 02949 8225.)

The fortress also houses a museum dedicated to the Emperor Maximilian of Mexico (brother of Emperor Franz Josef) and on the stairway leading to the crypt there is a cross carved from the mast of the frigate Novara on which his body was brought back to Austria. (Prince Khevenhüller-Metsch, owner of both Riegersburg and Hardegg had accompanied the unfortunate Maximilian to Mexico and was later sent to bring back his body.) In Hardegg 'town' see the twelfth-century church and charnel house.

Double back to Langau (interesting church and eighteenth-century St Nepomuk column) and from there follow directions for Drosendorf, first passing through **ALTSTADT**, the original settlement for the protection of which the fortress was built; it declined in importance as the village around the fortress grew. Note the parish church with its rich portal and very good frescoes, and the imposing parsonage.

The river Thaya makes an immense loop around **DROSENDORF**, surrounding it on three sides, before rushing off to Czechoslovakia and

returning to Austria once again near Hardegg. Drosendorf Fortress was first built in the twelfth century, on a steep escarpment to protect the country from the advancing Bohemians and, in 1278, only 1,000 men held up the 18,000-strong army of King Ottokar for 16 days, during which time Rudolf von Habsburg collected more troops for the decisive battle in which Ottokar lost his life. The Habsburgs showed their gratitude by granting Drosendorf the same town rights as Vienna in 1310 and Rudolf IV called himself Margrave of Drosendorf! Further evidence of Drosendorf's fierce spirit can be found on the inscription at Hornerstrasse 7 which says that Christian von Anhalt, known as 'dare-devil Christian', when beleaguering the town in 1620 achieved no more than 'scratching a pig's snout'. And during the Second World War there was a very strong anti-Nazi and pro-Monarchist resistance movement based on Drosendorf.

Drosendorf, the town hall

Today Drosendorf is a sleepy little village (pop: 700) of absolute picture-book quality, still surrounded by medieval walls. The once fierce fortress was converted into a rich Renaissance castle, promptly all but destroyed by fire and rebuilt in great splendour in 1694; now run as a *hotel garni* at very moderate prices. (Open between mid-June and mid-September 02915 219.) The main square—really an elongated triangle—is particularly charming with some exceptionally pretty houses, but see also Schlossgasse, the parish church and particularly the late-Gothic pillory, known as 'Roland's Column'. **Gasthof Feiler** (02915 327) serves exceptionally good food and wine (which can be enjoyed on a terrace overlooking the river or in a nicely-shaded garden) and also has some very pleasant rooms, all at reasonable prices.

Leave Drosendorf on 30 which runs along the river Thaya, following every twist and turn until **EIBENSTEIN** where river and road part company for a short while. Restoration work at the church above the river on the right uncovered some quite remarkable sixteenth-century frescoes. Fortress ruins on the other side of the river look wildly romantic and are best admired from below—unless you'd care for the view from the top which is pretty good too.

Continue on 30 to **RAABS** at the confluence of the Moravian and Austrian Thaya—which is known in Austria as German Thaya, presuming that if it could speak it would be gurgling away in German—as against the Thaya which comes from across the Czech border. Curiously enough, the 'German' Thaya (which has never been anywhere near Germany) starts its life as plain Thaya south-west of Raabs, adopts the 'German' a little further on, before the confluence with the Moravian Thaya—after which the combined river is once again known as Thaya—at least whilst in Austria. Having crossed the Czech border to the east it is known as Dyje—to return to Austria as Thaya, to cross again into Czechoslovakia . . .

Burg Raabs was built as one of the most important fortresses in eleventh-century Austria and the Herren (Lords) of Raabs were all-powerful (one daughter married a Zollern and was thus ancestor to the Prussian kings). Like all fortresses, and indeed towns, in the Waldviertel, it was repeatedly overrun, beleaguered—and rebuilt. Burg Raabs was also twice the scene of murder: in 1591 a neighbour whose servants had quarrelled with those of Niklas von Puchheim (then Lord of Raabs) appeared at the castle in disguise and shot Puchheim, whereupon the Catholic priest (the Puccheims were staunch Protestants) was arrested and kept in prison for years, whilst the murderer was allowed to escape. The priest was eventually released, but there is *still* a plaque in red marble branding him as 'a traitor and spy'. Just over 60 years ago there was another dramatic murder, when the wife of the residing count and her Russian lover decided to dispose of the husband, faking an accident. The shots misfired, barely touching the count—whereupon he turned round and shot the lover —after which the wife committed suicide.

In view of all this it seems highly appropriate that Burg Raabs now houses a fairytale museum (open May to October, otherwise by arrangement; 02846 659). See also the parish church and some nice old houses, ranging from Baroque to Biedermeier. **Hotel Thaya**, Hauptstrasse 14-18 (02846 202) is set directly on the river (pretty garden) with pleasant rooms, good food, and very moderate prices.

Still on 30, drive on to **KARLSTEIN** which at one time was a centre of horology, its speciality being carved wooden clocks (sadly overtaken by mechanised Black Forest clocks!) which started in 1750 and about a hundred years later there were about 300 families producing some 140,000 clocks every year. A special school for horology is still going strong however. Here the road meets up with the Thaya once more—the German one this time—and there is another mighty twelfth-century fortress guarding the river (it stood firm against the besieging Swedes and later on gave shelter against the Turks).

Leave Karlstein still on 30, through Göpfritzschlag and Riegers to **DOBERSBERG** (very impressive sixteenth-century castle, robbed of all furnishings after the Second World War, but parish church worth viewing) where turn left onto 36 for the lovely little village of **THAYA** (back to the river once more). You may be surprised by a few of the houses in Marktplatz and Hauptstrasse which appear to be rather grand and not quite in keeping with the sleepy little hamlet: in the last century Thaya was a centre for fabulously rich pig dealers (called 'Schweinebarone') who employed Italian builders for their little palaces. Swine fever, and resulting laws restricting imports, put an end to this lucrative business. See also the Romanesque parish church (rococo altar donated by the Tailors' Union); the Renaissance fountain; and a seventeenth-century pillory with the figure of a knight, fondly known as 'Pillory Hansl'.

There are two roads from Thaya to Waidhofen; it does not matter which one you take, but the road east of the Thaya, though slightly longer, is the prettier and sticks more or less to the river, leading through peaceful little **VESTENÖTTING** which lies cradled in a river loop (Baroque church reached by steps, sixteenth-century castle in village centre).

WAIDHOFEN AN DER THAYA

WAIDHOFEN AN DER THAYA (there is another one 'an der Ybbs' in Lower Austria) is a delightful and rather romantic country town, sitting very prettily on an escarpment above the river. Town rights were granted in 1230 and Waidhofen has always enjoyed special privileges such as market rights (much to the detriment of neighbouring Thaya which had its market rights taken away by Rudolf IV so as not to harm the prosperity of Waidhofen). Quiet and peaceful now, Waidhofen shared the fate of other settlements in the Waldviertel: overrun and beleaguered time and again (Bohemian King Ottokar set fire to the church, killing all those who had sought refuge there), pestilence and finally an enormous fire in 1873 which destroyed some of the old town. Many of the houses had so-called 'Fluchtkeller' (literally 'cellar through which to flee')—underground passages leading out of town. Wienerstrasse 14 (with sgraffito) houses the 'old' museum including 'black kitchen' and Fluchtkeller. (Open daily to 10 am to 12 pm during July/August, other months Sunday 10 am to 12 pm only. 02842 2621). There is plenty to see: Hauptplatz with Renaissance town hall: Pfarrgasse; parish church on highest part of town with stunning eighteenth-century interior; Bürgerspitalskirche (outside medieval fortifications); 'new' museum at Schadekgasse 4 in opulent house of a former 'pig baron' for whom Thaya was obviously too small; Schloss; and much, much more besides.

From Waidhofen take 5 to Pfaffenschlag, passing a small lake on the left (Jägerteich), and from there to **HEIDENREICHSTEIN**. Burg Heidenreichstein, surrounded by water on three sides and the grandest of all 'Burgen' in Austria, was built to frighten off invaders by sight and indeed no enemy has ever attempted to conquer it. During the Thirty Years War the village was attacked by Swedish troops, but the fortress was left severely alone. Some of the original furnishings are still 'in residence', including an enormous Gothic cupboard and a beautiful tiled stove, also paintings, arms, etc. Guided visits only (mid/April to mid/October, except Monday, every hour; 02862 2268). See also the parish church and seventeenth-century pillory with 'beer bell' once used to ring out closing hour!

Heidenreichstein is on the old Imperial road to Prague and the settlement grew around the fortress. At the end of the last century some metal works and textile mills were established which makes Heidenreichstein, somewhat surprisingly, a splendid place for 'ex-factory' shopping. The Tourist Office, Kirchenplatz 1 (02862 2336) will suggest suitable addresses. **Gasthof Grossmann**, Stadtplatz 9 (02862 2279) is a good little modern inn with pleasant restaurant; **Burgstüberl**, Waidhofener Strasse 1 (02862 3101) a cosy restaurant and **Gasthof Nöbauer**, Schremser Strasse 28 (02862 2237) another good modern inn, with roof terrace.

Leave Heidenreichstein on 30, direction Schrems, and at large junction outside Schrems follow signs for **GMÜND** (pop: 6,500), a sturdy and sedate small town at the confluence of Lainsitz and Braunau rivers. In a document of Emperor Barbarossa '*concursus duorum rivulorum*' was mentioned as being the border point between Bohemia and Austria, which Gmünd has remained to this day. Despite the ravages brought by fire (in 1473 Gmünd was recorded as 'ganz abgebrunnen', totally burned down), wars and pestilence—what one could call the 'usual' Waldviertel trials—Gmünd now presents a serene (not to say sleepy) appearance and the sixteenth-century main square (Hauptplatz) with its sgraffiti houses looks like an old print. Until the eighteenth century Gmünd was known as 'Gmünd near the Long Woods' and a nightwatchman rang the bells at 10 pm and again at 3 am for people 'lost in the woods'. See particularly: Hauptplatz with old town hall and Glass and Mineral Museum (No. 34, open May/September and by arrangement; 02852 2506); thirteenth-century castle (extended sixteenth and seventeenth centuries); parish church St Stephan. Tourist Office: Stadtplatz 19 (02852 3212).

Gmünd is also the beginning of the much-loved Waldviertler Schmalspurbahn (narrow-gauge railway) which trundles from Gmünd to Gross Gerungs via Weitra and charming little Langschlag, complete with old-fashioned dining car, serving all sorts of local specialities like poppyseed 'Zelten', beer brewed at Weitra, and fiery local Schnapps.

(A visit to the Blockheide—a huge nature park outside Gmünd—could also prove rewarding. It has stunning rock formations, and interesting flora and fauna. Information Centre: Eibenstein/Blockheide, 02852 3817, open 15 April to 30 September.)

Leave Gmünd on 41, driving along the river Lainsitz through **UNSERFRAU** (literally 'Our Lady'), once a famous place of pilgrimage—particularly in the seventeenth century—connected with miraculous healings at the local spa. It has a beautifully situated parish church (note the windows, pulpit, fourteenth-century statuary) as well as the original chapel where about 20 years ago some early sixteenth-century frescoes were discovered.

Further on 41 you come to **WEITRA**, a walled and attractive small town, built solidly on granite rock. Enter through the towered gate with its inscription 'Gott bewahr die Stadt' and you are well and truly in another world. Everything in Weitra is worth seeing: the ancient houses, the parish church and above all, the Renaissance castle with its own theatre (which pretends to be rococo but was built at the end of the last century—all the decorations are papier maché!). The Tourist Office at Stadtamt (02856 2378 and 2682) will ensure that you do not miss anything in Weitra. **Gasthof Waschka**, Rathausplatz 8 (02856 2296) is a good little inn, moderately priced.

From Weitra take direction Zwettl which leads through some very pleasant woods and past the occasional 'Wackelstein' and eventually through Jagenbach. About 2 km after Jagenbach turn right, signposted 'Schloss Rosenau 3 km', drive through Rosenau village and follow directions for Schloss Rosenau.

Schloss Rosenau (02822 8221) is another hidden treasure of the Waldviertel. Beautifully situated, originally a Renaissance castle, and completely rebuilt in 1740, it now houses the only Masonic museum in Europe. The castle is run as a hotel (rooms a little sparsely furnished), more than reasonably priced, with a very good restaurant. (It is a popular venue for conferences, so booking ahead is advised if you want to stay).

Leaving Schloss Rosenau, turn left, signposted 'Zwettl 8 km', and then right, again marked Zwettl.

ZWETTL (pop: 4,000) is the geographical centre of the Waldviertel, and one of the coldest spots in Austria. Do not let that—or the fact that Zwettl has had rather more than its share of the usual Waldviertel disasters like wars, fires and rebellions—deter you from exploring the town which has a great deal of hidden charm. Tourist Office, Dreifaltigkeitsplatz 1 (02822 2233) has a useful little booklet which pinpoints all the important buildings such as the Provost Church, town hall, parish church, and many fifteenth/sixteenth-century houses. There is also a rather unusual museum, sited in a twelfth-century tower, containing furniture, pictures, arms, and other relics collected by a local chimney sweep who saved them from destruction! It's called the 'Anton' Museum (02822 2343).

Leave Zwettl centre, taking direction Ottenschlag and Stift Zwettl, and follow signs for Stift Zwettl throughout. These are admittedly rather sparse and I can only hope that the authorities have done something about this since my last visit (and complaints!). Stift Zwettl is one of the oldest Cistercian monasteries in Austria (guided visits only, usually every hour, 02822 3181) with a particularly beautiful abbey church (rebuilt by Munggenast, statuary by Schletterer), but see as well the cloisters, chapter house (oldest in Austria), refectory with Troger paintings, library; and a visit to the **Stiftstaverne** could also prove most rewarding (02822 3174) since Zwettl Monastery is also famous for its vineyards!

About 3 km north of Zwettl on the 36 is **Dürnhof**, formerly the farm of Zwettl Monastery, built probably around 1200 and now the only Museum of Humanbiometeorologie—medicine/meteorology—in the world. (Open May to October, closed Monday, 02822 3180.)

Return to Zwettl Zentrum (which is infinitely easier than finding the way out to the Stift) and then follow 36 direction Ottenschlag. Drive south on 36 and after about 9 km at Frankenreith—if you feel that you could bear to visit another fortress (and if it is a Saturday, Sunday or holiday)—turn right for Rapottenstein and then left for Burg Rapottenstein. It's worth the short detour for not only will you see some rather impressive Wackel-steine on the way, but also twelfth-century Burg Rapottenstein with its Renaissance arcades and beautiful frescoes is particularly attractive. (Hourly guided tours, from Easter until 1 November, Saturday, Sunday and holidays only.)

Double back to 36, direction **OTTENSCHLAG** (sixteenth-century castle with beautiful Renaissance portal; now occupied by offices and flats) and continue on 36 for about 15 km to a junction where follow directions for **PÖGGSTALL**. This is another detour—albeit only about 4 km in all—well worth taking: to Schloss Rogendorf at Pöggstall. Local publicity points to it being a 'Heimatmuseum mit Folterkammer' (folklore museum with torture chamber) which comes close to suggesting that every well-equipped castle should have its own torture chamber! In fact the torture chamber is of secondary importance compared to the castle and particularly the barbican which was designed by Albrecht Dürer (or rather built according to plans laid down by Dürer in his book on fortifi-cations). (Open 1 March to 30 November or by arrangement; 02758 2349 and 2397.) See also the parish church St Anna and particularly Gothic St Anna im Felde.

Return the 2 km to the junction, then continue on 36 along the Ysper (be careful to keep to the right fork at Laimbach) to Altenmarkt. This is a very peaceful road with only a few scattered villages—lovely and relaxing after all the fortresses. **ALTENMARKT** is the oldest settlement in the Ysper Valley and was once called Ysper, which must have been slightly confusing as there is not only the river of the same name but also another village called Ysper on the other side. (However, when the 'new' Ysper had grown in size, the 'old' Ysper began to be known as 'alter Markt'— old market = Altenmarkt). There's a romanesque parish church in Alten-markt with Troger painting. 'New' **YSPER** is a lovely and sleepy little village with ancient trees, attractive church, fountain and pillory (on market days a long pole is put up to 'stake' market rights).

After Altenmarkt leave 36, taking a right fork marked Grein and also Persenbeug. It is not the best of roads, but very pretty, twisting and turning with the river, and it meets road 3 at Ysperdorf. Turn right on 3 driving along the Danube, direction Grein.

GREIN (pop: 2,800) just across the border in Oberösterreich (Upper Austria) is an enchanting place with many attractions, such as the town hall with the oldest theatre in Austria (performances during the summer). The theatre still has 'Sperrsitze' (lockable seats) and in the olden days the town lock-up was in the same building—prisoners could watch performances from their cells, asking 'legit' paying visitors for tobacco and food and if this was not forthcoming, they would interrupt performances!

While here see Schloss Greinburg, a magnificent castle high above the Danube, clearly built for comfortable living rather than as a fortress (in fact permission was granted in the fifteenth century specifically to build a 'Gschloss' = castle as against a fortress). Since 1826 it has been Saxe-Coburg-Gotha property and at one time Queen Victoria owned half the castle (none of which stopped Russian troops from occupying it at the end of the Second World War). It has a beautiful arcaded courtyard, Rittersaal and fountain, also Shipping Museum (1 May to 9 November, closed Monday). There's a lot more to see in Grein, as a short stroll through the tiny town will prove, but retire to Cafe **Blumensträussl**, (07268 380) Stadtplatz 6, for delicious cakes and coffee before exploring further. Afterwards you may care to see, for example, the seventeenth-century parish church, or the many old houses in Donaugasse and Hauptstrasse.

8 BURGENLAND

Quiet, peaceful and serene—not to say sleepy. That is Burgenland now. Yet this has been one of the most fought-over territories in Austria. Countless armies have passed—Roman, Mongolian, Magyar, Turkish, French, German and finally Russian, not forgetting fierce uprisings by Hungarian noblemen.

After the first Turkish invasion in 1529 the country was so emptied that settlers were brought in from Croatia and later from Swabia—in fact 10 per cent of the population still speak Croat as their mother tongue. German has always been the principal language—Hungarian counts for a mere 2 per cent even though the great landowners and ruling princes— the Erdödys, Nadasdys, Batthanys and above all, the Esterhazys—were Hungarian to a man. Indeed until the end of the Austro-Hungarian Empire the area was known as German Western Hungary. After the First World War and following a plebiscite it became Austria's youngest province in 1921—the choice of a name for the new province was somewhat rash however. It was to be called Vierburgenland not after the 'Burgen' (fortresses), of which there are many more than four in this land, but after four towns all ending in 'burg': Eisenburg, Ödenburg, Wieselburg and Pressburg—now known as Vas, Sopron and Moson in Hungary and Bratislava in Czechoslovakia. Which just goes to show that you should not count your towns (or name your provinces) before you have actually got them (or make sure that the plebiscite is not 'rigged' in places which this one certainly was . . .)

Burgenland, where the Hungarian plain gently moulds into the foothills of the eastern Alps, is quite unlike any other part of Austria. The landscape is largely true Hungarian Puszta with a climate to match— summers are exceptionally hot and dry, while winters are said to be moderate, though the wind that whistles round Lake Neusiedl seems to (and probably does!) come straight from Siberia. There are vast vineyards (well over a third of all wine produced in Austria comes from Burgenland), interrupted only by orchards and fields where maize, corn and sunflowers grow in profusion. In spring the gaunt fortresses are wreathed in blossoms and Linden trees; sage and ripe strawberries scent the air in summer. It's perfect country for touring, for lazing and sunbathing, for enjoying the shallow lake and the ancient, tiny towns—and for listening to good music (festivals at Eisenstadt, Mörbisch and Lockenhaus). Good

Burgenland

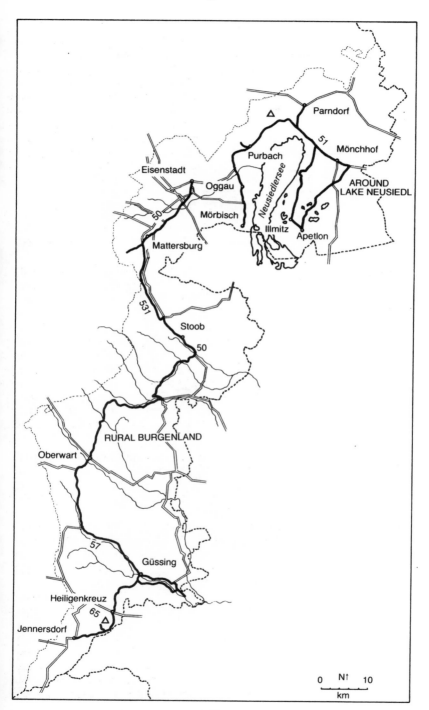

145

inns and good food abound—this is goose (and goose liver) country, but there's also plenty of excellent fish from the lake (local smoked eel is a rare delicacy since most of it goes to restaurants in Vienna), and game—everything spiced with the paprika which, together with apricots and cherries and other vegetables and fruit, grows in profusion under the hot sun.

Around Lake Neusiedl

1-5 days/about 105 km/from Parndorf to Mörbisch

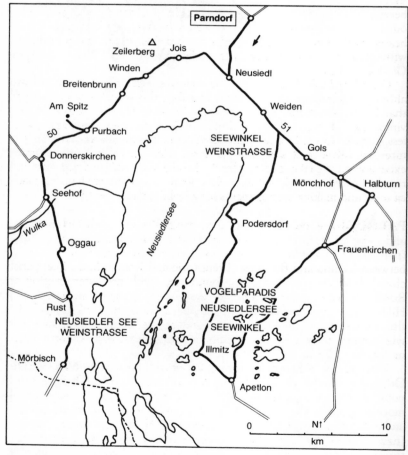

Lake Neusiedl is the largest steppe lake in Europe, measuring 36 km north to south and 5 km at its narrowest, the same width as the belt of reeds that surrounds it in places. Flat-bottomed and shallow, the wind rolls the water into the furthest corner—yet no-one knows where the water (and water with a high salt content at that) comes from in the first place. The river Wulka and other contributories account for no more than a quarter. And the rest? Mystery. Every hundred years or so the lake disappears completely—to re-appear with equal suddenness. Spur of the Asian salt deserts? Possibly, and this would explain the area known as Seewinkel on the lake's eastern shore: enormous flat marshes with warm salt lakes, exotic birds and flowers which can be found only in Asia.

The western shore presents a rather different picture—sheltered by the gentle Leitha Hills there are vast orchards and sturdy little villages poised prettily against the hillside or stretching out towards the lake.

Grapes grow well on either shore, the dense mist from the lake causing 'noble rot' and resulting in some superb Beerenauslesen and Trockenbeerenauslesen. 'I have come to the conclusion that the Burgenland has out-classed by far the Sauternes wines, that Chateau Yquem stands beaten by the finest of the Burgenland wines. There is no comparison.' So wrote that noted authority Fritz Hallgarten in *The Wines and Wine Gardens of Austria*.

Our route leads through the wine regions on either side of the lake and although it could be covered easily in a day, this would mean missing all that is best about that particular area: the leisurely drive through quiet vineyards and stopping in villages full of flowering oleander trees; the no less leisurely lunch in one of the small inns, arriving at yet another picturesque village and sampling the local wine—even an early morning excursion on the lake, gliding silently through the reeds in a boat to watch rare birds; and possibly falling in love with one of the enchanting places *en route* and making arrangements for a holiday there next year . . .

PARNDORF is on 10, about 40 km from Vienna's Schwechat airport and some 50 km from the centre of Vienna. Though only a small village (pop: 2,400), it was once an important coach station on the route between Vienna and Budapest. Prehistoric and Roman finds. See: parish church built on twelfth-century foundations with presbytery resting on Roman foundations; eighteenth-century nave designed by Lukas von Hildebrandt. Also charming Baroque chapel set in orchard. (Parndorf is the scene of Franz Werfel's daunting novel **Die wahre Geschichte vom wiederhergestellten Kreuz**—doubly daunting because it is mostly based on fact.)

Take 50 out of Parndorf, turning left at fork onto 51 to **NEUSIEDL**. Originally called Sumbotheil after the Saturday market which is still a popular feature in summer (also 'Krämermarkt' on first Monday in month) it was destroyed by Mongolian hordes in the thirteenth century and rebuilt almost immediately afterwards—hence the name Neusiedl (new settlement). Destroyed and rebuilt several times through the centuries, it is now a busy lakeside resort, long-stretched with a 2 km road leading out to the beach centre where there are excellent sporting facilities—bathing, surfing, sailing, tennis courts, fishing, etc. Its beach extends over 40,000 m^2 and is 500 m long. The climate supposedly is beneficial to asthma sufferers. **Hotel Wende** (02167 8111) is an excellent, moderately-priced family hotel with beauty farm and special therapy. **Barth Stuben** (02167 2625) Franz Lisztgasse 37 (road runs parallel to main street behind Post Office) is not only one of the best and most reasonably priced restaurants in Burgenland, but also one of the prettiest. See: Lake Museum next to beach centre (Easter/end October), with flora and fauna from around the lake, and recordings of birdcalls; the parish church—Gothic, baroquised with particularly interesting 'fisherman's' pulpit; Tabor (fortress) ruins on hill above town with good views over countryside; and the Folk Museum at Kalvarienbergstrasse 40, which is privately owned by enthusiast Karl Eidler—and you could well end up sharing bread and wine with him! Tourist Office: Hauptplatz 1 (02167 2229)

Continue on 51 to **WEIDEN** and its charming Sesselmarkt (chair market) at which fruit, vegetables and local basketware are displayed on chairs along the main street, under the watchful supervision of benevolent or fierce-looking women, clad in black, with kerchief firmly knotted under the chin. It's a rambling, old-fashioned village with good-looking holiday flats and houses—some of the best modern ones on the lake. Note the interesting Baroque parish church with treasures from the now defunct Augustine monastery at Bruck an der Leitha. Tourist Office: Gemeindeamt (02167 80311)

The road—still 51—moves farther away from the lake to **GOLS**, the largest wine-growing community in Burgenland. There is a grand nine-day festival in August when celebrations, including wine tastings, never seem to stop. **Weinbau Stieglmar**, Untere Haupstrasse 60 (02173 203) is a splendid place at which to sample the local wines at any time between Easter and end September (good food as well) or wine tastings only at **Allacher**, Winzergasse (sales of wine at both places). **Birkenhof** (02173 2346) is a pleasant family hotel, near the village green where the festival is held. Above all, do not miss a visit to **Lunzer**, known as the 'Blaue Konditorei' in the main street just opposite the church. It is one of the best patisseries in Austria! The church, first built in the thirteenth century, has been well restored, though little remains of the original.

Gols is the largest wine growing community in Burgenland, but **MÖNCHHOF**, the next village on 51, is the oldest, the first vines being planted by Cistercian monks in the thirteenth century. Its impressive eighteenth-century parish church was built immediately after the Turks had ravaged the place. Note particularly the painting on side altar by Altomonte (the main altar painting is by one of his pupils). **Marienkron**, a Cistercian convent, now includes an excellent hotel for Kneipp cures (02173 80205). It's usually booked for months, if not years ahead, and is excellent for an 'away from it all' holiday—with an easy escape route to nearby inns and vineyards in case you find the regime too strict.

Leave 51 at Mönchhof and take left fork to **HALBTURN**. This quiet little village has some interesting old houses, Tschardaken (storage barns for maize and typical of Burgenland) and an eighteenth-century parish church enlarged according to plans by Fischer von Erlach. But all this palls before **Schloss Halbturn**, one of the most beautiful Baroque castles built by Lukas von Hildebrandt. It is open between the middle of May and end of October, and special exhibitions and concert are usually held (02172 2237). See particularly: grand central hall with ceiling fresco by Maulpertsch (commissioned by the Empress Maria Theresia); and the beautiful park. The **Schlosskellerei** are also worth a visit—do not be put off by rather quaint names of wines such as Göttertrank (drink of the gods): the wines are from castle vineyards and are excellent.

Drive down through the small square leading from the castle, turn right at the bottom and then left for **FRAUENKIRCHEN** where the climate is like that of Heluan in Egypt and almond trees flourish. There's an outstandingly beautiful Baroque pilgrimage church by Martinelli—all white and gilt and gold (two previous pilgrimage churches were destroyed by the Turks). Note the statue of the medieval Holy Virgin carved in limewood. See also: Franciscan monastery (conducted tours every Sunday after mass), small Baroque castle (now school), Jewish cemetery with tombstones dating back to the seventeenth century (Frauenkirchen was one of the 'seven communities'—important Jewish settlements in Burgenland). **Altes Brauhaus** (02172 2217) opposite the church is a splendid old-fashioned restaurant (Baroque building, arcaded courtyard) serving good local dishes and excellent local wines (Franciscan monks had their own underground passage to the cellars). Tourist Office: Amtshausgasse 7 (02172 2300).

Turn left after Altes Brauhaus, direction Illmitz, Podersdorf, then follow sign 'Güterweg Apetlon' (there is a proper sign for Apetlon a little further on). This road is a little bumpy at first, but calms down later on and is certainly worth taking since it leads straight through the **Seewinkel**—enormous flat marshes dotted with warm salt lakes—about 80 of them, none more than about 1.5 m deep. The waters of the Darschosee (about 3 km before Apetlon on right) are exceptionally warm and supposed to have healing powers.

Seewinkel is at its most attractive in spring and early summer when the ground is covered with rare flowers, some of which can only be found in the Asian steppes. (The flowers are highly protected—you may think you have arrived at the end of the world, but cars have been known to be searched!) It is also a paradise for bird lovers with some 280 different species—avocet, redshank, bittern, spoonbill, purple, great white and squacco heron, about eight different kinds of duck, wild geese—whilst the great bustard has its own nature reserve a little further east near Andau.

After about 12 km the Güterweg will bring you to **APETLON**, a typically Hungarian Puszta village with reeded huts, draw wells, storks nesting on rooftops, and horses for hire should you wish to explore the Seewinkel in either a horse-drawn carriage or on horseback. If one of the gabled houses seems familiar, you are not suffering from *déjà vu*—it is featured in practically every brochure for Burgenland. Like all Seewinkel villages Apetlon has excellent wines. Their Muskat Ottonel is much recommended. Tourist Office: Kirchengasse la (02175 2220).

From Apetlon take road 12, first marked Neusiedl, Podersdorf and then, after a few metres, Podersdorf, Illmitz. For about 3 km it leads through what seems to be a single vineyard, pride and joy of Illmitz whose wine won the much coveted 'best wine in the world' medal for five years in succession. **ILLMITZ** is an exceptionally pretty village—Hungarian Puszta with a dash of Viennese coffee house atmosphere—witness the small main square with tiny park, art galleries and coffee house. If not all the houses are as genuinely old as they would like to appear, all is forgiven for the immensely pleasing effect. The St Bartholomaeus spring in the village centre supplies free mineral water. See also: reed-covered barn (Kreuzscheune) and Florianihof (Baroque with reeded roof), Baroque church. There is also a bird museum (02175 2209) and a biological station.

Rosenhof (02175 2232) is a charming small hotel with all that is typical of Burgenland: storks nesting on the roof, rose garden, restaurant with gipsy music, and superb wines from their own vineyards. Tourist Office: Obere Hauptstrasse 2-4 (02175 2383). (It is 5 km on the road out to the lake, through vineyards and reeds, perhaps best explored in a horse-drawn carriage.)

From Illmitz follow signs to Podersdorf which is in fact the Seewinkel weinstrasse (vineyard road). **PODERSDORF** is the resort closest to the lake and the only one entirely free of reeds which makes it the most popular for bathing and, alas, the most crowded during the summer months. The beach (follow signs 'Zum See') is pleasantly large however and there always seems to be plenty of parking space (though possibly not by the normal standards of Burgenland, where parking is never a problem!). **Strand Hotel Tauber** (02177 204) and **Haus Attila** (02177 415) are good family hotels and there are masses of small pensions, inns, apartments and other holiday accommodation. The Dutch windmill at Mühlstrasse 26 has an interesting interior (daily guided tours 02177 286). Tourist Office: Hauptstrasse 2 (02177 227).

Continue along the lake on a one-way street which bends to right and leads back to the main road, eventually joining 51 where turn left for Weiden and Neusiedl. After Neusiedl take left fork joining 50 for **JOIS** (Bronze Age graves, also an eighteenth-century parish church worth viewing for splendid altars and pulpit and if you have not sampled the wines at Halbturn, here is another chance to do so at the **Saliterhof**).

Stay on 50 for **WINDEN** where the oldest Roman wine press in Austria was found in a Roman farmhouse. (A small road out of Winden leads up to the Zeilerberg and the Ludloch, the only cave in Burgenland with fossilised fauna. The cave was discovered in the 1920s during a fox hunt, when the skeleton of an Ice Age cave bear was also found. The skeleton can now be seen in a museum in Eisenstadt, and Winden celebrates with a Bear Festival every August!).

Continue on 50 to **BREITENBRUNN** where a seventeenth-century tower looms high above the village. Built as a fortification against the Turks, its five floors now house the only museum in Austria set in a tower. There are lovely views from the balcony on top. The village has some very attractive houses, sixteenth- and seventeenth-century, with archways, mostly in Prangerstrasse. See also: parish church with underground charnel house. Quarries near Breitenbrunn supplied material for many of Vienna's famous buildings, including St Stephen's Cathedral.

The road continues through vineyards to **PURBACH**, known through centuries for the excellence of its wine. Ten barrels of it and forty oxen bought the local castle for a 'Count Nickolaus' in the thirteenth century and two centuries later it was recorded that a local judge fled before the rebellious Hungarians 'taking with him all his wine'. He also buried 18,240 gold and silver coins, which were found later and were the largest loot ever unearthed! Purbach's favourite legend concerns a Turkish soldier who hid in a chimney with a bottle (or two) of local wine, so as not to have to join his departing comrades. He was discovered later, fast asleep and pleasantly sozzled, and allowed to stay on, converting to Christianity and living happily ever after (history does not relate whether he married a local girl, but this is more than likely). See him peeping out from the chimney at Schulgasse 9 (you will have to go back to the main street for this, as he can't be spotted if you stand close to the house), a beautiful sixteenth-century building with wine cellar and arcaded courtyard. Legends apart, Purbach has some fine old houses within its fortification walls and one of the prettiest, also one of the oldest, is the **Nikolauszeche** (0283 5514), now an elegant, if rather expensive (for Burgenland) restaurant, with a short but delectable menu and an enormous wine list—as befits a 'country cousin' of Vienna's 'Zu den 3 Husaren' restaurant. Tourist Office: Schulgasse 19 (02683 5176).

For a large selection of local specialities in charming surroundings take the road to the right of 50, signposted **Am Spitz Hölzl-Schwarz** (02683 5519). You will think you have lost your way for it leads through seemingly endless vineyards—in fact only about 1 km—to top of a small hill from which you get a marvellous view across the lake. The restaurant building probably stands on the site of the old 'castrum' for which Count Nickolaus paid with wine. Replaced by a monastery later on, hence the label 'Kloster am Spitz' for wines from the Hölzl vineyards. Flowering oleander trees line the open terrace, portions are huge, prices very moderate and there is a pleasant small hotel next to the restaurant, owned by the same family. On the way back note the many reed-covered houses sunk into the hillside: wine cellars, some of which are open to the public.

About 4 km farther along 50 you come to **DONNERSKIRCHEN**, a picturesque little village nestling against the foot of the Leitha Hills. Follow signs to right for the centre. Like all the area surrounding the lake, this is ancient ground, with tumuli, graves from the Hallstatt culture, as well as remains of one of the oldest churches in Austria. But Donnerskirchen has another claim to fame: the first ever documented Trockenbeerenauslese was made from grapes grown in the Donnerskirchen vineyards in 1526 and called Lutherwein. Three centuries and three casks later the wine was still very much 'alive' and appreciated—any vacant space having been filled with gravelstones to prevent oxidation. St Marti-

nus, the Donnerskirchen wine co-operative still call their best wines
'Lutherweine' and they are immensely proud that one of those was
chosen 'best wine in the world' out of 1,300 competitors a few years ago.
Wine seminaries are held during the summer at the **Martinsschlössl**
(02683 8512), an enchanting Baroque manor, now headquarters of the
co-operative. From early July, Donnerskirchen seems to be permanently
en fête—there is a cherry festival, then a wine festival with gipsy musicians
playing in the streets and, for more serious music lovers, there are Haydn
serenades in the seventeenth-century parish church (St Martins). See also
the seventeenth-century pillory. **Gasthof Engel** (02683 8502) is a good,
old-fashioned inn (they also run the restaurant at the Martinsschlössl).
Tourist Office: Kiosk in Hauptstrasse during summer, otherwise at the
Martinsschlössl.

Return to 50 and turn right, direction Eisenstadt. After about 3 km
turn left, signposted Oggau, Rust and Mörbisch and then just Rust, Mörbisch. The road winds its way through numerous vineyards to **OGGAU**,
a pleasant little village noted for its velvety red wine called Blaufränkischer. On All Saints Day the children of the village call on their
relations, asking for an 'Allerheiligenstriezel', a plaited loaf made of
brioche pastry. The population of Oggau is 1,900, but on that day the
bakers sell more than twice that number of these loaves!

Drive through Oggau, following directions for Rust. **RUST** is proud
to be called 'the smallest town in Austria'. Its population totals 1,700, so
quite where this would leave Hardegg (in Lower Austria) which has a
population of just over 200 and is a town older than Rust, is a debatable
point. Rust is strikingly handsome and beautifully preserved, a town
grown rich on wine and spared by the Turkish invaders. In 1524 local
wine growers acquired the right to mark their wines with an R—probably
one of the earliest trademarks. Rust prospered tremendously after that.
Beautiful houses were built and many of its citizens ennobled, and in 1681
Rust was declared a Free Town, having bought its freedom from the
Habsburgs with 60,000 Gulden and 30,000 litres of wine. Two years later,
when the Turks invaded the country once more, the newly-created Free
Town sided with the Hungarian rebel leader Tököly who in turn sided
with the Turks—and Rust was spared destruction, unlike the rest of the
region. Impossible to pick out the many splendid buildings worthy of
inspection. (Austrian authorities when faced with a similar dilemma
simply declared the whole of Rust an ancient monument in 1963.) Better
by far would be to wander in the tiny central area—Rathausplatz, Hauptstrasse, Conradplatz, Kirchengasse and Haydngasse—though you may
care to note particularly the house called 'Zum Auge Gottes' (Rathausplatz 2) with its rich facade and bay window, or the Rathaus (town hall)
glowing in warm red. The **Rathauskeller** (in town hall) is an excellent,
reasonably priced restaurant with many local specialities and, of course,
superb wines. **Feiler-Artinger**, Hauptstrasse 3 and **Wenzel**, Hauptstrasse
29 should be noted not only for their splendid houses, but these are the
places to go for serious wine tasting—and buying. Above all, do not miss:
the twelfth-century parish church St Pankrazius and St Ägydius, known

as Fischerkirche with the thirteenth-century St Mary's chapel, medieval frescoes; seventeenth-century parish church Holy Trinity (worth climbing the impressive tower for the view from the balcony, particularly for observing the famous Rust storks at close quarters); eighteenth-century Protestant church with onion-domed tower. **Arkadenhof** (02685 246) and **Hotel Stadt Rust** (02685 268) are pleasant, typically local hotels with good restaurants. Just outside the town centre, towards the lake, there is the very modern and slightly pricey **Seehotel** (02685 381) in case one had forgotten that Rust is also a lakeside resort. Golden Wine week at end of July. Candlelight concerts at Fischerkirche. Tourist Office: Rathaus (02685 202).

If you can tear yourself away from Rust, take 52 (another 'wine road') to **MÖRBISCH** which is exactly the opposite of Rust. For this is just a typical wine village. It is immensely endearing with its white-washed houses and alleyways, courtyards full of flowering oleander trees and storks which, at least to me, always appear to be more genuine than the famous Rust storks who—I am sure—get knighted at the end of their term of office and retire on a state pension. A 1,700 m road leads through reeds to the lake and a small artificial peninsula with beach, **Seehotel** (02685 8217) and, quite unexpectedly, an enormous open-air theatre with stage set in lake and auditorium seating over 3,000. From mid-July to end-August operetta is performed there every weekend against the magnificent lake background, with the occasional stork winging its way home and a full moon lighting the scenery. Superb performances (most of

Mörbisch

the singers come from Vienna's Volksoper), but take a mosquito spray. Tourist Office: Hauptstrasse 28 (02685 8430).

Rural Burgenland

2-3 days/about 175 km/from Eisenstadt to Jennersdorf

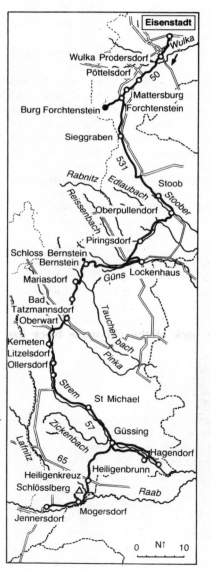

Vineyards and maize fields, sunflowers and tobacco plants, roads scented with lime blossoms and strawberries—and spattered thickly with cherries which even the birds have not bothered to pick (they know that there are even better cherries just around the next bend) . . . You will find all these on your journey to the southern tip of Burgenland. Plus ancient fortresses, romantic castles and a host of old legends—even the occasional ghost!

EISENSTADT (pop: 10,500) the capital of Burgenland is old, tiny and not only the smallest, but also—except for a few weeks in summer—the quietest capital of any Austrian province. Declared a Free Town in 1648, having bought its freedom with 16,000 Gulden and 3,000 buckets of wine from the Esterhazys whose magnificent castle stands somewhat surprisingly (and probably surprised) at the top of the High Street. Nelson and the Hamiltons stayed there, as did emperors and kings throughout the centuries. Josef Haydn called Eisenstadt the place 'where I wish to live and to die' a wish which was more-or-less granted: he was Court musician to the Esterhazys and although he did not die in Eisenstadt, he is buried at the Bergkirche (where his head joined his body only in 1954, having been kept by the Gesellschaft der Musikfreunde until then!).

Although Eisenstadt is only small, one could easily spend days exploring it, discovering new and hidden treasures, even staying on for an extra day for one of the concerts at the Haydnsaal at the castle (altered according to Haydn's specifications, so that the acoustics are marvellous). See particularly: Schloss Esterhazy (daily from 9 am to 4.30 pm) including Haydnsaal, Wildschweinsaal (with statue of Princess Leopoldine Esterhazy by Canova); Schlosskirche (where Beethoven's Mass in C Major, commissioned by Prince Esterhazy, was first performed); eighteenth-century Bergkirche and Calvary hill; Haydn's house, and also the charming little garden house in Bürgerspitalgasse where he spent many hours composing; seventeenth-century town hall; fifteenth-century Domkirche; Franziskanerkirche with monastery and Esterhazy mausoleum—and much more.

From the thirteenth century onwards Eisenstadt had a very large Jewish community, self-governed with its own Mayor and Notary (under the patronage of the Esterhazys). This was an unbroken tradition which continued until 1938, at which time of course it abruptly ceased. The posts which held the chains to close off the ghetto during the Sabbath are still visible. At Unterberggasse 6, in the former ghetto, there is now the only museum in Austria dedicated entirely to Judaica (02682 5145—Easter to October) and the ancient Jewish cemetery also warrants a visit.

Tourist Office (for Burgenland): Schloss Esterhazy
Tourist Office (for Eisenstadt): Town Hall, Hauptstrasse 35 (02682 250713).

Hotel Burgenland (02682 5521) is an excellent modern hotel, with superbly comfortable rooms (swimming pool practically suspended in the sky) and an elegant restaurant with good food, as well as a coffee shop for light meals, all most reasonably priced. **Parkhotel Mikschi** (02682 4361), at Haydngasse 38, is small, modern and very good indeed and backs on to the excellent **Patisserie Mikschi** in the Hauptstrasse. Wines from the Esterhazy vineyards can be sampled at the **Schlosstaverne** opposite the castle (Schlosstaverne restaurant at back of the old stable block has recently changed ownership—so it is too early to report on it.)

During the last week of August Eisenstadt celebrates the 'Feast of a Thousand Wines', an event no wine lover should miss, but book ahead as hotels tend to get crowded during that period.

Leave Eisenstadt on 50 (marked 59a and no doubt a few other numbers as well on different maps). Try not to stray onto the fast S4/S31—no great harm done if you do: simply leave again on the Mattersburg exit—but the country road is the prettier one. It leads through sleepy Wulkaprodersdorf, past Zemendorf and **PÖTTELSDORF** where you will see a large building on the left, proclaiming 'Fürst Bismarck—die grossen Weine' (with attached Weinstube for sampling). Pöttelsdorfer Blaufränkischer, a pleasant smooth red with low alcohol content (and reputedly no after-effects), is also known as Bismarckwein, since Fürst Bismarck is said to have preferred it to all other wines. 'Have we won a battle there?' was his first question when told the place of origin—and the great wine merchant

Sandor Wolf from Eisenstadt supplied him with it ever thereafter.

Follow 50 to **MATTERSBURG** (pop: 5,600) a pleasant little town at the foot of the Rosaliengebirge (see eighteenth-century plague column, wrongly dated 1614, also St Martin's on hill) which changed its name from Mattersdorf (Dorf = village) to Mattersburg (Burg = fortress) in anticipation of becoming capital of Burgenland, but lost out to Eisenstadt. Mattersdorf was one of the important Jewish 'seven communities' with a famous Hebrew school (now re-established in Israel). In the nineteenth-century the Jewish population constituted about a third of the total. The synagogue was totally destroyed and looted by the Nazis—all that is left are some old tombstones stacked against the cemetery walls and relics of Judaica at the Stadtmuseum (02626 2333, Hauptplatz 14, mid-April to mid-October).

In Mattersburg follow signs 'Schloss Forchtenstein 8 km', followed almost immediately by **FORCHTENSTEIN**, 5 km. The former goes to the castle, the latter to the village of the same name which really consists of two even smaller villages called Forchtenau and Neustift. The road rises towards the mighty Forchtenstein fortress. **Reisner**, Hauptstrasse 141 (02626 3139—closed Wednesday), is quite a remarkable restaurant, part village inn, with a tiny terrace set back from the road (more like a suburban residential street) none of which prepares for the cooking within which is simply superb. (Closed Wednesdays; booking advised at weekends.)

Drive up the hill to **Burg Forchtenstein** which—particularly in spring when wreathed in cherry blossoms and in summer when the air is thick with the scents of flowering sage and strawberries ripening in the fields below—looks much more like a fairytale castle than a fierce fortress. Yet its strength was proved in times of war; in fact, Forchtenstein was never conquered and gave refuge to countless people. As befits an ancient fortress, it is also surrounded by legends—one of them concerning the first owner, a Prince Giletus who had his wife Rosalia thrown into the dungeons for ill-treating the serfs during his absence. Her ghost then started to haunt the place, whereupon the prince built the Rosalienka-pelle (in the Neustift part of Forchtenstein) which soon became a place of pilgrimage. Not a very likely tale, since first mention of the chapel was made in 1614, by which time Forchtenstein (which had been built by the Counts of Mattersburg and changed hands several times) had become the property of the Esterhazys which it has remained to this day. Nevertheless Rosalia perhaps still haunts the castle which Prince Nicholas Esterhazy completely rebuilt in the seventeenth century, not at all as a forbidding fortress, but as his residence, until the rebuilding of Eisenstadt had been completed. Open all year. (Rosalienkapelle at Neustift also worth a visit for remarkable interior.) To see particularly: fantastic arsenal and armoury (enough to fit out a whole army) including flags, banners and standards; Turkish tent left behind after the second siege of Vienna in 1683; carriages; furnishings including family portraits of the Esterhazys; original seventeenth-century kitchens and 142 m deep well, dug by Turkish prisoners of war; and 'don't forget to take with you some of our wines' as it says rather endearingly at the entrance gate!

Retrace your steps down hill and into Mattersburg, then follow directions for Oberpullendorf and Sieggraben which will bring you onto S31. In this particular case the so-called schnellstrasse (fast road) is preferable to the old country road: sweeping along rather majestically with some lovely views on the way, not least of the tortuous turns of the picturesque country road below! Follow S31 to its end and then slip onto 50 (direction Oberpullendorf) to **STOOB** which was founded in 1250, near the old Roman settlement just east of the present village. Stoob has been known as the 'potters' village' for centuries, one shape particular to Stoob being the 'Plutzer', a narrow-mouthed jug or jar, almost as old as Stoob and said to have been used by field workers as it kept drinks cool when sunk into the ground (it is certainly an ideal receptacle for keeping the good Burgenland wine at an even temperature). There are still many potters in Stoob—witness the numerous showrooms where designs can often be made to order. During the summer pottery classes are held for visitors. See the Bergkirche (St John the Baptist), thirteenth century with later additions.

Konditorei Koth at Stoob (left on main road) serves the largest Danish pastries in captivity (except that they are not called Danish here), also delicious breads, snacks and other pastries.

Continue on 50 by-passing **OBERPULLENDORF** (very good restaurant **Zur Schmiede** in centre) past Dörfl and through **PIRINGS-DORF**, known for its basket weavers (and several spas), after which take a left fork to **LOCKENHAUS**, sitting rather sedately at the foot of the grand but sombre **Burg Lockenhaus**. The village, surrounded by the river Güns which wraps itself round the fortress as well, is a popular holiday resort, but it is the fortress—built to block the narrow valley—that deserves all the attention. There are two fortresses really: the 'Untere (lower) Burg' and the 'Hochburg' also known as Alte Burg. (Guide provided 02616 2394). See particularly: Rittersaal, running entire width of 'old castle' and probably used by the Templars; sixteenth-century well reaching right down to valley below (supposedly secret escape route with door and key at other end, though never discovered); St Nicholas chapel; thirteenth-century keep with Gothic hall and tower with Gothic frescoes. Also worth seeing is the parish church, with its burial crypt of the Nadasdy family (the most elaborate sarcophagus is the one for Franz Nadasdy who was beheaded for conspiring against the Emperor Leopold I, only to be buried with full honours in the

Burg Lockenhaus

presence of the emperor's representative!). During July there is an interna-
tionally acclaimed Chamber Music Festival at Burg Lockenhaus, but at
other times so-called Rittermahle (Knights' Feasts) are held (02616 2321
for details). Nowadays they have a strong touristy flavour, with a ghost
wafting in at midnight. (I think this is tempting fate a bit, since Erzebet
Nadasdy—grandmother of the Franz who was beheaded—was a sort of
female Count Dracula who murdered countless village maidens and is said
to haunt the place. Certainly one of my sanest, most sober friends swears
that he was touched by a ghostly hand at Burg Lockenhaus in broad
daylight!) There is a perfectly comfortable (though slightly pricey for
Burgenland) **Pension** at the Untere Schloss (02616 2394)—ghost not
guaranteed! Tourist Office: Hauptplatz 10 (02616 2203).

Retrace your steps to 50 for **BERNSTEIN** which at 619 m lies high for
Burgenland, where the highest point—the Geschriebenstein—is a mere
833 m. Bernstein is on the old Amber Road from which it probably
derives its name (Bernstein = amber) but 'the' stone of Bernstein is the
serpentine which is found and worked locally and known as 'Austrian
Jade' because of its colour which varies from deep dark to a light, almost
translucent green. The little Felsenmuseum, Hauptplatz 5 (03354 320
open daily, including Sunday) is a little 'gem' in many respects, an underground museum hewn into rock: a miniature mine, displaying minerals,
semi-precious stones and of course, serpentine. See too the eighteenth-
century parish church St Michael with particularly beautiful high altar.
Schloss Bernstein is one of the most impressive and romantic castles in
Burgenland and now run as a hotel (02243 220). Some parts are accessible and may be viewed during daytime (Rittersaal is also open for lunch
to non-residents, though infinitely more glamorous during candlelit
dinners), but it is worth staying at the Schloss if only to see the rooms
which are not open to merely passing mortals. Very reasonable prices, but
be warned though: Bernstein does have a fully acknowledged ghost, duly
registered not only with the former Imperial authorities, but also with
those of the two republics before and after the Second World War!

From Bernstein continue on 50. After about 4 km there is a sign to the
right to **MARIASDORF**—a detour of about 2 km each way, well worth
taking for the late-Gothic parish church.

Return to 50 and continue to **BAD TATZMANNSDORF**, a particularly pleasant little spa, completely unsophisticated, with lovely park and
open-air museum showing some of the interesting old Burgenland buildings. **Parkhotel** (03353 200) and **Kurhotel** (03353 428) are both effi-
ciently run, the latter connected to the treatment centre (in case you
want to be serious!)

Drive on to **OBERWART** on 50, second largest town in Burgenland
(pop: 6,200) which at first may appear just a small but busy modern town.
However there are some typical old Burgenland farmhouses here (many
with arcades), as well as several interesting churches, particularly the
Protestant one at the western end, with eighteenth-century arcaded
rectory.

At the fork after Oberwart take 57 to left, through Kemeten, Litzelsdorf and Ollersdorf to **STEGERSBACH** (museum in Renaissance castle; open Easter/end October) and **ST MICHAEL**. Through vineyards and orchards as well, to **GÜSSING**. Even in Austria Güssing is little known and hardly ever mentioned except for the sparkling mineral water (Güssinger) which originates there (mineral water museum in Güssing) and one must admit that Güssing looks slightly unreal—a fortress atop an extinct volcano, more often than not surrounded by a misty haze—in fact the whole of Güssing is like a Sleeping Beauty which no prince has kissed awake. The fortress (originally built wholly in wood and rebuilt in 1240), where Emperor Frederic III was elected King of Hungary in 1459, where Pieter Breughel painted and where Carolus Clusius wrote the first recorded book on botany in the seventeenth century (and a book about mushrooms) can be visited from 1 April to 31 October, except Monday (03322 2491). See particularly: Rittersaal; seventeenth-century chapel Maria Schnee; medieval keep; fortifications, fortress museum and also so-called 'open air theatre' with 'volcanic' seats. In Güssing itself there is the Romanesque parish church St Jakob; a Franciscan monastery (important library) with church (see paintings and also crypt of the Batthanys, particularly sarcophagus of Prince Karl Batthany); also seventeenth-century Kastell Batthany and Baroque castle Draskovich (not accessible, though the chapel, with the only Gothic altar in Burgenland, can be visited on application).

Leave Güssing on 57 towards Heiligenkreuz, but just outside Güssing (opposite large pond) turn left, along the little Strembach through St

Heiligenbrunn

159

Nikolaus and Gläsing to **HEILIGENBRUNN** where sweet chestnuts grow in profusion and where the Kellerviertel (wrongly named 'cellar quarters' as they are not cellars at all, but small vintners' houses with thatched roofs—mostly eighteenth-century) is rightly protected by the Hague Convention. Ideal time to visit the Kellerviertel is on Saturdays and Sundays, when wine and local snacks are served under old fruit trees—all very informal and utterly delightful (a little prompting will produce the same on weekdays, provided the owners are at home). There is also a little spa with supposedly health-giving properties near St Ulrich Chapel.

At the end of the Kellerviertel turn left across the fields and then right for **HAGENDORF**, where geese crossing the road still control the traffic. **Schwabenhof** (03324 333) is the most unpretentious little inn—behind the village petrol pump—and an oasis of peace and quiet. There is a tiny garden and an even tinier swimming pool. You can sit under fruit trees and the only disturbance will be on the occasional ripe fruit dropping into your drink. Cooking is simple, but absolutely genuine and the sunsets in this part of the world are unbelievably beautiful. Nearby **Hotel Krutzler** (03324 240) seems almost too fashionable in this setting.

Return to Güssing, following direction Strem (no need to go back to Heiligenbrunn), turn right at fork and then left for Strem and 56 which leads back to Güssing. At Güssing take 57 to **HEILIGENKREUZ IM LAFNITZTAL**. The river runs along by the road most of the way and Heiligenkreuz, which was almost entirely destroyed at the end of the Second World War, is now a pretty village, wreathed in flowers. **Gibiser** (03325 216) rewards a journey all the way from almost anywhere. It's a marvellous, reasonably-priced restaurant with excellent accommodation (in thatched little vintners' houses in the rather extensive grounds).

From Heiligenkreuz take 65 direction Fürstenfeld, but immediately outside village turn left direction Jennersdorf. Follow this direction. The road runs along the Austro-Hungarian border (with warnings in some places that the left side of the road is Hungarian!), giving a good view of the little Hungarian town of Szentgotthard (St Gotthard) where the great battle fending off the Turks took place in 1664. The road leads on to **MOGERSDORF** where turn right for a brief detour up to the **Schlössl-berg**; the great battle in which Turkish troops amounting to 100,000 were beaten by a mere 16,000 led by Montecuccoli, is known as the battle of Mogersdorf in Austria and on top of the Schlösslberg there is a 15m high concrete cross and a 1964 chapel (in place of the old one destroyed in the Second World War) to commemorate this victory. As well as—what else, in Austria?—a splendid inn called **Kreuzstadl** with small exhibition of battle relics. Return to Mogersdorf (pretty Anna chapel, built 1670, probably by widow of Count Trautmannsdorf who died in the battle) and turn right, following directions for Jennersdorf via Weichselbaum.

JENNERSDORF, at the foot of the little Tafelberg, is a pleasant little holiday village with the largest swimming pool in Burgenland — with its own restaurant, Lindenczarda, open in season also during the evening, complete with outdoor grill and gipsy musicians! It is however **Raffel** (03154 328) to which people flock from far and wide (same owners as the Lindenczarda), a restaurant where dishes come with a strong Hungarian flavour, again accompanied by gipsy music, and where portions (even by Burgenland standards) are gigantic. Prices are moderate and it is just as well that there are some very comfortable rooms upstairs (all fairly recently refurbished and at moderate prices).

The route ends here and you may well think I am leaving you in the middle of nowhere and at the end of the world. This is not so — Jennersdorf is at the southern tip of Burgenland, what they call 'three-country-corner' with both Hungary and Yugoslavia just a few kilometres away, but it is also only about 4 km to Styria, 14 km to Fehring, or return to Heiligenkreuz and take 65 for Fürstenfeld which leads on to the motorway for Graz.

GLOSSARY

Apotheke pharmacy
Ärztenotdienst emergency medical service, published in newspapers and available from local police station or telephone directory
Autobahn motorway
Brettljausn light meal, usually cold meats and sausage
Buschenschenken places (usually in vineyards) where local wine is served
Drogerie perfumery, chemist (*not* selling medicines)
Fremdenverkehrsverein Tourist Office
Frühschoppen a jolly Sunday-morning music session, held at a local inn
'ganztägig warme Küche' hot food served throughout the day, though not necessarily a full menu
Gasthof inn
gebührenpflichtig subject to a fee
Heiltherme healthgiving thermal spa
Heurigen, Heuriger new wine, "born" on 11th November when the wine harvested the previous year is first tasted. Also the place—often situated in a vineyard—at which you drink the locally grown wine.
Karte short for *Speisekarte*—menu
Kellerviertel 'cellar quarter', an area where many wine cellars are clustered together.
Kipfel, Kipferl Viennese version of croissant which is much crisper and drier.
Kirtag Kermes
Konditorei Patisserie
Kurdirektion Tourist Office in a spa
Kurzparkzone short term parking area
Menu fixed price set meal
Millirahmstrudel, Milchrahmstrudel Strudel pastry with soft curd and raisin filling
ÖMATC Austrian (Österreichischer) Automobile, Motorcycle and Touring Club
Obstler *see* Schnapps
Pension boarding house offering bed and breakfast (sometimes also serving other meals, to house guests only)

Pradikätsweine 'top of the list' wine (the list starts with Tafelwein (table wine) followed by Landwein (country wine—vin du pays), Qualitätswein, then Pradikätsweine)

Schilcher Styrian wine from the Wildbach grape, varying from pale to dark pink

Schnapps, Obstler, Eau de Vie liqueurs brewed from different kinds of fruit

Speisekarte menu

Steirergwand Styrian national costume which varies according to region. Quite often used as colloquialism for Austrian costume generally.

Steirisches Kernöl delicious dark brown oil pressed from green pumpkin seeds. If used in a salad with vinegar or lemonjuice, it turns dark green.

Tabak Trafik tobacconist, usually not only selling cigarettes and tobacco (State Monopoly in Austria), but newspapers, stationery and parking clocks for display on windscreens of cars.

Tageskarte Carte du jour, listing specialities of the day, usually also including the fixed price set meal.

Touristen Wanderkarten hiker's maps

Urlaub am Bauernhof holidays on a farm. List of farmhouses providing these are usually available at the local tourist office.

Verhackerts a country speciality claimed by more than one province: smoked pork, some crackling etc, chopped up (verhackert) and buried in rendered pork fat. Strongly spiced and absolutely delicious.

Vierkanthöfe literally 'four square courts': a type of building particular to Upper Austria

Wackelstein 'wobbly stone': huge slabs of granite so delicately poised on top of each other that they rock at a touch. Found only in the Waldviertel.

Wiener Früstück tea, coffee or chocolate, a splendid selection of breads and rolls, butter, jam or honey and a soft-boiled egg.

BIBLIOGRAPHY

For details of historic buildings etc:
Dehio (Die Kunstdenkmäler Österreichs) Each volume covering a
  province (separate volume for Graz). Niederösterreich at present being
  out of print.
Note: Some of the following are out of print, available only from libraries.
S.F. & F.L. Hallgarten: **The Wines and Wine gardens of Austria** (Argus
  Books 1979)
Stella Musulin: **Austria: People and landscape** (Faber and Faber 1971)
Jörg Mauthe: **How to be Viennese** (Amalthea 1977 and constantly
  reprinted)
Hans Weigel: **O du mein Österreich** (first published in 1956)
John Bourke: **Baroque churches of Central Europe** (Faber 1958)
Pia Maria Pechl: **Das Marchfeld** (Herold 1969)
Fritz Molden: **Die Österreicher oder Die Macht der Geschichte** (Langen
  Müller 1986 and 1987)
Franz Werfel: **Die wahre Geschichte vom wiederhergestellten Kreuz**
  (gesammelte Werke—Erzählungen aus zwei welten) (published
  Frankfurt am Main 1954)
Ernst Trost: **Die Donau** (Molden 1968)
Otto Stradal: **Es steht manch Schloss in Osterreich**
Fritz Judtmann: **Mayerling ohne Mythos** (Krenmayr und Scheriau 1968)
Eduard Vorbeck, Lothar Beckel: **Carnuntum—Rom an der Donau** (Otto
  Müller Verlag Salzburg 1973)
Franz Eppel: **Die Wachau** (St. Peter Salzburg 1964)
——— **Das Waldviertel** (St. Peter Salzburg 1984)
August Ernst: **Geschichte des Burgenlands** (Wien 1987)
Herbert Steijskal: **Kärnten—Geschichte und Kultur in Bildern und
  Dokumenten** (Universitätsverlag Carinthia 1987)
Josef Riedmann: **Geschichte Tirols** (Verlag für Geschichte und Politik
  1982)
Richard Rickett: **Österreich: Sein Weg durch die Geschichte** (Prachner
  1969)
Salzburg: Stadt und Land (Prestel Verlag, Munich 1972)
Gordon Brook-Shepherd: **Austrian Odyssey** (Macmillan)
Madeleine Duke: **A City built to Music** (Jonathan Cape 1961)

164

INDEX

Index